The
Fantastic Vampire

**Recent Titles in Contributions to the
Study of Science Fiction and Fantasy**

The
Fantastic Vampire

Studies in the Children of the Night

Selected Essays from the
Eighteenth International Conference
on the Fantastic in the Arts

Edited by James Craig Holte

Contributions to the Study of Science Fiction and Fantasy, Number 91
C.W. Sullivan, III, Series Adviser

GREENWOOD PRESS
Westport, Connecticut • London

Library of Congress Cataloging-in-Publication Data

International Conference on the Fantastic in the Arts (18th : 1997 : Ft. Lauderdale, Fla.)
    The fantastic vampire : studies in the children of the night : selected essays from the
Eighteenth International Conference on the Fantastic in the Arts / edited by James Craig
Holte.
        p.   cm.—(Contributions to the study of science fiction and fantasy, ISSN 0193–6875 ;
    no. 91)
    Conference held in 1997 in Ft. Lauderdale, Fla.
    Includes bibliographical references and index.
    ISBN 0–313–30933–7 (alk. paper)
        1. Vampires in literature—Congresses.   2. Fantasy fiction, English—History and
criticism—Congresses.   3. Fantasy fiction, American—History and criticism—Congresses.
4. Horror tales, American—History and criticism—Congresses.   5. Horror tales,
English—History and criticism—Congresses.   6. Vampire films—History and
criticism—Congresses.   7. Stoker, Bram, 1847–1912. Dracula—Congresses.   8. Dracula,
Count (Fictitious character)—Congresses.   I. Holte, James Craig.   II. Title.   III. Series.
PR830.V3I58   1997
820.8′0375—dc21   99–462052

British Library Cataloguing in Publication Data is available.

Library of Congress Catalog Card Number: 99–462052
ISBN: 0–313–30933–7
ISSN: 0193–6875

First published in 2002

Greenwood Press, 88 Post Road West, Westport, CT 06881
An imprint of Greenwood Publishing Group, Inc.
www.greenwood.com

Printed in the United States of America

The paper used in this book complies with the
Permanent Paper Standard issued by the National
Information Standards Organization (Z39.48–1984).

10 9 8 7 6 5 4 3 2 1

This book is dedicated to my parents, Fred and Marie Holte, who took me to The New York Public Library early and often and who encouraged me to move to the adult section before others thought I was ready. They also let me read anything I would bring home, even horror fiction.

This book is also dedicated to my wife, the Honorable Judge Gwyn Hilburn, who has put up with my interest in the creatures of the night for years and never once reached for a sharpened wooden stake.

Finally, this book is dedicated to my daughter, Molly Hilburn-Holte, who inspires me every day.

Contents

Acknowledgments

Very little of value is created in isolation, and *The Fantastic Vampire* is the product of the collaboration of a large number of people. I would like to thank the contributors first, without whose scholarship and enthusiasm for the project there would have been nothing to edit. Their patience as this volume moved through the various editing stages has been much appreciated. Second, I must thank the officers of the International Association for the Fantastic of the Arts and the Lord Ruthven Assembly, especially Bill Senior, Chip Sullivan, and Elizabeth Miller, who have been supportive of this project from the beginning. I would also be remiss without thanking the Department of English at East Carolina University. The support and encouragement of my colleagues has made this long and winding project possible. In addition, I want to thank Joanna Rohrbach, who assisted in the proofreading of the manuscript. Cindy Rayburn, who helped with the final editing, and Nicole Tipton, whose expertise salvaged the manuscript more than once. Finally, this book is dedicated to Gwyn and Molly, who put up with my unusual interests and without whose love my life would indeed be a dark and stormy night.

Introduction

James Craig Holte

Vampires have always been shape shifters, and vampires have always been popular. Throughout their long history vampires have been able to transform themselves to satisfy their own needs as well as the needs of readers and viewers. From their homeland in central Asia, vampires and vampire legends moved outward into India, China, Eastern Europe, Greece, Africa, and the Americas. Wherever they existed in the imaginations of people they adapted themselves to customs of the local culture.

In the Western tradition, folklore asserts that vampires can transform themselves into a variety of shapes, including those of the cat, dog, wolf, rat, and bat, all creatures associated with the demonic. In addition, it has been believed that the vampire can take the form of mist, smoke, and fog.

The literary vampire is also a shape shifter. In nineteenth-century British fiction there are a number of famous vampires, each unique. In 1819 in *The Vampyre*, John Polidori introduced Lord Ruthven, the vampire as typical gothic villain, and established the vampire craze of the nineteenth century that resulted in a flood of German vampire poetry, French vampire drama, and British vampire fiction. In the mid 1840s English readers were treated to *Varney the Vampire, or the Feast of Blood*, which appeared in 109 weekly installments and later was published in a single 800 page volume. Varney was far more cruel and bloody than the brooding Lord Ruthven. Sheridan Le Fanu published the famous story "Carmilla" in 1872, introducing readers to an erotic lesbian vampire. In 1897 Bram Stoker published *Dracula*, fixing the character of the Transylvanian nobleman as the archetypal vampire firmly in the public imagination.

The transformations of Dracula himself are equally dramatic. In Bram Stoker's novel Dracula is a white-haired Eastern European patriarch with bad breath and hairy palms. In the film adaptations of *Dracula*, however, the vampire continually shifts shapes, creating in the public imagination a composite Dracula who has become a cultural icon. The images of Stoker's vampire that have appeared on stage and on screen in the twentieth century are quite different from one another. Max Schreck's emaciated vampire in the 1922 *Nosferatu* is the antithesis of Bela Lugosi's Eastern European aristocrat in Tod Browning's 1931 *Dracula.* Christopher Lee's powerful Dracula from the popular Hammer films stands in sharp contrast to Frank Langella's romantic portrayal of the Count in the successful 1979 adaptation. And Gary Oldman plays Dracula as both a monster and handsome prince in Francis Ford Coppola's 1992 *Bram Stoker's Dracula*.

The vampires of contemporary fiction are equally diverse. The vampires who populate the neogothic world of Anne Rice's Vampire Chronicles are complex, erotic characters who brood on the undead condition. Chelsea Quinn Yarbro's Count Saint-Germain, the central figure in her series of historical novels, is a sensitive and intelligent romantic hero. Fred Saberhagen's vampire is a detective hero, and Stephen King's vampire is a monster. All of them, however, are popular.

The popularity of the vampire in contemporary culture is reflected in the critical and academic worlds as well. In the past several years international conferences devoted to the study of the children of the night have been held in Romania, the setting of Dracula's home in Stoker's novel; Dublin, Stoker's birthplace; and Los Angeles, the focal point of film and popular culture. In addition, scholars from a variety of fields and using a variety of critical tools have, like Professor Van Helsing, undertaken extensive studies of the vampire.

At the Eighteenth International Conference on the Fantastic in the Arts (IAFA), held in Ft. Lauderdale, Florida, in 1997, the centenary anniversary of the publication of *Dracula,* scholars examined the increasing popularity of the figure of the vampire in both literary and popular culture, remarked on the continued interest in Stoker's novel, examined the figure of the vampire in film and popular culture, explored the figure of the vampire in recent fiction, and studied the metaphor of vampirism in the age of AIDS. The chapters that follow, all presented at the Eighteenth IAFA Conference, chronicle the significant events of the Conference and demonstrate the many scholarly approaches to the study of the vampire that were in evidence there.

The Fantastic Vampire is divided into four general categories, reflecting the breadth of recent scholarship. In Part One, Studies in Stoker, Elizabeth Miller examines Stoker's own editorial changes to the novel in "Shapeshifting *Dracula:* The Abridged Edition of 1901." Raymond McNally argues that *Dracula* is actually about the political situation in nineteenth-century Ireland in "Bram Stoker and Irish Gothic." Katie Harse examines the relationship between two of Stoker's works in *"Dracula's Reflection: The Jewel of Seven Stars."* William Pencak observes significant similarities between the work of Stoker and Oscar Wilde in "'Appalling in Its Gloomy Fascination' Stoker's *Dracula and* Wilde's *Salome."* Scott Vander Ploeg compares *Dracula* to other works of gothic literature in "Stoker's *Dracula:* A Neo-Gothic Experiment." And Suzanna Nyberg looks at the depiction of women in late-nineteenth-century art in "Men in Love: The Fantasizing of Brain Stoker and Edvard Munch."

In Part Two, The Vampire in Film and Popular Culture, Tony Fonseca charts the influence of goth and vampire music in contemporary culture in "Bela Lugosi's Dead, but Vampire Music Stalks the Airwaves." Leslie Tannenbaum examines the popular recent vampire film *Vampire in Brooklyn* in "Policing Eddie Murphy: The Unstable Black Body in *Vampire in Brooklyn.*" James Craig Holte examines the renewed interest in the film vampire in "Resurrection in Britain: Christopher Lee and the Hammer Draculas." And Margaret Carter studies the appearance of the vampire in role playing games in "I, Strahd: Narrative Voice and Variations on a Non-Player Character in TSR's 'Ravenloft' Universe."

In Part Three, Modern Vampire Fictions, Bette Roberts observes the similarities between popular female vampires in "The Mother Goddess in H. Rider Haggard's *She* and Anne Rice's *The Queen of the Damned.*" Heidi L. Nordberg looks at the work of two successful contemporary writers of vampire fiction in "Blood Spirit/Blood Bodies: The Viral in the Vampire Chronicles of Anne Rice and Chelsea Quinn Yarbro." Stephanie Moss provides a close reading of Yarbro's recent novel *Kelene* in "Kelene: The Face in the Mirror." And Sharon A. Russell examines Yarbro's creation of her vampire hero in "The Construction of the Vampire in Yarbro's *Hotel Transylvania.*"

In the final part, Contemporary Issues in the World of the Undead, Teri Ann Doerksen provides a feminist reading of the vampire in "Deadly Kisses: Vampirism, Colonialism, and the Gendering of Horror"; and Jeane Rose discusses the use of vampirism as a metaphor for disease in "'A Girl Like That Will Give You AIDS': Vampirism as AIDS Metaphor in *Killing Zoe.*"

This volume presents a diverse collection of observations on the nature of the vampire and its place in literature and culture at the end of the twentieth century. Enter freely and of your own will.

Part One

Studies in Stoker

Chapter 1

Shapeshifting *Dracula*: The Abridged Edition of 1901

Elizabeth Miller

> We were struck with the fact, that in all the mass of material of which the record is composed, there is hardly one authentic document; nothing but a mass of type-writing.
>
> —Stoker,
> *Dracula, 444*

When we speak of *Dracula,* we are usually referring to the book first published in 1897, which has reappeared in many editions. But the story of the text of Bram Stoker's novel is more complex. For one thing, there is a considerable (and re-traceable) pre-textual stage: Stoker's own notes, the manuscript, and the dramatic version. Then we have the shapeshifting that has occurred with the published text, including countless revisionist versions, prequels, sequels, adaptations and mutations. This chapter will focus on a considerably abridged edition that appeared in 1901 from Constable, the original publisher.

Until recently this text has gone virtually unnoticed.[1] Martin Riccardo's bibliography, *Vampires Unearthed,* lists it as just another reprint, while Richard Dalby calls it merely "the first paperback edition" (27). Yet it is a very different text. Constable published it as a cheap "popular" book, aimed at a less affluent, less sophisticated readership. As was often the case with these books, *Dracula* was reduced in length both to keep down production costs and to make the text more accessible for the general reader. Whether the revisions were made by Stoker himself, by an editor, or by both is not certain.[2] What we know is that the original text was reduced by about 15 percent (approximately 25,000 words). Every chapter of the novel is affected: some undergo only minor alterations, while significant cuts are made in others. In his Foreword to the 1994 reprint of the 1901 text, Robert Eighteen-Bisang notes that most authorities agree that the revised edition of *Dracula* is more readable and, hence, more enjoyable than the common, well-known text. Raymond McNally concurs, commenting in his Introduction to the same text that "the abridgment reads better than the original." I disagree. The novel loses much of its texture, resulting in what I consider a vastly inferior book.[3]

True, we might have done without some of Stoker's lengthy descriptions and conversations, which dominate the first edition. Few would mourn the loss of such passages as Professor Van Helsing's detailed analysis of Dracula's "child-brain" (361, 402) and the "bloom and blood" account given by the captain of the *Czarina Catherine* (376 –77). Nor would the absence of the following upset anyone but the "trivial pursuit" enthusiast: that Dracula does not smoke (25), the routes taken by the steamers *Emma* and *Scarborough* (101), tea at Robin Hood's Bay (119), lunch at Mulgrave Woods (124), the fact that Van Helsing was staying at the Great Eastern Hotel (148),[4] four tidbits about Thomas Bilder and his wife (175), Mr. Hardy's broken finger (197), the list of attendees at Mr. Hawkins's funeral service (214), and the illness of the Vice-Consul at Galatz (410). Except for the purist for whom every scrap of text is sacred, these are dispensable.

I am certain the novel could have survived with other minor deletions, albeit these do add in some small way to its texture: allusions to Spohr and MacKenzie, Disraeli, Ellen Terry, and Hans Andersen (124, 142, 221, 401); Van Helsing's references to Jonathan Harker's "true grit" and Quincey Morris' head "in plane with the horizon" (277, 350); the "white lady" at Whitby Abbey and the hundreds of steps leading up to East Cliff (84, 86), "Count de Ville" (3 –6); the beautiful girl in a big cart-wheel hat (215); and Renfield's exclamation "Damn all thick-headed Dutchmen!" (308). Much of the legal material in the text was eliminated: Dracula's questions about British solicitors and the disposition of property (43–44), the ramifications of a ship's tiller being held by a dead hand (106), the regulations of the Board of Trade (108), and the disposition of Mrs. Westenra's estate (210). While the removal of these passages has no effect on the plot, it lessens the richness of the text by eliminating details about contemporary Victorian England.

The scissors did yeoman work on the numerous literary allusions that dot the original, resulting in the loss of much of the novel's intertextuality. Significant among such deletions are the quotation from Burger's poem "Lenore" (15) and the line "As idle as a painted ship upon a painted ocean" from Coleridge's "The Rime of the Ancient Mariner" (103). Into the discard heap went the majority of the Shakespearean intertext, including several references to *Hamlet, Macbeth, Othello, Romeo* and *Juliet,* and *King Lear.* Some of these we would today consider vital, such as Harker's misquotation of Hamlet—"My tablets! quick my tablets!/'Tis meet that I put it down" (50)—while others (for example, the allusion to Malvolio on page 321) are insignificant. Stoker, or his editor, does not seem to have drawn such distinctions. Other somewhat erudite allusions are also cut: a brief mention of *Arabian Nights* (42), the Latin phrase from Tacitus (375), the short reference to Archimedes (402), as well as lines from Thomas Hood and Byron (202, 240).[5] Biblical allusions, on the other hand, fared better, with most of them remaining intact. Obviously, someone considered much of the intertext expendable for the projected readership. Unfortunately, the result is an inferior piece of work.

We are considering much more than elimination of relatively insignificant details and esoteric allusions. While most of the memorable scenes in the novel are left intact

in the 1901 abridgement (Jonathan's seduction by the three vampire women, the
Count crawling headfirst down the castle wall, the ship's Log, the blood transfusions,
Lucy's appearances as the "bloofer lady" and her subsequent staking, Mina's "baptism
of blood," the final chase), there are a few notable exceptions. The role of bats and rats
is diminished. Gone is Quincey Morris's anecdote about the vampire bat on the
Pampas (191), as well as a scene at Carfax that presents one of the most horrifying
images in the novel:

A few minutes later I saw Morris step suddenly back from a corner, which he was examining.
We all followed his movements with our eyes, for undoubtedly some nervousness was growing
on us and we saw a whole mass of phosphorescence which twinkled like stars. We all
instinctively drew back. The whole place was becoming alive with rats.
    . . . in the minute that had elapsed the number of the rats had vastly increased. They
seemed to swarm over the place all at once, till the lamplight, shining on their moving dark
bodies and glittering, baleful eyes, made the place look like a bank of earth set with fireflies. . . .
The rats were multiplying in thousands, and we moved out. (303–4)

Significant deletions occur in the early part of the novel (Chapters 1–4), Jonathan
Harker's journal of his sojourn in Transylvania. What may be seen as Stoker's over-
reliance on his sources (he squeezes much detail into those four opening chapters)
may well be their strength. Details about the history, geography and local customs not
only give the text its richness but successfully ground it in the real world. Transylvania
is both real and mysterious, setting up the central dichotomy of the novel. Much of this
effect (though not all) is lost in the 1901 text as a result of deletions. Most conspicuous
is the disappearance of the following: the references to various local dishes (4), some
of the history of Bistritz (6), the entire entry on the "robber steak" (9), the "Cszeks and
Slovaks, all in picturesque attire" (12), the leiter-wagon with its "long, snake-like
vertebra calculated to suit the inequalities of the road" (13), and the custom of the
gypsies to "attach themselves . . . to some great noble or boyar" (57). Gone also is the
description of the Carpathians as "endless perspective of jagged rock and pointed
crags . . . lost in the distance. Where the snowy peaks rose grandly" (12).
    There are two significant deletions from the concluding chapter. The first occurs
immediately after Van Helsing stakes the three female vampires: "For, friend John,
hardly had my knife severed the head of each, before the whole body began to melt
away and crumble into its native dust" (438). This prepares us for a similar occurrence
in the case of Dracula, though one could argue that its deletion improves the text,
reserving this special method of disintegration for the Count alone. Secondly, and this
is certainly no improvement, a decision was made to delete the references to the "look
of peace" on Dracula's face at the final moment and the last image of Castle Dracula:

I shall be glad as long as I live that even in that moment of final dissolution, there was in the face
a look of peace, such as I never could have imagined might have rested there.
    The Castle of Dracula now stood out against the red sky, and every stone of its broken
battlements was articulated against the light of the setting sun. (443)

While the removal of the former may help to eliminate any possible ambiguity
concerning the evil nature of the Count, the latter is a major loss.

It has often been stated that the characters in *Dracula* (with the exception of the Count and possibly Mina and Renfield) are flat and uninteresting. If that is the case, then the 1901 text makes them even more so. Several nuances that introduce ambiguity into the characterization are missing. Jonathan Harker, for example, no longer makes the condescending comment about the peasant women, that they "looked pretty, except when you got near them" (5). Nor, having admitted to a "wicked, burning desire" while being seduced by the three female vampires, does he think "It is not good to note this down, lest some day it should meet Mina's eyes and cause her pain" (51). Arthur Holmwood loses his line "I would give the last drop of blood in my body for her" (159), as well as his melodramatic outcry "Oh, Jack! Jack! What shall I do! The whole of life seems gone from me at once, and there is nothing in the wide world for me to live for" (211). Dr. Seward's momentary longing for the "modern Morpheus" (134) is removed. Quincey Morris is made even more insignificant, with the removal of Seward's observation that he is a "moral Viking" and that if "America can go on breeding men like that she will be a power in the world indeed" (217). The complexity of Renfield is lessened with the exclusion of Van Helsing's astute observation the "Perhaps I may gain more knowledge out of folly of this madman than I shall from the teaching of the most wise" (307).

In fact, a somewhat different Van Helsing emerges. In the revised text he has lost much of his sense of humor (along with his entire "King Laugh" speech). On the other hand, the removal of the insensitive remark (made in Mina's presence) "Do you forget . . . that last night he banqueted heavily, and will sleep late?" (351) takes some of the edge off his abrasiveness. We lose that tantalizing allusion to his wife, "dead to me, but alive by church's law, though no wits" (219), as well as the indication that he has also lost a son.

Some of the deletions render the band of vampire hunters somewhat less reprehensible. Dr. Seward no longer offers to falsify Renfield's death certificate by claiming the cause of death a "misadventure in falling from bed" (346). Nor does Quincey Morris offer the employee at Doolittle's Wharf "something from his pocket which crackle as he roll it up" (375). And Harker does not make the comment in Varna that "this is the country where bribery can do anything. . . . Judge Moneybag will settle this case, I think!" (395). On the other hand, some examples of questionable ethical behavior do remain. Although Lord Godalming retains his reservations about Jonathan's involvement in the breaking-and-entry scheme because of possible censure by the Incorporated Law Society, he is still not averse to using his title "to make it all right with the locksmith, and with any policeman that may come alone (355).

Count Dracula, too, is affected. He loses the line "Come in: the night air is chill, and you must need to eat and rest" (23), as well as the following eloquent passage with its Shakespearean resonance: "The warlike days are over. Blood is too precious a thing in these days of dishonourable peace; and the glories of the great races are as a tale that is told" (42). He no longer gives his fascinating explanation of the blue flame" (30). Lost is his association with "the strangeness of the geologic and chemical world" (378). We are given less information about his past with the removal of the following remarks by Van Helsing:

I have studied, over and over again since they came into my hands, all the papers relating to this monster; and the more I have studied, the greater seems the necessity to utterly stamp him out. All through there are signs of his advance; not only of his power, but of his knowledge of it. As I learned from the researches of my friend Arminius of Buda-Pesth, he was in life a most wonderful man. Soldier, statesman, and alchemist —which latter was the highest development of the science-knowledge of his time. He had a mighty brain, a learning beyond compare, and a heart that knew no fear and no remorse. He dared even to attend the Scholomance, and there was no branch of knowledge of his time that he did not essay. (360)

More crucial is the effect this has on the reader's response to the Count, especially with the disappearance of Van Helsing's assessment that "[Dracula] was in life a most wonderful man." When one couples this with the elimination of Mina's earlier comment "I suppose one ought to pity any thing so hunted as is the Count" (277), much of the potential sympathy for Dracula is lost.

The character altered the most by the deletions is Mina. Much of the interpretation of her character rests on the occasional touches of ambivalence that the text supplies. For example, both of her references to the "New Woman" are removed (119–20), and along with them the enticing possibility that Mina may have felt an affinity with the "New Woman." Neither does she retain her desire to "practice interviewing" (226) or her interest in Seward's phonograph (269). But some of the changes may be for the better. She no longer is concerned about being seen with bare feet (123). She is spared the line "I went to bed when the men had gone, simply because they had told me to" (309), as well as her comment about "some of the taste of the original apple that remains still in our mouths" (227) and her observation that "We women have something of the mother in us that makes us rise above smaller matters when the mother-spirit is invoked" (278). The perceptive reader need no longer be doubtful about her declaration that "I felt a thrill of joy through me when I knew that no other woman was a cause of trouble" (138). And, as noted above, her sympathy for Dracula also takes a direct hit, with the removal of her statement "I suppose one ought to pity any thing so hunted as is the Count" (277).

Occasionally, a deletion actually improves the text. One example is the elimination of Van Helsing's use of "my child" in reference to Arthur Holmwood, a wise decision considering that the professor is about to ask Arthur if he can "cut off the head of dead Miss Lucy" (251). But other changes are more puzzling. Why, for example, was Dracula's straw hat removed? The "hat of straw," which the Count is seen wearing as he hurries to make preparations on the *Czarina Catherine* (376), becomes in the 1901 text merely "a hat"—a peculiar omission, as it renders the next phrase "which suit not him or the time," rather meaningless. Another minor inconsistency resulted from the decision to remove Van Helsing's statement to Arthur that "You shall kiss her once before it is done" (159) but to leave in on the following page "You may take that one little kiss."

The preceding discussion has focused primarily on deletions. But in a few cases there were changes and even additions. Most of these were occasioned by the need for new transitions to accommodate the removal of portions of text and do not merit any comment. However, that Stoker (or his editor) read at least parts of the text carefully for this abridgement is evident in the fact that some of the errors are corrected: "Hopwood" (82) is corrected to "Holmwood" and "gloated" (302) to "gorged."[6] That

Dracula no longer addresses his newly arrived guest as "Mr. Harker" (23) may indicate a realization that at this stage the Count was still expecting Mr. Hawkins and not his employee. Somebody caught the inconsistency in the journal entries for 30 September: in the original text Seward had stated that the Professor had called a meeting for "nine o'clock" while Mina had said "two hours after dinner, which had been at six o'clock" (286); the first reference appears in 1901 but is changed to "eight."[7] Unfortunately, these errors remain in later editions that followed the 1897 text or its successors.

Had the 1901 text of *Dracula* been the one that went into hundreds of reprints, the whole course of *Dracula* scholarship might have been altered. New historicists would have a text without the two references to Charcot (235). With the removal of the Hebrew with "a nose like a sheep" (413), those who see the text as anti-Semitic would have a weaker case. Lucy's racist remark that she sympathizes with "poor Desdemona [in *Othello*] when she had such a dangerous stream poured in her ear, even by a black man" (76–77) is no longer there. Post-colonialist criticism would be affected with the elimination of some of the condescending remarks about Transylvania: that the women were "clumsy about the waist" (5), that the dinner at the Golden Krone in Bistritz was "in the simple style of the London cat's-meat" (5, 9), that the trains were late and the roads bad. Also removed was of one of the key lines of text —the oft-quoted "The impression I had was that we were leaving the West and entering the East" (1). Likewise a great impact would have been made on feminist readings. Not only were all references to the "New Woman" removed, but so was that famous declaration made by Lucy: "Why can't they let a girl marry three men, or as many as want her, and save all this trouble?" (78).

Is it possible that Stoker or his editor was aware of the subtexts in his novel and was deliberately eliminating some of them? This could explain the removal of a line such as "as it would have been to have stripped off her clothing in her sleep whilst living" (242) and the omission of Van Helsing's reference to Lucy as a "polyandrist" (a euphemism for "prostitute" in Stoker's time).[8] Yet one of the most erotic sections of the novel, Jonathan's seduction by the three voluptuous females, is left in. An examination of the changes suggests that the decisions were somewhat arbitrary, with no clear rationale beyond cutting text that was (at least at that time) considered expendable. Ultimately, it is immaterial. For what we have are two texts of *Dracula*, each the product of a Bram Stoker and hence each equally valid. Regardless of the fact that it is an abridged (and inferior) text, the 1901 edition stands on its own. Although it went into obscurity and has never been in contention (as in the case of *Frankenstein)* as the definitive text of *Dracula*, its resurfacing opens up the potential for readings of the novel that conflict with each other.

NOTES

1. It was reprinted in 1994 by Transylvania Press, with a Foreword by Robert Eighteen-Bisang and an Introduction by Raymond McNally.

2. That Stoker himself made the changes has been claimed by Ludlam (136) and reiterated by Eighteen-Bisang in his Foreword to the 1994 reprint. I have not been able to substantiate this.

3. I would make one qualification: the superb cover illustration, which depicts Count

Dracula crawling, bat-like, down the castle wall.

4. Though in this instance, maybe someone had a flash of insight and noted the inconsistency (drawn to our attention by Leonard Wolf, *Essential Dracula* (149, n.22) that later on the professor is at the Berkeley.

5. Fortunately, one key Byronic reference remains: the phrase "decay's effacing fingers" (207) is from *The Giaour,* the poem that contains Byron's famous "vampire curse."

6. This latter change solves the mystery alluded to by Leonard Wolf. —"This is a strange use of the word 'gloated,' which normally is the past tense of the verb to 'gloat.' Stoker may have written 'bloated,' which would make the 'g' a typographer's error" *(Essential Dracula* 302, n.5).

7. However, the same "somebody" missed the dating error of Seward's diary entry of "25 April" (80).

8. *OED* cites from the *Pall Mall Gazette* 14 July 1887 a reference to "attempts to make the regulation of the movements of female polyandrists a police function."

WORKS CITED

Dalby, Richard. *Bram Stoker: A Bibliography of First Editions*. London: Dracula Press, 1983.

Ludlum, Harry. *A Bibliography of Bram Stoker, Creator of Dracula*. 1962. London: New English Library, 1977.

Riccardo, Martin. *Vampires Unearthed: The Complete Multi-Media Vampire and Dracula Bibliography*. New York: Garland Publishers, 1983.

Stoker, Bram. *Dracula: The Rare Text of 1901*. Ed. With Foreword by Robert Eighteen-Bisang. Introduction by Raymond McNally. White Rock, BC: Transylvania Press 1994.

Wolf, Leonard, ed. *The Essential Dracula: The Definitive Annotated Edition of Bram Stoker's Classic Novel*. New York: Penguin, 1993.

Chapter 2

Bram Stoker and Irish Gothic

Raymond T. McNally

At the outset I would like to clarify what I am not going to do and what I am going to try to do in this short chapter: my approach is that of an historian and not that of a literary critic. In addition, my field of specialization is not Irish history, nor Irish literature. I am somewhat familiar with Russian and East European history, especially the life of the Romanian ruler Vlad Dracula, nicknamed "The Impaler" (1431–1476), and I do know a little bit about the life of Bram Stoker (1847–1912). (The latest and best biography is Barbara Belford, *Bram Stoker: A Biography of the Author of Dracula* [Alfred Knopf: New York, 1996]).

In general, I have been greatly influenced by the works of the so-called revisionist of Irish history, R. F. Foster, especially his book *Modern Ireland 1600–1972*, published in 1988. (Although I must agree with the criticism by my colleague at Boston College, Professor Kevin O'Neil, that Foster's "attitude towards the Irish abroad is paranoid, especially when compared to his general 'moderate' tone. He finds the 'Irish identity of emigrant communities "anachronistic" and "fiercely unrealistically obsessive".'" [First published as "Revisionist Milestone" in the *Irish Literary Supplement*, Fall 1989, pp. 1, 39 and reprinted in *Interpreting Irish History: The Debate on Historical Revisionism 1938–1994*, Ciaran Brady, ed. (Dublin: Irish Academic Press, 1994, p. 221)]. However, in particular, I do agree with Foster's "hope of a more relaxed and inclusive definition of Irishness" (Foster 596), thus including the so-called Protestant Anglo-Irish,—a hope exemplified, in my opinion, among other things, by the plaques recently erected in memory of the places associated with Bram Stoker in the city of Dublin. (Brendan Behan when asked to define a city said that it was a place where one stands in little danger of being attacked by a wild sheep; I feel it's as good an Irish definition of Dublin as any other.)

My slender hope is that I may be able to view this complicated topic with fresh eyes, especially as I plan to compare briefly the situation of the Russian gentry and that of Ireland during the late nineteenth century. I shall begin by defining what I mean by the word "Gothic," used in this case as an adjective to describe a specific type of literature that arose during the late eighteenth century and flourished in the nineteenth century, especially among Irish authors writing in English. Then I shall attempt to clarify its connection with the adjective "Irish," which I use not in a racial or ethnic sense or quasi-religious notion of Catholic, but rather in a cultural context, though I realize that to some even today to be Irish is to be Catholic and vice versa, much in the way that some Poles think that to be Catholic means to be Polish,—as the current pontiff sometimes seems to imply. Behind all these issues is the central question: Why do Irish authors so dominate the Gothic in English literature?

In the late eighteenth century during the heyday of Neoclassicism, art critics invariably used the term "Gothic" in a pejorative sense, referring to medieval cathedrals with their apparent lack of architecturally classic balance so unlike the Parthenon. The French *philosophes* used the term "Gothic" to label certain art or literature as coarse, uncouth and barbaric. The eighteenth century critics also favored Aristotle's *Poetics* as a model for drama, with its emphasis on evoking pity and fear by depicting the fall of a noble man through a 24-hour setting on stage and with all action necessarily confined to the same place.

The Romantic breakthrough of the late eighteenth century was an actual revolution in literary taste that challenged these values, which were based on an assumption of basic uniformity among humans. Instead, the Romantic opted for diversity, the strange, the unusual, and often even the grotesque. Emphasis shifted away from the expectations of the audience to the unleashings of the creative geniuses like Beethoven, whose symphonies were often branded as cacophony or "bad vibes." What many critics failed to understand is that from the outset Gothic literature was aimed not at an aristocracy but at the widest audience possible. It was often light reading not only for women but also for men of the new rising literate middle class.

Gothic literature often sought to create a sense of dread, combined with mystery, miracles, and wonderment. Horace P. Walpole (1717–1796), a tall, slender English bachelor of pale complexion, often dressed in partridge-colored silk stockings, gold buckles, and a lavender suit, actually began the trend. After attending Eton and Cambridge University, he went on the traditional Grand Tour of Europe to France and Italy in the company of his old Eton schoolmate Thomas Gray, "the graveyard poet." Walpole, a victim of gout, had plenty of time and money on his hands to indulge his fantasies. He devoted two decades and a good deal of cash to constructing an imitation medieval castle on his estate called Strawberry Hill. In a way, Walpole was the Walt Disney of his day, as his estate was an early version of a private Disneyland where almost anything could happen. The style inspired the buildings of Trinity College, Yale, and Boston College in the United States, to name but a few constructed in "bastard Gothic style."

Walpole decided to try his hand at being a writer. His inspiration, he says, came from a nightmare; he wrote: "I waked one morning, in the beginning of last June [1764] from a dream, of which all I could recover was that I had thought myself in an ancient castle . . . and that on the upper-most banister of a great staircase I saw a gigantic hand in amour. In the evening I sat down to write," and with that Walpole set off the opening salvo in the Gothic revolution. The subtitle that he bestowed on his book *The Castle of Otranto* was, significantly, *A Gothic Story*. Initially somewhat unsure of his talents, he did not identify himself as the author. Like so many other later Gothic writers, he maintained the fiction in the book that it came from an old manuscript that he had turned up and that it was hence based on real people and actual places, as in Bram Stoker's *Dracula*. The emphasis on arcane or antique documents thus became a staple in many subsequent Gothic tales; in addition, the following elements are often part of the definition of a Gothic story:

1.   the ominous, vast, ancient castle as the setting with its long deserted wings and damp corridors;
2.   the darkly handsome, tyrannical, dangerous evil nobleman as the seeming villain;
3.   the insipid, virginal, and generally naive heroine who is pursued by the handsome villain who appears to threaten her "with a fate worse than death";
4.   the valiant hero who ultimately saves the girl and generally also solves the entirely awkward situation;
5.   the convention of foreign names for many of the characters, thereby adding an exotic, alien atmosphere to the story; and
6.   the miraculous occurrences, as lamps suddenly go out, trap doors are found, and secret passageways appear as props.

Two major trends developed in the Gothic tradition: to depict the miracles as part of acceptable, everyday life; or else to explain away the seeming miracles on rationalistic or scientific grounds. Walpole presented the strange happenings as real, and that is the style inherited by Stoker and other Irish authors; whereas the Scotsman Arthur Conan Doyle, famed author of the Sherlock Holmes series, was more in the tradition of Ann Radcliffe and Clara Reeves in which the seemingly miraculous was explained away.

In my opinion, Irish writers turned out to be some of the best authors of Gothic tales partly because fantasy always was a traditionally strong element in most Irish story telling since time immemorial. I would classify these Irish writers into three groups: the Irish who stayed home, those in exile, and those who found their way back home. What makes the Gothic of these writers Irish is that there is generally no interest in past medieval times; instead, as W. J. McCormack points out, "Irish gothic fiction is remarkably explicit in the way it demonstrates its attachment to history and to politics" ("Irish Gothic and Beyond" 833). It is my theory that there was no interest in medieval horrors in Ireland because the horrors of the day sufficed; the case, I think, was similar in Russia and Eastern Europe.

In my mind three Irish authors form what I consider to be the Unholy Trinity of Irish Gothic: namely, Charles Robert Maturin (1782–1824), Joseph Sheridan Le Fanu (1814–1873), and Bram Stoker (1847–1912); but they obviously had their precursors and descendants. One significant forerunner who deserves a bit more research was William Hamilton Maxwell (1792–1850). After service in the British army, he became a Church of Ireland clergyman and was shipped off to remote Ballagh in County Mayo. Maxwell wrote *The Fortunes of Hector O'Halloran and his Man Mark Anthony O'Toole*, published in 1842. (In my opinion, such funny names are usually found in the writings of either Irish or Russian authors; an example in the latter group is Nikolai Gogol in the latter group whose anti-hero in the *Overcoat* is named Akakii Akakievich, which is a funny name to Russian readers. O'Halloran's dog in Maxwell's story is named, as you might guess, Caesar. And no one need remind you of Caesar's accounts of the barbarous Brits?)

Maxwell's novel is set in 1795 just after the Irish had stirred up a great deal of trouble and caused worries among the Anglo-Irish landowning class. Here the "Big House" dominates, a characteristic of Irish Gothic. (By the way, significantly, in American dialect, "the Big House" is a slang expression referring to a prison.) There is a lot of ethnic and religious ambiguity in the story, typical for Victorian Ireland. For example, the hero's mother is an English Catholic and his father is Protestant but with an old Gaelic family name.

Most Irish Gothic writers were tied to the old Established Church of Ireland, which was quickly unraveling in their day. Both Maxwell and Maturin were ordained ministers in the Church of Ireland (in fact, Maturin rejected a career open to him as a civil servant to become a clergyman in the Anglican church); Le Fanu was the son of a Church of Ireland dean. Class and religion often went together, but sometimes in peculiar ways. Most of these writers were from the Irish middle class, not from the old landowning class. They were no living vampires, sucking the life's blood from Irish peasants as the Ascendancy types often appeared to the common people. Maturin and Le Fanu came from Huguenot merchant class roots, not landed gentry. Stoker's father was a stolid bureaucrat, a clerk in Dublin Castle, as was Bram himself until he chose to manage the affairs of Henry Irving. Stoker's brother was a medical doctor who became head of the Irish Royal College of Surgeons and was knighted by Queen Victoria in 1895, and, of course, Oscar Wilde's father was a medical doctor. In short, there was no long pedigree of landowning status among most of these writers, which might explain how many of them, like Bram Stoker, could find joy in taking pot shots at the dominating class. Charles Maturin, who attended Trinity College, Dublin, like Bram Stoker and Oscar Wilde, published his first novel, *Fatal Revenge*, under the pseudonym Dennis Jasper Murphy in 1807 and *Melmoth the Wanderer* in 1820. Once a very popular Romantic novel, *Melmoth* is still read by students on the continent. It is partially based on the old legend of the Wandering Jew, particularly the version that a Jew who was asked to help Christ carry his cross refused, and so Christ condemned him to perpetual wandering.

Melmoth, himself a Trinity College student, goes to his uncle's County Wicklow estate, which is falling apart. The hero recalls that "The first of the Melmoths . . . who settled in Ireland, was an officer in Cromwell's army, who obtained . . . the confiscated property of an Irish family attached to the royal cause." His dying uncle has lost all faith in the old order; his mind is as disorderly as his house. Eventually, through perusing an old document meant to "verify untrue things" in the language of Dogberry, the Melmoth descendant finds out that this other Melmoth has sold his soul to the devil for 150 years of life. But there is a typically Irish escape clause: Melmoth can get released from his contract with the devil and avoid damnation provided that he can find someone worse off than himself and hence willing to take his place in the devil's bargain for his soul. In the Ireland of his day one did not have to look for such a type. Melmoth finds unfortunate people on the edge of complete despair, but ironically he can find no one willing to accept his offer. In the end, after a significantly final visit to his ancestral home (Irish Gothic characters, like Irish Americans, often return home for farewell visits), he disappears over a cliff.

Joseph Sheridan Le Fanu's first story appeared in the *Dublin University Magazine*, a publication with no connection to Dublin University and of which Le Fanu later became the main editor (from 1869 to 1872). Le Fanu's short story "A Chapter in the History of a Tyrone Family," published in the October 1839 issue of the *Dublin University Magazine*, contained a plot that is almost the same as that of Charlotte Brontë *Jane Eyre*, which was published eight years later in 1847 (although I am not thereby suggesting that she stole it). In Le Fanu's famous short story "Green Tea," published in *In a Glass Darkly* in 1872, we encounter a clergyman "with a natty, old-fashioned, high-church precision," Mr. Jennings, who is haunted by a malignant monkey on his back. Dr. Martin Hesselius, who is one poorly equipped doctor, thinks that it's all in Jenning's mind, a mere ghost. He is not one to worry—until Jennings is driven to suicide. Written in the year Gladstone abandoned the Church of Ireland, the story is full of anxiety. Especially when the monkey interferes with Jenning's attempts to do his job, we can see reflections of the traditional *Punch* magazine drawings of the Irish as the missing-link ape-men. In the end the clergyman feels wholly abandoned in the hands of an incompetent doctor, much in the way that the Anglo-Irish felt abandoned by their incompetent British counterparts. It is possible that the ineffectual medical doctor in the story, Dr. Hesselius, a psychic investigator, may have been one of the many inspirations for Bram Stoker's only slightly more competent Dr. Abraham Van Helsing. (Van Helsing is probably as responsible for Lucy's death as Hesselius is for Jenning's demise; in Van Helsing's case, although medical doctors of his day did not know all about blood types, any physician should have realized that too many blood transfusions would result in the death of the patient.)

In Le Fanu's tale "The Familiar," supposedly taken from notes given to Dr. Hesselius by a "venerable Irish clergyman," poor Captain Barton, after serving in the British navy on a frigate during the American War, has returned to Dublin in 1794, fearful of a Demon or Watcher haunting him. After trying unsuccessfully to shake off the Demon by fleeing to England, Barton returns again to Ireland and, due to his unstable mental situation, is removed by relatives to the house of Lady L——— "in the neighborhood of Clontarf." There, confined to this Big House, another case of the garrison mentality of the so called Anglo-Irish, the unfortunate Barton "never daring to cherish a hope of his ultimate emancipation from the horrors under which his life was literally wasting away" encounters the Watcher in the form of an owl, which drives him to inevitable suicide (cited in Tremayne, 95).

But it is in Le Fanu's great novelette *Carmilla* that we find the flowering of the peculiarly Irish Gothic. (In fact, I was so impressed by that work that I included it in my anthology *A Clutch of Vampires*, which contains what I consider to be the best vampire stories from history and from literature over the past two thousand years.) The heroine, Laura, tells us at once that "My father is English, and I bear an English name, although I never saw England." Is this not also the case for many of the Anglo-Irish?

Sadomasochism is linked up with colonial exploitation in Le Fanu's story as it is in Stoker's novel, as the strange elder vampire comes to dominate the young girl. As Laura put it, the elder Countess would often hold her hand, "Blushing softly, gazing in my face with languid and burning, eyes, and breathing so fast that her dress rose and fell with tumultuous respiration. It was like the ardour of a love . . . and she would whisper almost in sobs, 'You are mine, you shall be mine," steamy lines that could have been written by Stoker. (You may recall Stoker's depiction of Jonathan Harker's erotic encounter with the vampire women in Castle Dracula, where one of them goes down on her knees, and, as Stephen King has pointed out, a girl who goes down on her knees is not likely to be one whom you would bring home and introduce to mother!)

Finally, we come to Bram Stoker's Irish Gothic style. First of all, Bram thought of himself as deeply Irish. In fact, letters in the archives of Trinity College, Dublin, provide evidence that Bram suffered an Irishman's feeling of being shamed by the British overlords. When his brother, William Thornley, head of the Irish Royal College of Surgeons, invited the new British lieutenant governor to dinner, the stupid Brit refused on the basis that he could not accept a "personal" invitation. As Bram pointed out, this was no "personal invitation," but one from an official head of the Irish Royal College of Surgeons; so, to Bram, this was just another typical example of how the British disdain the Irish and do not treat Irish properly as British citizens.

It is not my purpose here to recount the Dracula story but only to point out that Transylvania is, in my opinion, really Ireland. Stoker never even visited Transylvania, except through travel books, whereas he was raised and grew up in Ireland, and there is a critical consensus that if he had set his popular novel in the west of Ireland he would be recognized as one of Ireland's major writers.

It is well known that Stoker's mother, who was from Sligo, told him stories from her native land, especially tales of cholera, when people were sometimes buried alive, and they fed his boyhood imagination in a way which was never possible for that other devotee of the occult, W. B. Yeats, who only first encountered fairies in the reading room of the British Museum.

Transylvania is at a minimum a metaphor for Ireland, as both Transylvania and Ireland are frontier territories on the fringes of the empire, fought over often by foreigners. The term "the land beyond the forest" has the meaning of the unknown "land beyond the clouds" where almost anything can happen. The common people are as superstitious and as "wild" as Irish peasants were thought to be. The dominant class to which Dracula belongs is alien to the common people. He claims that he is different ethnically from his subjects: he belongs to "a great and noble race" of conquering Szecklys tracing lineage back to Atilla the Hun. He disdains his native peasants as cowards.

Similarly to both vampires and werewolves the Transylvanian landowning aristocracy fed on their subjects. Stoker often laughed about the Dracula character with his friends, as if it were an Irishman's revenge on the British landowning aristocracy. Stoker particularly enjoyed the fact, as he said that "he made his vampire monster wait hand and foot on Jonathan Harker . . . at the castle." After all, in life turn about is fair play! Even when the evil Count opens the door to invite Harker out to face a pack of hungry, howling wolves, the aristocrat still talks, as Harker put it, "with a sweet courtesy which made me rub my eyes it seemed so real." Oh, how Anglo-Irish landowners could speak the King's English in mellifluous tones as they invited the sheep out to be slaughtered and noted the silence of the lambs!

It is widely known that it was a Dubliner who looked the Big House in the eye and exposed it for the corruption and decadence which it had enjoyed and flaunted over the yokels and rustics for over a hundred years. The Anglo-Irish fostered a sometimes confused identity that was often more class conscious than ethnic. The term "Protestant Ascendancy" was first systematically used in the early 1790s, according to Foster (*Modern Ireland*, 170). The designation meant specifically the exclusivity of Anglicanism, which formed a social not an ethnic elite both in England and Ireland. In Ireland the Anglo-Irish had a "complex relationship to England—stemming from their position of conscious but resented dependence" (*Modern Ireland*, 173). (However, it seems to me important to recall that the dictionary generally defines "ascendancy" as "domination" and, as an example, quotes Churchill, who said, "Germany only waits trade revival to gain an immense mercantile ascendancy.") There is no doubt that the Protestant dominant group often felt themselves superior to the Irish and somehow destined to try to control the wild natives, whom the Brits considered as either childlike or animal-like.

Certainly after 1720 most educated Anglo-Irish often thought of themselves as Irish, though there was some doubt as to whether they wished others to call them Irish. As for the writers from that general group, literary historians have labeled this group of writers the Ascendancy because labeling them as a group reduces them to manageable proportions. This label is also given to those writers who have persued the most characteristic genre of Anglo-Irish literature, the novel of the Big House.
The Big House, the home of the landlord, dominated the Irish countryside for so long it became a symbol of grandeur, oppression, superiority, cruelty, attainment, or decline, depending one the writer's point of view.

The focus was Trinity College, but getting an education at Trinity did not insure becoming a member of the ruling elite known as the Ascendancy. Two examples of two widely divergent paths may suffice here: Edmund Burke (1729–1797), born in Dublin, father Protestant and mother Catholic, educated at Trinity, a radical in his youth, and, frightened by the excesses of the French Revolution, somewhat conservative in his old age, especially in his *Reflections on the Revolution in France* (1790); Theobald Wolfe Tone (1763–1799) born in Dublin, educated at Trinity, leader of abortive French expeditions to Ireland in 1796 and 1798, and a revolutionary who, when captured, committed suicide on being refused a soldier's death.

As early as the eighteenth century in his infamous "Modest Proposal," Jonathan Swift (1667–1747), whose book popularly known as *Gulliver's Travels* embodied more than a few covert references to Ireland, had English civilians dining on the flesh of native Irish children in a tasty stew, much in the way that Dracula sucks the life's blood from his peasants. William Blake (1757–1827) is another Irishman but in exile in England, as his parents were Irish; in fact, his father, John O'Neil, changed his name to Blake when he married his fiancee Ellen Blake, in order to escape money problems. The American writer Edgar Allan Poe was of Irish parentage, and his parents, in fact, brought him to Ireland as a boy. We all know about Poe's uncanny gift for fantasy and horror short stories.

The Brontë sisters, who were Irish, published their famed novels in 1847, the year Stoker was born: Emily Brontë's *Wuthering Heights* and Charlotte Brontë's *Jane Eyre*. Surely the wild, attractive Heathcliff of *Wuthering Heights* and the mysterious, somber, tall, dark, and handsome Mr. Robinson of *Jane Eyre* are literary ancestors of Dracula; and Mr. Robinson's insane wife is actually compared to the awful presence of a vampire in that novel.

Other Irish in exile, contemporaries of Bram Stoker, come also to mind: not only Oscar Wilde, author of *The Picture of Dorian Gray*, first published in July 1890, but also Bernard Shaw and later James Joyce and Samuel Beckett. Fitz-James O'Brien (1828–1862), born in Limerick, went to Trinity, then joined the American army during the Civil War along with thousands of other Irish immigrants forming the Union Army's Irish Brigade, and he met his untimely death in one of the bloodiest battle of that bloody war. And one strange Irish fantasy writer who belongs to those rare ones who found their way home was M. P. Shiel (1865–1947), born of Irish parents in the West Indies; his father was a Methodist preacher who took the family back to Ireland.

Dracula resides in his decaying Big House with its battered battlements. Dracula embodies the kind of isolated "garrison mentality" common to the English landowning class in Ireland. His days of glory and colonial type of exploitation are over. So now, he, the alien, plans to reverse the colonial process and conquer England. So, in a strange way, he also embodies the English fear of reverse colonialism, like that Irishman Stoker who came to London and took over the management of its most illustrious theater and most notable actor.

Times were tough for the English in Ireland, beginning in 1717 with the abolition of the Penal Laws, which had once secured Protestant dominance. The rising of the United Irishmen in 1798 renewed the fears. Catholic Emancipation in 1829 and the Disestablishment of the Church of Ireland signified the demise of the Old Order. Bram Stoker was born in 1847 during the worse year of the potato blight known as the Great Famine. The Ascendancy was slowly losing control of the land. Stoker's reference to the wonders of the Ordinance maps re-echoed the Ordinance Survey campaign designed to help bring law and order to the "wild natives" of Ireland. And the popularity of social Darwinism sent many British in search of natural laws to define and justify both Englishness and Irishness.

A comparison between the Russian gentry and the Anglo-Irish aristocracy reveals significant similarities and differences: during the late nineteenth century the Russian gentry feared a massive, bloody peasant uprising led by what they called a "Pugachev a l'universite," referring to the mass peasant uprising led by the uneducated Pughahev during the time of Catherine the Great with the warning that it would be worse if led by some educated rebel in the near future. As we have seen, the Anglo-Irish ascendancy had similar fears about an Irish peasant uprising led by those educated in the principles of the French Revolution. The main difference between the situation of the Russian gentry and that of the Anglo-Irish landlords is that in Russia both peasants and gentry came from the same ethnic stock, whereas in Ireland the general situation was sometimes different.

The British overlords, many infected with social Darwinism, claimed that

Englishmen were manly and adult in behavior, whereas the Irish were childish and feminine, and notoriously disloyal, like most women of their day, much in the same way that the British depicted the Hindus of India whom they had to dominate as part of The White Man's oh-so-reluctant Burden. As Declan Kiberd put it, "at the root of many an Englishman's suspicion of the Irish was an unease at the woman or child who lurked within himself" (87).

Stoker's novel echoes this sexual ambiguity and its fears. For example, need I remind you that Dracula attacks Harker, a male, first. In many ways, Dracula is both a woman and a man. The late Gothic specialist Sir Devendra P. Varma hit on the Gothic writers' "feelings of nostalgia and terror," (217), how those feelings are so characteristic of so many Anglo-Irish writers. What terrible things were bound to happen once the Irish, who were obviously so unfit to rule themselves, quite like the French, ever got infected with the French madness. As Varma pointed out, "writers were conscious of the decadence of the old order, the future seemed to offer them no hope" (218).

One later Irish writer who retreated into inner exile was Lord Dunsany (1878–1957). Born of an Ascendancy family claiming the second oldest title in the Irish peerage, Edward John Moreton Drax Plunkett was an odd ball, an atheist who did not conform to the common image of the Ascendancy landowning cast of Anglicans. His family heritage is a revealing one: the Plunketts had stuck to Catholicism throughout the worst persecutions until in 1713; the then Baron Dunsany of County Meath converted to Protestantism. If traditional Irishness left out the Anglicans, then what about the atheists? In 1932 when Yeats founded the Irish Academy of Letters he foolishly, in my opinion, omitted Dunsany on the puerile grounds that up to that point Dunsany had not written about Ireland but about imaginary places. (What more imaginary place could you write about than Ireland?) But Dunsany had his revenge on Yeats when Dunsany publicly announced the formation of an a society to honor Italian writers and deliberately omitted Dante because "Dante did not write about Italy, but of a very different place. Most unsuitable."

One of my favorite Dunsany tales is "The Ghost of the Valley," which successfully combines both fantasy and humor, as I think Brain Stoker did in his *Dracula*. In "The Ghost of the Valley," the writer encounters a ghost and asks:

"Who are you" and so small and shrill was the answer, that at first I thought it was birds of the reeds and water that spoke. "A ghost," it seemed to be saying. "What?" said I. And then more clearly it said, "Have you never seen ghosts before?" . . . "And you?" I asked. "I am going," it said. "Why?" I asked it. "Times are changing," it said. "The old firesides are altering, and they are poisoning the river, and the smoke of the cities is unwholesome, like your bread. I am going away among unicorns, griffons, and wiverns." "But there are such things?" I asked. "There used to be," it replied. But I was growing impatient at being lectured to by a ghost and was a little chilled by the mist. "Are there such things as ghosts?" I asked then. And a wind blew then, and the ghost was suddenly gone. "We used to be," it sighed softly. (35)

Similarly, as a Dracula expert, I am frequently asked, "Are there really such things as vampires? or, more poignantly, "Do you believe in vampires?" To which I often reply, "What do you think I am anyway? I'm a teacher, not a preacher. In my life

I have never met an undead, so until I do, I cannot personally believe in such a thing. But I do listen when other people tell me that vampires exist, because they are usually describing something that is real to them, so I try to figure out what they mean. It's like detective work. Some people still like to believe in Santa Claus and the Easter Bunny. They need myths."

Stoker's Dracula is, after all, not a very versatile sexual figure; in fact, he or she is quite limited sexually. All he or she can perform is oral sex; it's as if he or she were sexually paralyzed from the waist down, or perhaps there is no penis. Dr. Van Helsing often refers to Dracula as having a child's mind; Dracula is a child halted at the oral stage of sexual development; he or she gets thrills only through the mouth. As McCormack puts-it in a vernacular phrase that I normally would not dare use, but which I now can, as McCormack has put it down in print: "the tragedy of the Count lies in the fact that he is compelled to bite off more than he can screw." Dracula's victims are subjected to "the zipless fuck," to borrow a phrase from Erica Jong's *Fear of Flying*.

Dracula is basically a parasite, not a productive contributor to society. He takes the life's blood from living human beings, as do the living vampires of Ireland, the landowning declining class in the people's imagination. He has no sense of community. He is the ultimate loner. That is why he is bound to fail, especially when the vampire hunters form a community against him. I think Stoker in his way was warning that some day the Irish would band together and destroy the alien vampiric aristocracy in Ireland. Hence, in my opinion, in more ways than one, Stoker's novel *Dracula* is Irish.

WORKS CITED

Day, William Patrick. *In the Circles of Fear and Desire*. Chicago: U of Chicago P, 1985.

Deane, Seamus. "Civilians and Barbarians." in *Ireland's Field Day*, ed. Seamus Deane, et al. London: Hutchinson, 1985.

Dunsany, Edward, John, Moreton, Drax, Plonckett, Baron. *The Last Book of Wonder*. Boston: J.W. Luce, 1916

Foster, R. F. *Modern Ireland 1600–1972*. London: Allen Lane, The Penguin Press, 1988.

Hatlen, Burton. "The Return of the Repressed/Oppressed in Bram Stoker's Dracula." In *Dracula: The Vampire and the Critics*. Ed. Margaret Carter. Ann Arbor: UMI Research Press, 1988.

Kiberd, Declan. "Anglo-Irish Attitudes." In *Ireland's Field Day Anthology of Irish Writing*. Ed. Seamus Deane, et al. Derry, Northern Ireland: Field Publications, 1991.

Le Fanu, Joseph Sheridan. *In a Glass Darkly*. New York: Oxford UP, 1993.

———. *Uncle Silas*. New York: Arno Press, 1977.

Maturin, Charles Robert. *Melmoth the Wanderer*. London: Oxford, UP, 1968.

McCormack, W. J. "Irish Gothic and Beyond." *In The Field Day Anthology of Irish Writings*. Ed. Seamus Deane, et al. Derry, Northern Ireland: Field Day Publications, 1991.

———. *Sheridan Le Fanu and Victorian Ireland*. New York: Oxford UP, 1980. Sage, Victor. *Horror Fiction in the Protestant Tradition*. New York: St. Martin's Press, 1988.

Swift, Jonathan. *Swift's Irish Pamphlets*. Ed. McMinn. Gerrards Cross, Buckinghamshire: Colin Smythe, 1991.

Tremayne, Peter. *Irish Masters of Fantasy*. Dublin: Wolfhound Press, 1979.
Varma, Devendra P. *The Gothic Flame*. Metuchen, NJ: Scarecrow Press, 1987.

Chapter 3

Dracula's Reflection:
The Jewel of Seven Stars

Katie Harse

In the introduction to his edition of *The Jewel of Seven Stars*, Clive Leatherdale suggests that "Egypt . . . mirrors the Transylvania of *Dracula*" (11); although Phyllis Roth contends that *Jewel* is a "paler copy" of *Dracula's* "sharply-etched original" (74), the mirror metaphor is more appropriate. A mirror-image is a reversal, and a mirror can also magnify, distort, or obscure. Indeed, *Jewel* plays all these tricks with themes apparent in *Dracula*, which, on the surface, it resembles: there is the same group of stalwart, middle-class men, plus one good, and sometimes imperiled, woman—Margaret Trelawny, daughter of the group's leader, the Egyptologist Abel Trelawny. They are also confronted by a supernatural aristocrat, in this case the ancient Egyptian Sorceress—Queen, Tera, whom the protagonists will attempt to resurrect according to instructions taken from her tomb.

However, where *Jewel* is most interesting in its own right is precisely where it reflects and diverges from *Dracula*: namely, in its treatment of otherness, which is more ambiguous and potentially more subversive. What was perceived as its disturbing lack of clarity is evident in the reviews that greeted *Jewel's* publication in 1903. *The Spectator* disparages the novel's "contradictory mysteries," and suggests that "what happens in the last scene only Mr. Bram Stoker can understand" (298), while an otherwise positive review in the *New York Times* admits, nonetheless, that "it would be impossible to say just what one really does think of . . .'The Jewel of Seven Stars'" (157).

To return to Leatherdale's statement about Egypt and Transylvania, this is perhaps the most obvious site of comparison as the two settings do, indeed, reflect each other in reverse. While Tera is "other" in that she is not English, her otherness differs from that of Dracula, who originates in "one of the wildest and least known portions of Europe" (Stoker, i), a place that is, as Burton Hatlen notes, both "primitive" and "barbaric" (126) in contrast to English "technology, rationality, and progress" (125). While Tera's Egypt is unmistakably exotic, it is also, as David

Glover notes, "surprisingly advanced" (*Vampires*, 85), even in comparison to modern England. Abel Trelawny observes that "the Egyptians knew sciences, of which to-day, despite all our advantages, we are profoundly ignorant" (Stoker, 175) and his aim is to "let in on the world of modern science such a flood of light from the Old World as will change every condition of thought and experiment and practice" (106). Ancient Egypt is, significantly, a source of knowledge and "light" in direct opposition to unknown Transylvania's "vast darkness" (Hatlen, 125).[1]

The protagonists' faith in, and admiration for, Egyptian learning, is not simply a matter of belief in occult possibilities, akin to Van Helsing's instructions to "have an open mind" (193). While Van Helsing criticizes Seward's refusal to believe anything but scientific evidence, and confirms the folk beliefs of Transylvanian peasants, Trelawny and his followers consider Tera's arts, not in relation to the "superstitious fears" (119) of the twentieth-century Egyptians whom the archaeologists employ, but explicitly as science, albeit indistinguishable from magic in a culture that is less technologically advanced, in this case—surprisingly—England.

If Egypt is technologically superior, however, it is not necessarily morally so, a distinction that is, ironically, revealed when Trelawny takes pains to establish that Tera has "foresight far, far beyond her age and the philosophy of her time" and "seems to have seen through the weakness of her own religion" (173). Thus, he sets the queen apart from what Roth calls "the heated passion and violence of the desert" (73). Trelawny claims that "all [Tera's] aspirations were for the North, the point of the compass whence blew the cool invigorating breezes" (173), but the protagonists' projection of this dream of Northern purity onto the Egyptian queen serves, in turn, to justify their own imperialist project: the removal of the queen's mummy to England (not only a robbery, but an act of kidnapping, as she, like Dracula, is not dead in the conventional sense), and the appropriation of her "Great Experiment," which, as the narrator, Malcolm Ross, notes "was [intended] to be accomplished in the lonely tomb" in Egypt (216), for all Trelawny's rationalization.

These questionable actions compound what Leatherdale calls "the question of evil" (12). Like *Dracula*, *Jewel* does not always present its protagonists in the most favorable light; Trelawny's colleague Corbeck, for example, openly admits to being a thief and a desecrator of tombs and wonders "if indeed, there be any graves for us who have robbed the grave" (144). However, *Jewel* undermines the distinction between "self" and "other" from both sides, presenting Tera as something other than unequivocally evil.

Margaret Trelawny, "born of a dead mother during the time that her father [was] in a trance in the tomb" (213), resembles Tera in an uncanny way and exhibits a "dual existence" (215) that will be familiar to readers of *Dracula*, as it parallels Lucy Westenra's alternation between angelic victim and demonic vampire during her transformation; however, despite the fact that Margaret is occasionally possessed by the spirit of the Egyptian queen, the relationship between the two women is not a simple binary opposition. Margaret resembles Mina Harker, who herself cannot be defined as unproblematically "good," and Tera is no threatening vampiress. First, she literally lacks the physicality necessary to be sexually threatening or seductive; for the most part, she is even more conspicuously absent—at least in body—than Dracula himself. In fact, Margaret's Tera-manifestation disturbs Ross, who is in love with her, in part because of her "intellectual aloofness" (211); not only does he feel he no longer has sole possession of his woman, but he can no longer talk to her!

As Tera does not present the same sexual threat as the voluptuous female vampires in *Dracula*, so her project does not seem to threaten the dominant society as a whole. Although Tera can compel Margaret "to speak or act as instructed" (215), a power similar to Dracula's, her influence is not, properly, contagious and only Margaret's identity is in danger. Tera does not terrify because, in Leatherdale's words, although "England may have feared a vampire epidemic[,] it did not fear being overrun by mummies" (12).

Leatherdale also notes the novel's tendency to portray Tera "as victim, not oppressor" (12). In her own time she was persecuted by priests who feared her as a powerful, educated woman. She has also suffered at the hands of archaeologists, beginning with the Dutch explorer Van Huyn, who was the first to rob her tomb, and whose written account of his discovery prompts Trelawny and Corbeck to begin their quest (117ff), which in turn victimizes Tera. While Ross notes that "nine men that we know of have been slain by her own hand or by her instigation" (217), Margaret argues that the deaths "justly came from meddling with her arrangements and thwarting her purpose. . . . Remember she was fighting for her life!" (220). The queen acts in self-defense, then, or in defense of what is hers.

Thus, Tera may be dangerous, but she is not necessarily evil. Regarding her control of Margaret, Ross notes that, if Tera is "just and kind and clean, all might be well. But if not! . . . The thought was too awful for words" (216). The fact that he even considers the prospect of Tera having noble intentions is enormously significant. In *Dracula*, by contrast, the destruction of the vampires is "necessary" (319) and the vampire-hunters justify their actions in the name of "high duty" (216).

The scene of the "Great Experiment" in the cavern under Trelawny's ancestral home resembles that which takes place in Lucy's tomb in *Dracula*, again seen through a distorting mirror. In both scenes, a group of men surrounds an unconscious woman, but *Jewel* disrupts the symmetry with the presence of Margaret, who calls attention to herself, to the men's actions, and to Tera's position of helplessness. She objects to the unwrapping of Tera: "a woman! All alone! In such a way! . . . It's cruel, cruel!" (236). Trelawny answers that Tera is "not a woman dear [but] a mummy" (236), to which his daughter replies "what does that matter? . . . A woman is a woman, if she had been dead five thousand centuries" (236). Here, Margaret refuses to let the objectification of the woman go unnoticed, and, although her father dismisses her objections with the old stand-by "it is necessary" (237) and the patronizing remark that "they didn't have women's rights or lady doctors in ancient Egypt, my dear!" (236), her protest on Tera's behalf informs the entire scene.

In addition, the object of this gathering obviously differs greatly from that in *Dracula*, which violently suppresses the woman "other" in order to reinscribe the dominant social order. The Great Experiment's purpose is not murder, nor even exorcism, but resurrection. Rather than being contained, the other is unleashed.

The final outcome of the Great Experiment is also *Dracula's* ultimate mirror image and the most obvious instance of ambiguity in *Jewel*. Just as the resurrection is presumably under way, a shutter breaks, interfering with the progress of the magical cloud of green vapor, and filling the room with black smoke. All the lights fail, and Ross carries "a body" (249), which he fears is Margaret's, out of the cavern. Returning with candles, he discovers that "her body was not there. But on the spot where I had laid her was Queen Tera's bridal robe. . . . Where the heart had been, lay the Jewel of Seven Stars" (249). He returns to the cavern to find his companions dead, "gazing upward with fixed eyes of unspeakable terror" (250).

Even at the plot level, the cause of the catastrophe is not clear. The storm could be natural, which would still perhaps indicate the folly of conducting the experiment in Cornwall, rather than Egypt. Otherwise, it may be the work of vengeful Egyptian deities; the priests' inscription on Tera's tomb reads "hither the Gods come not at any summons. . . . Go not nigh, lest their vengeance wither you away!" (132). The text also allows for the possibility that it is the Christian God who is offended here, as Ross speculates as to whether there is "room in the universe for opposing Gods" (191); and Trelawny's single-minded pursuit of knowledge, so focused on "the end of [the] undertaking that all else is of secondary importance" (233), is indeed "Faust-like" as Glover notes ("Introduction," xiii). Finally, the agent of the disaster may be Tera herself, in which case the question is whether she really is evil, or if, rather, she simply resents the indignities she has suffered at the hands of the protagonists.

Perhaps, then, the issue is to what extent the experimenters are responsible for their own demise and why Ross alone survives. Leatherdale implies that Ross's Christian faith saves him (248, n.88); but, although he is shown kneeling in prayer (224), Ross also states that "the moral aspect of the case, which involved the religious belief in which I had been reared was not one to trouble me" (221, emphasis added). The *New York Times* finds fault with Stoker's "giving his narrator the most unadvantageous place, from which it was impossible to see all the proceedings" ("An Egyptian Mystery,"157), but this may be what saves him. Certainly the others have suffered in the time-honored tradition of those who look on the forbidden. Similarly, Ross does not participate in either the violation of Tera's tomb or the disrobing of her person; nor does Margaret, but she, as Tera's double and Trelawny's daughter, is doomed.

Ross is, indeed, the only participant to question the wisdom of the experiment, which he calls "so unnecessary!" (191), and his response to the unrolling of the mummy is equally sensitive. Although he cannot help gazing with desire at Tera's "beautiful form," he also notes that "it was not right that we should be there, gazing with irreverent eyes. . . . it was indecent; it was almost sacrilegious" (241). His shame seems to indicate more than fear and loathing of the female body; he refuses to see Tera as an object, and refers to her as "this woman—I could not think of her as a mummy or a corpse" (241). The possible reasons for Ross's survival, then, are multiple, although Margaret's demise calls most of them into question.

In any case, this much is apparent: the protagonists, including the good woman, die in their attempt to resurrect the Egyptian queen, who seemingly survives. In this— the fact that the "other" is not destroyed—and in its open ending, *Jewel* resembles not *Dracula* but *Frankenstein*. While Ross perceptively notes that what is at stake in the Great Experiment is " the resurrection of the woman, and the woman's life" (218),

Trelawny has loftier ambitions: "what is a woman's life in the scale with what we hope for! . . . . we can be placed on the road to the knowledge of lost arts, lost learning, lost sciences" (218–19). For the furthering of knowledge, and for his own glory, Trelawny proposes to keep Tera as a sort of pet oracle, a personal reference library, and it may be that he and the others perish because they presume an authority they do not have, either over Tera's experiment, or over forbidden knowledge more generally. By contrast, Tera, who would otherwise have been Trelawny's creature, is allowed to escape and becomes a subject in her own right. While the heroes in *Dracula* successfully contain the vampire other, Tera is not even contained by the narrative!

The lack of closure, as well as the lack of clarity, and perhaps its ambivalence regarding the relative positions and fates of the self and the other, proved disturbing enough to readers of *Jewel* that the original ending was not reprinted in the second, or subsequent, editions, but was replaced by one in which Margaret and the others survive, while all that remains of Tera is "a scattering of black ashes" (255). However, although the revised version appears to offer a final scene of domestic bliss comparable to that of *Dracula*—Ross and Margaret live happily ever after—it actually makes no more sense than the original. Even Ross admits "we never got a clue to what had happened" (255); no storm interrupts the experiment, but still it fails, producing a morally acceptable anticlimax, rather than a satisfying resolution.

If the 1912 ending is inconsistent, and the 1903 version hopelessly obscure—at least in the minds of reviewers—it is interesting to note how the confusion of the reader over the narrative's content, which either "resists interpretation" (Glover, "Introduction," ix) or generates "multiple interpretations" (Leatherdale, 250, n.99), mirrors that which the characters experience at the level of the plot. The text is full of gaps, instances of interrupted speech, and deliberate omissions. Secrecy abounds in *Dracula*, but the sheer, vast number of secrets in *Jewel* is nothing less than inspiring. Although, even more so than the earlier novel, which contains more action, *Jewel* relies on narrative and dialogue to propel the plot forward, it seems that no two characters can have a conversation in which they share the whole truth. The result is that no one ever really knows exactly what is happening, and this lack of knowledge affects the reader as well.

However, as "secrecy is everything" (94), so "ignorance [is] helplessness" (90)— the novel's fundamental contradiction. Even "reality is suspect" here, as Leatherdale observes (11), but the characters frequently take refuge in scientific details, or in scientific method, as an antidote to much larger issues of confusion: to Ross the very act of "analys[ing] the evidence before [him]" (213) is as important to soothing his doubts concerning Margaret as the facts themselves, while Trelawny demonstrates and copes with his "harrowing anxiety" by "ever explaining things" (192) and even turns to a discussion of "the process of embalming" (242) in order to diffuse the tension surrounding the unwrapping of Tera's mummy and her resemblance to Margaret.

As The *New York Times* claims, "there are chapters where a little less minutiae might not have marred the telling of the story" ("An Egyptian Mystery," 157), but such details appear to act as a last defense against the chaos of unknowing, for *Jewel* is ultimately a narrative about the failure of knowledge. Ross looks for simple binaries in the belief that "all things . . . are finally resolved into direct opposites" (210), and, as Glover notes, "the pathos of [the novel] lies in [his] vain struggle to find an explanation, any explanation, that will set his fears to rest" (*Vampires*, 87); he finds only disillusionment and doubt. Likewise, Trelawny seeks knowledge and finds only death, as the reader pursues a satisfactory resolution, and finds only uncertainty.

While it is difficult to tell how much of this ambiguity is simply the result of flawed writing—as the reviewers obviously believed—it is worth noting that Stoker deliberately has his characters employ metaphors of storytelling and that these usually relate to a postponement of narrative satisfaction, the promise that all will be revealed later. Trelawny, for example, initially refuses to answer Margaret's questions about Tera's sarcophagus because "the story is not yet told, as I hope to tell it to you" (100). Although this particular story does get told, as the text of *Jewel*, Trelawny's death prevents him from revealing still other secrets to which he refers, but never explains (206).

The general impression, then, is one of total epistemological meltdown, which may contribute to the anxiety of reviewers with negative opinions of the novel's first edition; although *Jewel* is not necessarily subversive in its intent, its insistent uncertainty indicates subversive potential. Part of this may relate to religious doubt, an issue which Ross addresses directly in the other excised chapter, "Powers—Old and New." Glover compares the resurrection scene to "a grand séance" ("Introduction," xiv) and discusses the position of spiritualism as a zone of mediation between late-nineteenth-century religion and science"(xxii). More interesting, however, is Patrick Brantlinger's connection of spiritualism and, paradoxically, science to a more political issue in what he terms "imperial Gothic," which "combines the seemingly scientific, progressive, often Darwinian ideology of imperialism with an antithetical interest in the occult" (227). One of the themes of imperial Gothic is "the diminution of opportunities for adventure and heroism in the modern world" (230); occultism becomes relevant here in that "just at the moment actual frontiers were vanishing, late Victorian and Edwardian occultist literature is filled with metaphors of exploration" (249). This may explain the frequent contrast, in *Jewel*, of the wonders of ancient Egypt with "this prosaic age"—the phrase occurs no less than three times in the text itself (1, 128, 169).

Brantlinger notes that "imperialism and occultism both functioned as ersatz religions, but their fusion in imperial Gothic represents something different from a search for new faiths" (229); rather, these late nineteenth-and early-twentieth-century texts express anxiety over the decline of empire (229). Although both *Dracula* and *Jewel* are examples of imperial Gothic, here, too, they relate to each other as in a mirror. While *Dracula* clearly addresses "the ease with which civilization can revert to barbarism or savagery" (Brantlinger, 229), the threat of reverse imperialism or colonial revolt is dissipated by the protagonists' violent suppression of the vampire other, thus reinscribing the imperial social order. The 1903 edition of *Jewel* is complicated by the apparent victory of the foreign or colonial other and by the protagonists' demise, which may, admittedly, be read as a type of dreadful warning about "the weakening of Britain's imperial hegemony" (Brantlinger, 229). Glover links this possibility with "fears of degeneration at the fin-de-siecle" (*Vampires*, 93), the danger that a weakened empire could no longer control its colonies.

However, several aspects of *Jewel* point towards another, more radical interpretation. Tera as foreign or colonial other hails from a more technologically advanced society, rather than from Brantlinger's realm of "barbarism and savagery" (229). Further, she is not seen as completely evil, thus reducing the imperialist anxiety, while the actions and fate of the British imperialists led by Trelawny suggest a critique of the empire itself. Finally, the ambiguous ending, which appears to transform the other into an autonomous subject, further destabilizes established categories of self and other, which are never re-inscribed. Indeed, the novel is conceivably subversive in its very ambiguity. In any case it may be time to move Tera out of the Count's shadow, or his looking-glass, and to consider the text in its own right, as it certainly generates interpretive possibilities at least as interesting as those of its predecessor.

NOTE

1. Indeed, Tera's skin is described as "like ivory," (241) both exotic and unmistakably fair in comparison even to the English Egyptologist Corbeck, who is "brown as a coffee berry" (87), and certainly to Dracula, who, although European, is called a "dark stranger."

WORKS CITED

Brantlinger, Patrick. *Rule of Darkness: British Literature and Imperialism, 1830–1914.* Ithaca, NY: Cornell UP, 1988.

"An Egyptian Mystery." Rev. of *The Jewel of Seven Stars*, by Bram Stoker. *New York Times Saturday Review of Books*, 5 Mar. 1904: 157.

Glover, David. Introduction. *The Jewel of Seven Stars*, by Bram Stoker. Oxford, England: Oxford UP, 1996.

———. *Vampires, Mummies, and Liberals: Bram Stoker and the Politics of Popular Fiction.* Durham, NC: Duke UP, 1996.

Hatlen, Burton. "The Return of the Repressed/Oppressed in Bram Stoker's *Dracula.*" *Dracula: The Vampires and the Critics.* Ed. Margaret L. Carter. *Studies in Speculative Fiction* 19. Ann Arbor, MI: UMI Research, 1988. 117–35.

Leatherdale, Clive. Introduction and notes. *The Jewel of the Seven Stars.* By Bram Stoker. Westcliff-on-Sea, UK: Desert Island Books, 1996.

Roth, Phyllis A. *Bram Stoker.* Twayne's English Author Series 343. Boston: Twayne, 1982.

Stoker, Bram. *Dracula.* Ed. A.N. Wilson, Oxford, England: Oxford UP, 1983.

———. *The Jewel of Seven Stars.* 1903. Westcliff-on-Sea, UK: Desert Island Books.

Chapter 4

"Appalling in Its Gloomy Fascination": Stoker's *Dracula* and Wilde's *Salome*

William Pencak

On the initial appearance of Bram Stoker's *Dracula* in 1897, reviewers were simultaneously attracted and repelled. "Weird, powerful and horrible," wrote the critic in the London *Daily Mail*, comparing *Dracula* to Mary Shelley's *Frankenstein*, among other works, as "appalling in its gloomy fascination" (Farson, 163). "A summary of the book would shock and disgust: but . . . we read nearly the whole with rapt attention," the *Bookman* reported (Senf, 61). Reaction to Oscar Wilde's *Salome*, written in French and performed in Paris in 1892, was similar. (Censorship prevented its performance on the English stage until 1931.) As Romain Rolland wrote to Richard Strauss when Strauss was thinking of turning *Salome* into an opera: "There is an undeniable dramatic power in Wilde's poem; but . . . Salome, and all those who surround her, except that poor creature Jokanaan, are unwholesome, unclean, hysterical, or alcoholic beings, stinking of sophisticated and perfumed corruption" (Myers, 82–83).

Salome and *Dracula* have a lot in common. Royce MacGillivray writes that even people who have never heard of Stoker know Dracula: "a myth comparable in vitality to that of the Wandering Jew, Faust, or Don Juan" (519). This is equally true of Salome's Dance of the Seven Veils if not of the damsel herself. The briefest possible descriptions of both works present interesting parallels. Dracula is an (Un-)dead man who sucks the blood out of living women and "dies" when he no longer can so sustain himself. Salome is a living woman who sucks the blood on the lips of a dead man and dies because she does. Both tales deal with the night, moonlight, and blood; mysterious, dark, hidden places; severed heads, exotic lands, and voluptuous women who drive men wild with desire. There are also deeper meanings concerning the struggle of Christianity and paganism and the questions of what are life, death, and immortality. Salome even provides a further hint of vampirism when King Herod says to his stepdaughter, "I love to see in a fruit the mark of thy little teeth" (32).[1]

It is tempting to speculate that Wilde's play influenced Stoker's product in some way, although conclusive proof is lacking. Although Stoker began work on *Dracula* in 1890, before *Salome* appeared, he continued with it several years thereafter. Henry Irving, the charismatic actor and impresario for whom Stoker arranged tours and worked incessantly, has sometimes been considered one of the models for Dracula. Irving led the successful campaign to have *Salome* banned from the English stage at the time Stoker was writing *Dracula*. Thus, on a symbolic level, Dracula/Irving, as the emanation of Stoker, kills Salome, the product of Wilde, in the world of the theater. Similarly, as the women Dracula seduces and murders in the moonlight, who come alive only at night, are reminiscent of Salome, Irving/Dracula's murder of Salome/the women would be sweet symbolic revenge for Stoker against Wilde. Significantly, Wilde had first proposed marriage to Florence Balcombe, who later married Stoker. Despite his predominant attraction to men, Wilde retained his affection for Florence and sent her copies of his works, including *Salome*. Needless to say, his relations with Bram Stoker were distant. However, so many sources have been linked to *Dracula*'s composition that the Wilde connection must remain speculative (Farson, 38–39; Skal, 26–27, 36).

Like *Dracula*, *Salome* clearly fits the genre of the fantastic, manifesting three traits Brian Attebery summarizes: "the deliberate violation of consensus reality"; "the placing of fantasy stories in temporal settings other than the present day"; and "the borrowing of motifs and story structures from folk tradition" (4). Both works hover "between a natural and a supernatural explanation of the events described," causing us to question the very nature of the real, as Tzvetan Todorov writes in *The Fantastic* (33). In fact, E.T.A. Hoffmann's beautiful yet horrible "Princess Brambilla," whom Todorov uses as his principal illustration of the fantastic, could well have been a model for the Salomes Wilde probably used: the character described by J. K. Huysman in *A Rebours* and the subject of a painting by Gustave Moreau (Praz, ch. 5; the painting is on exhibit at the Armand Hammer Museum in Los Angeles).

The supernatural appears at once in Wilde's play. He frames it by personifying the moon and identifying it with the young princess. As *Salome* opens the characters compare the moon to "a dead woman," who, "one might fancy . . . was looking for dead things." and to "a little princess who wears a yellow veil. . . . one might fancy she was dancing" (1–2). The play ends when a beam of moonlight illuminates Salome in the darkness as she is kissing the head of John the Baptist (the prophet Jokanaan as Wilde refers to him), which she obtained by performing the Dance of the Seven Veils for Herod. Viewing this act of necrophilia, Herod commands his soldiers to "kill that woman!" (69). They crush her with their shields as the play ends. Salome is now the dead woman in the moon, or the dead thing the moon has found.

Salome's final scene also hints at supernatural intervention in human affairs. It fulfills the prophecy of Jokanaan, which Wilde bases on the Book of "Revelations." He predicts that "the wanton one! the harlot," terms he applies to Salome, will be crushed beneath soldiers' shields, and "the moon shall become like blood" (42–44). Also, throughout the play, Herod senses "an ill omen . . . a beating of giant wings in the air" (31, 49), which could be the Angel of Death. The moon plunges into darkness just before Salome's death. Such imagery recalls the horrific storm that accompanies Dracula's journey to England and the symbolic appearance of the vampire as bat to signify death.

Salome, like a vampire, only comes alive in the moonlight. Before she emerges from the interior of Herod's palace into the courtyard, other characters remark that she has never seemed so pale. They compare her appearance to the shadow of white roses shining in a mirror and her hands to white butterflies. When she enters, she exclaims: "How sweet is the air here! I can breathe here!" and then praises the moon repeatedly as a virgin who "has never abandoned herself to men, like the other goddesses" (3–11). Salome herself is a virgin who only tastes love, blood, and death simultaneously, thus completing her identification with the moon and its virgin goddess.

Salome's appearance is thus similar to Jonathan Harker's first vision of the vampire women in *Dracula*: "In the moonlight opposite me were three young women . . . . I felt in my heart a wicked, burning desire that they would kiss me with those red lips" (35). And of course, the close relationship of sucking blood, sexuality, and moonlight is pervasive in both works. For instance, when Dracula bites Mina Harker, "the moonlight was so bright" that he was "forcing her face down on his bosom . . . his eyes flamed red with devilish passion . . . and the white sharp teeth, behind the full lips of the blood-dripping mouth, champed together like those of a wild beast" (262–63).

Lands and customs alien to the modern West also characterize the milieus in which both *Dracula* and *Salome* take place. Stoker begins his novel by stressing that polyglot Eastern Europe is the home of the vampire. *Dracula* opens as Harker crosses the Danube. Harker asserts that "we were leaving the West and entering the East" before describing the variety of peoples he finds intermingled there (1–3). Van Helsing tells us that vampires are found everywhere: they "follow the wake of the berserker Icelander, the devil-begotten Hun, the Slav, the Saxon, the Magyar" (222). They emerge from settings of imperialism where societies mix and values are uncertain, a context effectively compared by Stephen Arata (621–45) to the late Victorian Empire in which Stoker and Wilde lived.

Salome's Judaea at the time of Christ is also a melting pot of the ancient Roman empire. "Within" the palace she finds Jews "tearing each other in pieces over their foolish ceremonies, and barbarians who drink and spill their wine on the pavement, and Greeks from Smyrna with painted eyes and painted cheeks . . . and Egyptians silent and subtle . . . and Romans brutal and coarse." She makes a special point to say "how I loathe the Romans! They are rough and common and they give themselves airs of noble lords" (10). Indeed, representatives of most of these groups, and a few others, appear in *Salome* to confirm such stereotypes.

All these elements combine in an atmosphere of perversity and decadence that, with Salome's final striptease and her fondling of John the Baptist's severed head, explains why Wilde's play took nearly four decades to be performed in England. A drunken, incoherent Herod lusts after the princess, his stepdaughter, in the presence of his wife. Queen Herodias, in turn, demands Jokanaans's death because he criticizes her for marrying her first husband's murderer. A court page is in love with the young captain, who, in turn, kills himself when Salome spurns him.

Salome, like Dracula, is a terrible simplifier. She, too, cuts the Gordian Knot of moral uncertainty running rampant amid imperial diversity by wholeheartedly espousing the forces of night and passion. Rome, like Western Europe in the era of

Nietzsche and Freud, Stoker and Wilde, was master of much of the world but was in doubt as to what values it represented. Various characters in *Salome* embody this confusion. As the play opens, a Nubian complains that "the gods of my country are very fond of blood. . . . But I am afraid we never give them enough." A Cappadocian responds, "in my country there are no gods left." Four Jews dispute unpleasantly over the meaning of Jokanaan's prophecies and argue with Herod over whether Caesar is the Savior of the World. Only two alternatives remain: the Messiah heralded by Jokanaan and the moon goddess made incarnate through Salome.

Salome represents magical, irresistible beauty and instinctual, insatiable passion. She drives the young Syrian captain to kill himself and Herod to offer her half his kingdom for a dance, but she cares only about conquering her one true adversary, Jokanaan. "I would speak with him" and "Thou wilt do this thing for me" are her demands of the captain, who is under pain of death to keep the prophet in a cistern. She does not argue; she merely repeats her wishes over and over until she gets what she wants. The captain finally agrees when she promises him a mere smile.

Salome is equally insistent yet unargumentative with Herod, repeating several times, "I want the head of Jokanaan." She refuses his offers of material wealth and objects of great beauty from all over the world. Symbols of conventional religious authority—Herod will grant her the "mantle of the high priest" and "the veil of the sanctuary" (62)—are also irrelevant in what the king himself recognizes is the titanic struggle between the prophet, whose moral wrath he fears, and the girl, who represents the passions that dominate his life.

Similarly, as Joel N. Feimer has noted, "Bram Stoker was cautioning his contemporaries and their posterity against too rigorous insistence on the rational against the tyranny and arrogance of the normal" (171). Lucy Westenra—almost literally, "the light from the western ray" (Wasson, 25)—grows pale as Dracula sucks her blood. Blood from four men, Dr. Van Helsing and the three who loved and courted her—the British Lord Godalming, Doctor Seward, and the Texas millionaire Quincey P. Morris—fail to revive her.

All these names are significant, ironic commentaries on the pride in ancestry, elitism, science, and wealth of fin-de-siècle Britain as well as America, a country Stoker visited and knew well. They also reflect the moral confusion of that world, pulled in various directions much like Salome's Judaea. "Godalming" could be a play on words of either "God Almighty" or "gold mine," pointing to the material underpinnings of an elite convinced its rule served morality and justice whereas it rested on who was lucky enough to find or inherit the gold mine.

A third possibility, "God damning" (Hatlen, 830), draws a lesson from the other two: the God-damning effects of the gold mine on the human soul. "Seward" can stand for either "see ward"—the doctor's job is to oversee a ward of mental patients— "sewer"—a fit metaphor for the places modern society hides those who cannot deal with its stresses—or "sea ward"—the Western imperialist urge to "civilize" the world, which contemporary science backed as progress. "Morris" literally can be pronounced "more is," with the old-fashioned family name of Quincey and the initial "P" perhaps tacked on to mock the aristocratic pretensions of American arrivistes. For example, shortly before *Dracula* appeared on stage, New Yorks's Jennie Jerome had married Lord Randolph Churchill and then given birth to the child who would one day vanquish another central European monster.

Representatives of the tradition, reason, and wealth valued by the modern world are as afraid and helpless when confronted with primeval forces represented by Dracula as Herod was with a John the Baptist whom he tried to keep out of sight in a cistern. Only Van Helsing can defeat Dracula. His name is also apt: he literally makes "hell sing." He revives ancient lore scorned as pagan or superstitious, severing heads, driving stakes through hearts, and surrounding people with garlic to defeat the vampire on his own terms. He brings good out of barbaric punishments and a foul-smelling spice, revealing *Dracula* as a latter-day *Divine Comedy.*

Lucy, the woman to be saved, resembles Salome in that she is irresistible to several men. She is also extremely passionate, as her letters to Mina show (52–56). But Lucy is also a good Victorian lady, who only plans on surrendering her love through marriage. Lucy resists both her other suitors and the vampire much as Jokanaan, the white, moral, and conventionally "good" figure in Salome, is impervious to the princess's charms. He is pale from his stay in an underground prison—Salome goes on at length that "there is nothing in the world so white as thy body" (22). Lucy and the prophet both literally lose their heads to save their souls, signifying again the irreconcilable differences between the world of Christianity, morality, and spirit and the forces of paganism, depravity, and body (Wasson, 24–27).

For all their ability to titillate and outrage conventional folks, both Stoker and Wilde were telling us that an interior world western civilization has desperately attempted to suppress and sublimate is instinctual and almost unbearably seductive. It can only be ignored at our peril. But *Salome* and *Dracula* are no more immoral than Camille Saint-Saens's nearly contemporaneous opera *Samson et Dalila* or, to jump ahead, Cecil B. DeMille's *The Ten Commandments*—where the bad folks have all fun. Sigmund Freud, in fact, was saying the same thing at the same time when he warned us that the superego only represses the id at the expense of the ego. Theorist T. E. Apter, in his critique of Freud's theories, has made the astute point by arguing that "psychoanalysis is . . . more similar to a rich and complex fantasy work than to a series of explanatory theories" (150).

Brian Attebery notes that fantasy's "most profound political statement is to let the Other become a self" (10). In *Dracula* and *Salome*, Bram Stoker and Oscar Wilde give voice to a world we fear stirring within ourselves. The vampire and the princess, driven irresistibly on their destructive courses, are far more fascinating than the conventional forces that try to thwart them. As we at the end of the twentieth century confront not only the tension of Eastern Europe and the Middle East but cities and psyches in our postmodern society filled with the same strains between respectable conformity and demonic frenzy, we can learn no easy lessons from these two masterpieces. Or, as Emily Dickinson also wrote in the late nineteenth century: "Much madness is divinest sense (1. 337)." Let us not forget she too shunned the light.

NOTE

1. All references to Bram Stoker's *Dracula* and Oscar Wilde's *Salome* are by page only to the editions cited below.

WORKS CITED

Apter, T. E. *Fantasy Literature*. Bloomington, IN: Indiana U P, 1982.

Arata, Stephen D. "The Occidental Tourist: *Dracula* and the Anxiety of Reverse Colonization" *Victorian Studies*, 33 (1990): 621–45.

Attebery, Brian. "The Politics (If Any) of Fantasy," in *Modes of the Fantastic; Selected: Essays from the Twelfth International Conference on the Fantastic in the Arts*. Eds. Robert A. Latham and Robert A. Collins, Westport, CT: Greenwood Press, 1995: 1–11. Previously published in *The Journal of the Fantastic in the Arts* 4:1 (1991): 7–28.

Dickinson, Emily. *The Poems of Emily Dickinson*. Ed. Thomas H. Johnson. Cambridge, MA: The Belknap Press of Harvard Univ. 3 vols., 1963. Poem cited is #435, written about 1862.

Farson, Daniel. *The Man Who Wrote Dracula*. London: Michael Joseph, 1975. Feimer, Joel N. "Bram Stoker's *Dracula*: The Challenge of the Occult to Science, Reason, and Psychology." In *Contours of the Fantastic: Selected Essays from the Eighth International Conference on the Fantastic in the Arts*. Ed. Michelle K. Langford. Westport, CT: Greenwood Press, 1990, 165–171.

Hatlen, Burton. "The Return of the Repressed/Oppressed in Bram Stoker's *Dracula*," *Minnesota Review*, 15 (1980): 80–97.

MacGillivray, Royce. "Bram Stoker's Spoiled Masterpiece." *Queen's Quarterly*, 79 (1972): 519–28.

Myers, Rollo, ed. *Richard Strauss and Romain Rolland & Correspondence, Diary and Essays*. London: Calder and Boyers, 1968.

Praz, Mario. *The Romantic Agony*. Trans. Angus Davidson. London: Oxford UP, 1970.

Senf, Carol A. *The Critical Response to Bram Stoker*. Westport, CT: Greenwood Press, 1993.

Skal, David J. *Hollywood Gothic: The Tangled Web of Dracula from Novel to Stage to Screen*. New York: Norton, 1990.

Stoker, Bram. *Dracula*, 1897. Garden City, NY: Doubleday, 1973.

Todorov, Tzvetan. *The Fantastic: A Structural Approach to a Literary Genre*. Trans. Richard Howard. Cleveland: Case Western Reserve U P, 1973.

Wasson, Richard. "The Politics of *Dracula*." *English Literature in Transition*, 9 (1966): 24–27.

Wilde, Oscar. *Salome*, 1894. Translated from the 1892 French edition by Lord Alfred Douglas. Repr. with original pagination and illustrations by Aubrey Beardsley. New York: Dover, 1967.

Chapter 5

Stoker's *Dracula*:
A Neo-Gothic Experiment

Scott Vander Ploeg

For every fan of contemporary vampire-genre stories, there is easily a coven of readers who find them silly and automatically reject them beforehand. Perhaps part of the reason for such strong aversion is that today's vampire is a modern product that has little in common with the creature that emerged from Stoker's imagination. Vampire stories created toward the end of the twentieth century have added significantly to the creature that Stoker adapted from Polidori-Byron and Le Fanu in the late nineteenth century.

Even in their earliest avatars, the vampire was an abnormal creature. Its taboo-transgressive diet separated it from common humanity. But now we find recent vampires full of God-like abilities. They fly by their own powers or transform themselves into bats or fogs—or whatever creatures seem useful at the moment. They have incredible mental powers of control, telepathy, telekinesis. They are immortal. They battle with demons and alien gods that are intent on earth's destruction. Often, they become characters meant to elicit the reader's sympathy—protagonists instead of antagonists, heroes who advance a moral code of honor and integrity.[1] Typically, they are invulnerable to physical assault and in strength can match their antagonists (e.g., the vampire—as Batman?—vs. Superman). They are represented on stage and in film by the most popularly charismatic of actors. They are great seducers. They have culture and discernment and style. Our authors encourage us to admire them. In sum, the vampires of recent coinage are imbued with an incredible array of powers. They are also vastly different from the vampire of Stoker's creation.

According to Nina Auerbach (1983), Stoker's Dracula possesses many supernatural characteristics:

The master-mesmerist Dracula seems a derivation from Svengali, with his powers still further extended over time and space. The spell he casts . . . includes the animal kingdom, whose power he draws to himself at will, and at times the elements as well . . . his monstrous immortality aligns his power with time's. Svengali and Dracula are endowed with a magic beyond their own:

they possess the secret traditions of their culture. (16)

In degree and emphasis, Dracula is rougher, less refined, more bestial than is the modern vampire. Stoker's descriptions dwell on Dracula's strength and predisposition toward rapacious violence. Yet, despite his considerable power, and ironically through the agency of that power, he loses dominance toward the end of the novel and is virtually paralyzed in his little box of earth. It is hard to imagine the vampire of more recent vintage meeting such a simple end. Contemporary authors have chosen to aggrandize these supernatural powers and graft onto Stoker's concept the comic-book capacities of fantasy heroism.

All too commonly, the novel *Dracula* is referred to as a Gothic tale. While such classification is only a label—one of the assumptions on which critics rely—our pervasive unconscious acceptance of this term's appropriateness has occluded our view of the novel, thereby misrepresenting the origins of the vampire context. By such convenient negligence we have validated an error. Sullivan correctly identifies the distinction between Stoker's concept and its predecessors: "The modern [i.e., Victorian] ghostly tale is as much a reaction against the Gothic as an outgrowth of it" (5). *Dracula* is less Gothic than most recognize.

Leonard Wolf offers the traditional definition of the Gothic, first showing its derivation from architectural features, then dwelling on its affective dimension:

The novels were called Gothic because they had scenes set in ruined castles, monasteries, and convents. Characteristically, they featured tall, dark, Italian villains who pursued beautiful young women. . . . What distinguishes Gothic fiction from mainstream literature is that its goal is to delight the reader by creating fear . . . the aim of Gothic fiction is limited to the arousal of terror. (75–76)

Although quite common, this definition of the Gothic fails to indicate how that fear is created, and it implies, rather blandly, that the setting itself has something to do with this. It is true that Stoker set his novel in part among ancient castles, but these scenic elements are not alone sufficient to cause fear. Stoker does try to cause an "arousal of terror" in his readers, but not through the traditional Gothic strategy.

This view is corroborated by Stoker's nephew, who in his biography of Stoker offers, in opposition to Wolf, that "*Dracula* succeeds partly because it is not Gothic; to the Victorian it must have seemed daringly modern" (Farson, 142). In fact, this story has far more in common with the developing genre of the crime story.[2]

What the Victorian reader would have found to be "daringly modern" about Stoker's novel is that it eventually denies the validity of the supernatural as the central tenant of Dracula's existence. Instead of repeating romantic superstition, it raises science to the level of religious belief—or at least to the degree of a pragmatic faith. A true Gothic story owes much of its underpinning to a question of epistemological certainty that developed from Kantian theories of a priori knowledge. In opposition to the prevailing mechanistic and experience-based systems, Kant offered that there are certain essential axioms that we know to be true before evidence "proves" them. This view unsettled philosophical thinking in curious ways, especially empiricist belief in the sanctity experience, and it produced surprising results. One such result was the realization that the a priori truths might not be explicable by scientific law. Some things might be beyond investigation. This conceptual frame allowed for the creation of Gothic structure.

Writers grasped this philosophical quandary and saw the opportunity to incorporate such into their stories. The supernaturalism found in the works of Goethe and E.T.A. Hoffman are perhaps the most immediate literary offshoots of Kantian principles, and these in turn influenced Anglo-Romantic writers such as Coleridge and Byron, Hawthorne and Poe. Glover observes, "It is precisely this demarcation between the real and unreal that is at issue in *Dracula*" (*Vampires*, 64). Stoker chooses to make his vampire a real creature, a result of natural effects.

Stoker, writing at the conclusion of a century that made so much of the supernatural, ends in denying the importance of this lurking uncertainty and offers rational experience as the best weapon for defeating the threatening presence of the unknown. Van Hesling is the foil for Victorian rationality. This constitutes a rejection of much of what had devolved into an attenuated Romantic claptrap that was inconsistent with the Victorian faith in a predictable science. Such is Van Hesling's constant refrain: he incites the afflicted group of Victorians to oppose the seemingly supernatural evil of Dracula by relying on knowledge and reason. He "proves" how unsupernatural—and thus knowable and therefore mortal—Dracula is.

Most recent writers do not observe a difference between Gothic structure and Gothic elements. Gothic elements consist primarily of the aforementioned setting, a castle or monastery, typically a medieval context full of gloom and nascent dread. A strong religious element is often combined with the threat of imprisonment. Characters must travel through exotic landscapes to save maidens in distress. The formulaic approach to writing a Gothic vampire story might suggest that the writer only include all of these sensational trappings, but a more correct use of the genre would demand that the writer also tap into the supernatural world. It is this latter strategy that produces Gothic dread. The assumption is that these Gothic elements, the backdrop and window dressing, are found in Stoker's *Dracula* and therefore are what constitutes the Gothic. But, ironically, Stoker's use tends to diffuse the essential Gothic structure, eventually to ignore the supernatural agency. As a result, today's vampire story is often more Gothic than is its most famous forefather.

Walpole's *Castle of Otronto* is perhaps the prime example of a story in which the Gothic structure derives from such epistemological incertitude. In sum, there occur strange phenomena in that novel—a gigantic helm that appears *ex nihilo* and crushes one character, unknown and unknowable "things that go bump in the night"—and these events are entirely inexplicable. This story is set in the medieval context of a castle. The action involves the characters in confronting the unknown, often with a sense of dread and the foreboding of impending death and dissolution. In Stoker's *Dracula*, Van Helsing presents this perplexity of uncertainty for us midway into the novel when he reveals to John Seward the awful truth of what has killed Lucy Westenra and which threatens to turn England into a nation of vampires:

You are clever man, friend John; you reason well, and your wit is bold; but you are too prejudiced. You do not let your eyes see nor your ears hear, and that which is outside your daily life is not of account to you. Do you not think that there are things which you cannot understand; and yet which are; that some people see things that others cannot? . . . Ah, it is the fault of our science that it wants to explain all; and if it explains not, then it says there is nothing to explain. (213)

Van Helsing's gentle remonstrance faults Seward, a man of science, for disallowing the obvious conclusion resulting from the evidence; his error is in discounting a conclusion he does not wish to accept. Ironically, for all his protesting of the inscrutability of the unknown, Van Helsing's ability to deal with Dracula is predicated on his knowledge about that unknown. This suggests a duality that Rosemary Jann has explored, a recognition or internal contradiction, for though the story is a reaction "against materialist science, Stoker's narrative is also heavily invested in valorizing the rationalistic authority conventionally associated with scientific thought" (271).

Van Helsing's is a pragmatic Victorian mind, and he has a partisan audience in Dr. Seward, due to his medical training, and John Harker and his associates, due to their familiarity with law. Once Van Helsing convinces the inexperienced to accept the fact of the vampire, they quickly move on to dealing with its consequences. This is perhaps the modernity to which Farson alludes. Soon, the supernatural is marginalized by this avid quest for containment. It is consistent with this action that the story is told entirely through journal entries—the same evidence that Mina Harker and her cohorts use in binding this monster. As Auerbach puts it, Dracula is defeated by "the modern weapons of committee meetings and shorthand minutes" (16). The vampire hunters are able to control the supernatural through mundane means, implying that man has some power to contend with unimaginable forces. Such pretty well negates the Gothic underpinning.

To summarize at this point: Although *Dracula* is full of Gothic conventions, Stoker does not rely on Gothic belief in the supernatural to structure the novel.

The earliest overt Gothic stories were written in the mid 1700s. Stoker's *Dracula* was first published in 1897, nearly a century and a half after the Gothic became a literary reality. In that time, much had changed, and it is perhaps best that we recast this novel for what it more appropriately is—a crime/detection story.

Edgar Allan Poe was certainly no stranger to the Gothic, and it is also to him that we credit the development of the detective story and thence the crime story. The detective in his most un-Gothic tales, one August Dupin, is able to solve mysterious crimes of murder and theft in a curiously ironic way. Like the later Sherlock Holmes, Dupin relies on "ratiocination" to deduce certain truths, but he also admits that there are some things that can not be known. In "Murders in the Rue Morgue," it is by recognizing the irrationality of the act that Dupin correctly guesses that an irrational beast is the culprit. In "The Purloined Letter," it is by a lack of logical connection that the letter is found. Both stories imply that reason, alone, is insufficient. Holmes, however, is built differently. Arthur Conan Doyle creates a character who can solve the most difficult quandaries by combining sufficient rationality to his keen perspicacity. Like Doyle's, Stoker's concept rejects the earlier supernatural and eventually proves that reason is clearly able to cope with the unknown.

Jann points out that it is Dracula's inability to match the deductive logic of the vampire hunters that is his fatal flaw (281). Although believing that the novel retains its mystery, Cawelti admits that the "alien being is dealt with by a more or less rationalistic-religious technology of vampire control" (44). He is a creature that would be supernatural in an earlier context, but in late Victorian habit becomes a mostly explicable phenomenon—still a threat, but one that can be deduced and defended against, if sufficient rationality is applied. "It is science as the rigorously tested accumulation of evidence that ultimately guides the novel's construction" (Glover, *Vampires, Mummies, and Liberals*, 252).

The degree to which the novel is based on faith in science is evident in the arrangements that the group of would-be heroes make before they confront Dracula. In chapter 18, after having disposed of the Lucy Westenra vampire, and partly because her condition proved the existence of Dracula as their nemesis, they convene to discuss plans for opposing the irrefutable evil. First, Van Helsing lists Dracula's powers—this act itself a kind of reduction and demythologizing by definition—and after the members then swear to defeat the vampire, Van Helsing offers a brief catalogue of the Count's limitations. This is the first formal grouping of restrictions on Dracula's supernatural powers, though such limits have been previously hinted. A more detailed list of abilities and their limits follows some four chapters later. When the group soon after takes action, Dracula's powers are further restricted. What we see, then, is an ever greater diminution of the monster's otherworldly powers, and this suggests a crimping of his Gothic connections. For at first, in the early scenes when Harker is at the Count's home, a paradigmatic Gothic-convention castle, Dracula seems nearly omnipotent, but later we learn that he is only at full power during specific times of the day. The group plans to catch him in the open during the day, when he is virtually powerless.

The novel's ending is anticlimactic. After accepting the fact of the creature, and spending considerable narrative energy in producing that acceptance, the vampire hunters have merely to arrange the details of his defeat. The story no longer is concerned over the fact of his arcane power, but is instead focused on using it against him. The greatest ally of the vampire hunters is an appropriated power found in Mina, whose telepathic connection allows the troop to chase him down and end his cursed immortality.

Before this ending, Dracula enters into a contest with the entire group of crucifix-wielding, garlic-adorned heroes. He threatens them with his revenge, but his exit has all the markings of an escape, a point that Van Helsing asserts and Stoker emphasizes by capitalizing the word "ESCAPE"; it appears that the heroes have thwarted Dracula in his bid to control events locally in England. Whatever supernal powers he taps, they are unavailable to him in this group confrontation scene. Afterwards, he is a criminal on the run. Stoker attempts to complicate the resulting chase by granting Dracula the modest advantage of unpredictability, but this meager power is frustrated by Mina's telepathic tracking. The vampire hunters follow him to just outside of his castle in Transylvania, block his access, and thrust knives into his still corporeal form. Some (e.g., Cawelti) may believe that his end is ambiguous that he might be able to re-assemble himself; but Van Helsing's concluding comment— that even Dracula's face was beatific in release from the hellishness of his existence— would seem to suggest that the story is ended.

Recent scholarship has brought to light the fact that Stoker drafted a slightly different ending, then canceled two short paragraphs of manuscript before allowing it to be published. This material would have added description of an impressive consequence of the party's success. When Dracula "dies" after Morris stabs him in the heart with the bowie knife, the monster's body crumbles to dust, and the narrator notes his enigmatic smiling expression. The canceled continuation describes how suddenly the castle itself explodes in a volcanic-like eruption and more than implies that this is nature's revenge on Dracula (Auerbach and Skal, 325, n.5).

No records explain why Stoker chose to delete this material, but we may nominally conjecture that it too strongly indicates a supernatural link between Dracula and his castle. How would the castle be aware of his death? Was nature to be thought of as a sentient entity, one that seeks revenge? What would have triggered the explosion except a mystical link between the creature and its home? It is worth considering that not only did Stoker conceive of the more mystical ending, but that he consciously rejected it. Again, this suggests how much the author wanted to distance his story from Gothic romanticism.

Three chapters before the conclusion, having vanquished the enemy from English soil, Van Helsing reveals certain facts about Dracula that have been held back from the reader. These he has communicated to the other characters, but when forced to encourage their pursuit, he reveals this information to Mina and to the readers. In relation to the narrative, this information is not necessary, but in terms of the Gothic context, such is crucial—for here is given the probable explanation for the vampire's origin:

I have told them how the measure of leaving his own barren land—barren of peoples—and coming to a new land where life of man teems till they are like the multitude of standing corn, was the work of centuries. Were another of the Un-Dead, like him, to try to do what he has done, perhaps not all the centuries of the world that have been, or that will be could aid him. With this one, all the forces of nature that are occult and deep and strong must have worked together in some wondrous way. The very place, where he have been alive, Un-Dead for all these centuries, is full of strangeness of the geologic and chemical world. There are deep caverns and fissures that reach none know whither. There have been volcanoes, some of whose openings still send out waters of strange properties, and gases that kill or make to vivify. Doubtless, there is something magnetic or electric in some of these combinations of occult forces which work for physical life in strange way. (354)

This reveals that Dracula is a unique phenomenon. An army of vampires is not waiting to invade the homeland—except for those that this lone creature has infected. A second development from this is the recognition that Dracula is more of an accident of nature than a supernatural entity. In referring to the magnetic and electric and chemical and gaseous agents at work in producing him, Stoker puts in Van Helsing's empirical paradigm scientific beliefs that were current in the Victorian period. In effect, these pieces of the puzzle explain away the residual tatters of the supernaturalism that begin the novel.

The detective/crime story is one that relies on the resolution of a mystery, the solving of the crime; the Gothic story relies, instead, on the indeterminancy of the resolution—on its ambiguous assent to potential truths that are not accommodated into current understandings of the nature of reality. The quest for truth through detection undermines the mysterious and horrific. This is a basic tenant of William Patrick Day's study, wherein he observes that horror ends where the detective novel begins. We should grant that the novel offers many unanswered questions concerning the mechanisms of Dracula's powers, but we should also agree that the central concept of Gothic mystery is finally reduced to a negligible theme. The Gothic structure is supplanted by the penultimate cops-n-robbers chase scene.

In conclusion, the contemporary vampire story seems even more Gothic than is Stoker's creation. Our recent tales are the true neo-Gothic, not *Dracula*. This seems an odd feature of our modern world. Is it due to a kind of literary one-upmanship, a matter of having to produce a story that supersedes its predecessor? Possibly so, though the recent vampire mania seems to be due to other non-literary factors. For Stoker, modern science was something on which one could rely for us, perhaps not? Instead, we call our psychic advisors for reassurance.

NOTES

1. This view is corroborated by Glover in *Vampires, Mummies, and Liberals*: Modern writers see "the past as a domain of scandal and error awaiting exposure by a franker, more enlightened gaze. [Recent writers] all adopt a variant of this stance, rescuing their de-repressed monsters from the dead weight of inherited ignorance and superstition, flaunting their guilty secrets and endowing them with a romanticized humanity" (2). This provides an explanation for how contemporary vampire storytellers justify expanding the Gothic powers of their imagined creatures. These fantastic vampires should not be mistaken as having much in common with Stoker's creature. Moreover, we should be wary of presuming anything about Stoker's story on the basis of the popular contemporary view.

2. Patrick Brantlinger, in *The Nineteenth-Century Novel and Empire*, ed. John Richetti, et al., New York: Columbia UP, 1994, 577, posits the interesting thesis that a large portion of the anxiety *Dracula* generated in Victorian readers was due to their latent xenophobia combined with their increasing awareness of declining international dominance.

WORKS CITED

Auerbach, Nina. *Woman and the Demon. The Life of A Victorian Myth*. Cambridge, MA: Harvard UP, 1982.

Auerbach, Nina and David J. Skal. *Dracula. Authoritative Text—Backgrounds. Reviews and Reactions, Dramatic and Film Variations, Criticism*. Norton Critical Edition. New York: Norton, 1977.

Cawelti, John G. *Adventure, Mystery, and Romance: Formula Stories as Art and Popular Culture*. Chicago: U of Chicago P, 1976.

Day, William Patrick. *In Circles of Fear and Desire: A Study of Gothic Fantasy*. Chicago: U of Chicago P, 1985.

Farson, Daniel. *The Man Who Wrote Dracula: A Biography of Bram Stoker*. New York: St. Martin's Press, 1975.

Glover, David. "'Our Enemy Is Not Merely Spiritual':Degeneration and Modernity in Bram Stoker's *Dracula*." *Victorian Literature and Culture*, 22 (1994): 249–65.

————. *Vampires, Mummies, and Liberals: Bram Stoker and the Politics of Popular Fiction*. Durham, NC: Duke UP, 1996.

Jann, Rosemary. "Saved by Science? The Mixed Messages of Stoker's *Dracula*." *Texas Studies*

    in Literature and Language, 31.2 (Summer 1989): 273–87.
Stoker, Bram. *Dracula*. New York: Dell, 1984.
Sullivan, Jack. *Elegant Nightmares: The English Ghost Story from Le Fanu to Blackwood*.
    Athens, OH: Ohio UP, 1978.
Wolf, Leonard. *Dracula: The Connoisseur's Guide*. New York: Broadway Books, 1979.

Chapter 6

Men in Love: The Fantasizing of Bram Stoker and Edvard Munch

Suzanna Nyberg

Artists of the 1890s belonged to a turbulent generation, and no other artists have used the resources of fantasy and suspense to such effect as the novelist Bram Stoker and the painter Edvard Munch. Using these examples to encourage comparison and contrast between late nineteenth-century fantasists, in this chapter I hope to find a common pattern and strengthen the thematic coherence between artistic disciplines. David Glover in *Vampires, Mummies, and Liberals* writes that "Stoker's narratives are best understood as fantasies, as their frequent evocation of states of reveries, unconsciousness, dream and daydream ought perhaps to suggest" (15). Munch's works give the sensation of being transported to another world; Reinhold Heller says he belonged to a group who "announced the independence of their art from all verifiable reality" (43).

Love for the two artists was a matter of life and death, and the way they fantasized about it was unorthodox and often frightening. Both were overwhelmingly concerned with the state of the soul in love, its moods of anxiety, sorrow, and melancholy. Vampires, madonnas, and saints, women larger than life itself, abound in their imaginations. Demons torment these two men, demons that need to be exorcised. Stoker fantasizes about woman as vampiress, who in her capacity to drain men, justifies male fears. She poses a challenge to the pattern of culture itself. Munch, in paintings that hint at the sensuous movements of a woman but avoid clearly defining her, confers visibility on the lust of the vampire and the torment of the man in love. Their worlds converge: the techniques differ but the problems, concerns, and intentions are similar. Sexuality is always threatening, never comfortable.

The biographical elements in Stoker and Munch make them combinations.[1] Both men experienced illness and death in their childhood homes. Arne Eggum has noted that "Munch had a sensitive mind, and the agonizing experience of illness and death in his childhood home left their mark on him" (155). As a child, Stoker was so sick that he rarely left his room. Biographer Daniel Farson wrote that the more he learned of his great-uncle Bram, "the more schizophrenic he appeared" (19).

But these artists had much in common besides symmetries in life. Both evoke moods of premonition, Stoker through novels and Munch through a landscape. Both imagined a world of greater erotic freedom. They showed how women, assuming unprecedented liberties, eroticized men's worlds and, devoid of any ridicule, they paid tribute to the power of sexuality. The works of both artists have been illuminated by psychoanalytic techniques.

Stoker brings the supernatural into sex, using it to develop ideas he could not have developed in some other novel.[2] In *Dracula*, as a point of method and of honor, he hides the erotic in letters, journals, and diaries; the theme may be the fantastic, but the imagery in which it is expressed is sexual. Whereas other writers' erotic fantasies are domesticated or enjoined with matrimony, Stoker's, tied to the supernatural, are isolated from other aspects of human life. The supernatural banished a host of cultural proscriptions and taboos. Women initiate sex and men might acknowledge a variety of sexual pleasures. For a man hedged round by Victorian morality, the supernatural offered a mask to disguise sexual fantasies. Vampires were capable of liberating modern oppressed man from his narrow and confined milieu. Mina Harker describes Dracula's most salacious adventure in imagery appropriate to that of a lover:

He pulled open his shirt, and with his long sharp nails opened a vein in his breast. When the blood began to spurt out, he took my hands in one of his, holding them tight and with the other seized my neck and pressed my mouth to the wound, so that I must either suffocate or swallow. (Stoker, *Dracula*, 351)

The supernatural served as a veil for elaborating a scene that was otherwise considered taboo; repressed desire found representation through a vampire.

Stoker's imagination stamps marks of horror on sexuality. Dracula, although little more than a shadow in the background of the action, introduces the erotic to the English middle class. He is simply the icon of transgressive desire: gratification is not possible for him. Capering with him had strong appeal because of sexual overtones. The emphasis on sharp teeth and red lips was part of his power to excite; the little love bites he left on the neck were a new source of erotic stimulation. Dracula titillates; and the novel constantly flirts with the suggestion of an erotic basis for the attraction to vampires. Farson says that the "vampire superstition is riddled with sexuality; indeed it is dependent on it, with all the sucking, the flowing of blood and the love-biting" (211).

Jonathan Harker's diary opens the novel and it is the story of the beast within. All the phantoms of the male imagination grow in Stoker's alter ego. Biographer Barbara Belford notes that Dracula's "genesis was a process, which involved Stoker's education and interests, his fears and fantasies, as well as those of his Victorian colleagues. He dumped the signposts of his life into a supernatural cauldron and called it *Dracula*" (256). While in real life, Stoker had few external indulgences, in his imagination, lascivious fancies ran riot. He imagined the sexual as having its origin in an exotic land, creating situations where men were open to all kinds of temptations. Here Harker meets himself, his darker side, his hidden thoughts and repressed forbidden fantasies. In the West, he wore a mask: his unassuaged desires went concealed; in the East, the great resources of fantasy, long damned up in him, were unleashed.[3]

Harker is fascinated with three nameless women as objects of desire, yet he also fears erotic femininity. An encounter with them would be thrilling, but dangerous. Although he is a willing victim, the desire to submit was countered by the desire to resist. Harker, remote from his own sexuality, puzzles over his feelings. Describing his desire as wicked, he thinks guiltily of sin; uneasiness and desire commingle in him. Guilt and shame are brought to the pleasure Harker desires:

There was some longing about them that made me uneasy . . . I felt in my heart a wicked, burning desire that they would kiss me with those red lips . . . They all three laughed—such a silvery musical laugh . . . The fair girl shook her head coquettishly, and the other two urged her on. One said, "Go on! You are first, and we shall follow; yours is the right to begin." The other added: "he is young and strong; there are kisses for us all." I lay quiet, looking out under my eyelashes in an agony of delightful anticipation. The fair girl advanced and bent over me till I could feel the movement of her breath on me . . . Sweet it was, honey-sweet . . . The girl went on her knees, and bent over me, simply gloating. There was a deliberate voluptuousness that was both thrilling and repulsive, and as she arched her neck, she actually licked her lips like an animal . . . Lower and lower went her head as the lips went below the range of my mouth and chin and seemed to fasten on my throat. (Stoker, *Dracula*, 48)

Harker saw pleasure as being derived from evil.[4] Clearly, he likes the idea of not just one, but three women working with him. This fantasy of women freely and easily giving their love is also a fantasy of sexual possibility for the Victorian man. Harker is all too ready to allow himself to be passively seduced, to be dominated sexually. His fantasy was a flight from the culturally preordained into a new realm of pleasure where women are granted erotic autonomy and the masculine privilege of erotic choice. Stoker recognized that the beauty of woman acted on men with a strange and almost incredible power; sexuality was both a force within man and beyond his control, and man was drawn to woman in spite of himself. Harker is at the women's mercy until Dracula materializes; he avoids having to grapple with sexual pleasure. Yet the passivity Harker allowed himself paradoxically suggested sexual liberty. Lulled into a liaison for which he can deny any responsibility, the phantoms of his imagination provided access to a sensual realm where he could not be held responsible. Harker never really goes after anyone, including his wife. Ultimately, he is a fantasist, far more excited by idea than by performance.

The desire to love eventually mutates into the desire to kill. The three women, still nameless, also illuminate Van Helsing's erotic consciousness, and he almost falls prey to the same temptation. There is a note of ecstasy in Van Helsing's account of the three ladies, whose omitted names are all the more striking due to the detail with which Stoker fills the book. They, too, appeal, and Van Helsing, too, fights seduction, as much attracted to the three ladies as Jonathan Harker: "She was so fair to look on, so radiantly beautiful, so exquisitely voluptuous, that the very instinct of man in me, which calls some of my sex to love and protect one of hers, made my head whirl with new emotion" (451). Then he resists his sexuality and stakes her. In his world, giving in to desire is tantamount to capitulation. As Martin Tropp has noted in *Images of Fear*, it is sexual power "which infects the women in the book and which the men fight manfully to suppress" (138). Stoker imagines the male struggle with sexuality as ending only in death. Sex as an enjoyable human activity is cut short and sexual expression that involves more pain than pleasure is pursued. We need not look so much at the act, but at the perceived threat that is its source. Intense physical and spiritual torment create a state of near-madness where only a staking can bring relief. The literal act has a metaphorical function.

Lucy Westenra is marked from her first lush entrance in the novel. Three men propose to her in one day, and she greedily wants them all. She clearly has an effect on men long before she becomes a vampire. Mandy Merck quips in *Perversions* that "it's not difficult to predict which woman will end up with a stake through her heart" (212).[5] One night of love transforms Lucy into a grotesque, albeit voluptuous, monster, someone from whom men recoil. Recoil, not tenderness, plays a more decisive part in the reaction of the suitors to an erotic woman. Stoker condemns her ambitious sexuality, even imagining her as a nymphomaniac haunting Hampstead Heath after her death. In *Woman and the Demon*, Nina Auerbach sees the novel's women as heroines, not likable but pathetic victims. She reads it as a "myth of newly empowered womanhood, whose two heroines are violently transformed from victims to instigators of their story" (24).[6]

Lucy is more than killed; she is erotically conquered by the man she was to marry. Her staking is clearly sexualized. There is a brutal agony in the union of Arthur Holmwood, Lord Godalming, and Lucy; their first intercourse is nightmarish, and it is the only time Arthur really gets close to her. Arthur's act of love for Lucy highlights the possibilities for violence and cruelty in sexual behavior. The question implicitly raised, "How is it that one person can be in the presence of another in pain and ignore it, ignore it to the point where he will go on inflicting it," has an answer: Lucy is no longer a human being. We are kept from sympathy for this woman by the fantasy that demonizes her.

The ominous nature of women's sexuality also appears in *The Lair of the White Worm*, another Stoker novel about sexual failure. Lady Arabella, like Lucy, has disturbing powers: she is a white worm, a giant monster who attacks children. The imagery surrounding her is soft and liquidy. Stoker conceptualizes her body as a swamp, a pit of muck that threatens to engulf and annihilate. It is a place of perdition with which it was better to have nothing to do. Auerbach says that Arabella's "metamorphic power seems darkly intrinsic to womanhood itself" (25).[7] Both Lucy and Arabella are fantasies of feminine power and immortality. The vampiress and serpent are vividly sexual, and it is impossible to separate their sexuality from the dangers they present. A snake, like a vampire, bites, and is as much a source of terror.

Adam Salton, like Harker, is distanced from any semblance of sensuousness in his love relationships; he is sentimental and trite with Mimi. Acceptance of sexual feelings is impossible for him, and he must fight the threat of submersion, blowing up all that is wet and luscious. Unlike staking, dynamiting Arabella's home, "Diana's Grove," aims at total annihilation.

Sexual feelings undermine Stoker's notion of manliness: when a man's guard is lowered by sensuality, he is in danger. The upshot is that sexual desires are violently persecuted and they earn a tremendous death. The more desirable a woman is, the more threatening she becomes and the more she must be destroyed. The men in Stoker's novels are both fascinated with women as objects of desire and riddled with fear of their sexuality. Instead of a robust sensuality, there is a general creepiness. The iconography of the femme fatale, the woman who is willing to use her unbridled sexuality to control men, pervades the novels. The femme fatale, notorious not only for the insatiable passion she inspires in men, but for her own voracious sexuality, is both the quintessential object of male desire and the embodiment of the desiring female. Sexual feelings appear as a sharp crisis in Stoker; the feeling of intense attraction mingles with its opposite: death and sexuality, love and fear, depend upon each other. Male characters bear the cross of sexual misgivings; they simply cannot accept human sexuality. Instead of either sexual decency or raffishness, there is desire without consummation, longing mingled with dread.

Further, male desexualization is accompanied by a murderous aggression. One is not sure if the men who figure as heroes in *Dracula* and *The Lair of the White Worm* want so much to keep their women—as they are careless in their vigilance of Lucy, Mina, and Mimi—as they want to pursue monsters. It's they who do the killing. Although chauvinist and bourgeois in their ability to piece together movements, they resemble witch-hunters more than detectives. They relinquish their own livelihoods and identities to chase phantoms. They seem to relish their work, and in their mad pursuits, they avoid an intimacy they find terrifying. Staking, tracking, and dynamiting, acts of mammoth proportions, are really acts of terror that spring from profound desires, desires lent to the creation of death.

In "The Dream in the Dead House," a deleted chapter from *Dracula* turned into a separate short story, the narrator's fantasies are cloaked until he wanders to a crossroads on Walpurgis Night. At the entrance to a tomb, he has a nocturnal vision:

I saw, as my eyes were turned into the darkness of the tomb, a beautiful woman, with rounded cheeks, and red lips, seemingly sleeping on a bier. Just then there came another blinding flash . . . ..the dead woman rose for a moment of agony, while she was lapped in the flame, and her bitter scream of pain was drowned in the thunderclash. (Stoker, *Midnight Tales*, 25)

The erotic woman ceases to exist before the narrator can have contact with her. Desire, again marginalized, becomes a fantasy of separation and lack. Violent natural elements sever the narrator from the woman and from his own longings. Were it not for the flash, one wonders if the narrator would have been the consenting victim of his own fantasies.

Stoker's men have nothing sexually to do with women; they feel entirely comfortable with women except for the purpose of sexual pleasure. His work suggests that a more ethereal form of love should exist over the sexual. Only relations with vampires or monsters are eroticized: Stoker recommends chastity between normal mortals. When Harker marries Mina, he is an invalid in the hospital; there is no wedding night. A hospital wedding is a non-love fantasy; patients, never really alone, are reduced to the status of powerless children. Harker clearly prefers a platonic relationship with Mina; his love story reads more like comradeship. More drawn to the pursuit of Dracula, Jonathan appeals oblivious to Mina's sexuality. His marriage has fended off an erotic life; the only time Stoker describes him in bed with Mina, he is in a deep sleep and she is, in effect, cuckolding him. We marvel at the childbirth at the novel's end, wondering what led up to it.

In refusing to describe Mina, Stoker deprives her of sensuousness. She is good, not passionate, like the child, Zaya, in "The Spectre of Doom." In this short story, a fantasy based on Stoker's mother's experience of the cholera plague in Ireland, Zaya is also devoid of an erotic life. She is a little maid, who "made flowers of many kinds, roses and lilies, and violets, and snowdrops, and primroses, and mignonette, and many beautiful sweet flowers" (*Midnight Tales*, 33). Innocent, although not ignorant of evil, she strives to save her town. Mina's and Zaya's sexlessness is expressed in their iconography: the angelic woman and the pure little girl. Mina's sexuality is extinguished; Zaya is too young to have it emerge.

Based on Stoker's trip to Nuremberg's torture tower, "The Squaw" is his most sadistic fantasy. The Nuremberg Virgin, no more than butchery, is a medieval torture chamber, especially designed to pierce the heart. Her spikes were "square and massive, broad at the base and sharp at the points" (*Midnight Tales*, 95), symbolically a grotesque means of sexual expression. Elias P. Hutcheson of Nebraska wanted to sit on her lap; it seems to inflame his passions: "the custodian completed his task by tying the American's feet together so that he was now absolutely helpless and fixed in his voluntary prison. He seemed to really enjoy it, and the incipient smile which was habitual to his face blossomed into actuality" (*Midnight Tales*, 95).

Stoker tantalizes the reader by gradually leading Hutcheson more deeply into the chamber. In a state of repressed erotic emotion, Hutcheson sees his pleasure to be had with a machine shaped like a woman, ecstasy to be found with an instrument of torture. The supercharged narrative culminates in physical contact. Stoker has resorted to an excess as horrific as that found in any modern novel. Sitting in the chair, Hutcheson calls for the greatest intimacy possible, penetration between him and the Virgin: "Now, Judge, you jest begin to let this door down, slow, on me. I want to feel the same pleasure as the other jays had when those spikes began to move toward their eyes" (*Midnight Tales* 95). The cat, whose kitten he accidentally killed springs on the custodian, who in turn, drops the rope holding back the iron door. Hutcheson and the Nuremberg Virgin consummate their relationship.

Although Stoker wrote tales of horror, he was engaged in an exploration of sexual life. He turned to woman as a sensual being, but he did not develop her full potential for pleasure and life.

Munch shared aspects of Stoker's way of looking at sexuality. Many critics, such as Kirk Varnedoe, have concentrated on the social criticism in Munch's works, those "structures of perspective and narrative organization that are ultimately derived from Realist pictorial strategies" (24). Yet the social painter was also a painter of sexuality, forbidden emotions, and the feminine. As Stoker created fantastic women, so did Munch's paintings abound with them, women who are neither ravishingly pretty nor unquestionably beautiful. Both fantasize about Woman as a predator of robust spirit who pursues men with gusto and inflicts traumatic sexual experiences on them. As Stoker was attracted to the notion of death and its linkage to eroticism, so Munch, too, found the conjunction of women and corpses alluring and wrote that he was captivated by the sensations he got from a corpse. Both artists demonstrate that sexual attraction, while overpowering, was fused with anxiety.

Although the sexualized woman can become a monster, Munch eroticized her in a variety of ways. While many of his images elicit fearful responses and love for him was often synonymous with suffering, Munch never eroticized pain, and physical hurt was never treated as a matter of love. As Jean Selz has noted, "Munch's disturbed, anxious, pessimistic nature was constantly in evidence, but it was not violent" (76). Stoker's men defend themselves against intimacy; Munch also depicted couples who have lost their hearts to each other. His paintings reflect feelings connected to a loving sexuality, where men find it enjoyable, not dangerous, to give way to passion. Stoker feared dissolution through union; Munch embraced it. In his Saint-Cloud Manifesto, written while on fellowship in France, Munch glorifies sexuality: "These two in that instant when they are no longer themselves, but only one link in the thousands of links that bind generations to one another. People should understand the sanctity, the might of this, and remove their hats, as if in a church." Sexuality was not quite like any other bodily function: it was holy. Love with its lustful component was a virtuous emotion; the two feelings were eminently compatible and affirmed life in its mysterious totality.

The ideas that Stoker embodies in his fiction, Munch forces in front of our eyes. In "The Vampire" and "Madonna," Munch painted the overpowering eroticism of Stoker's works. Strong in their power, whether stark in black and grays or stunning in brightly hued colors, they affirmed the pleasures of a woman's body, while recognizing that pleasure can lead to frenzied jealousy and despair. Robert Rosenblum points out that Munch constantly recreated woman:

Munch was obsessed with the concept of the femme fatale, whom he reincarnated in multiple guises; a modern Eve, a blood-sucking vampire, a flamelike bacchante, an archetypal murderess . . . a demonic temptress disguised as a consoling Madonna. (*Munch*, 4)

Confronting the excesses of woman's sexuality, Munch's picture "Vampire" was first exhibited under the title "Love and Pain." The myth of the vampire proved a powerful means for drawing the sexual life. Munch used horizontal lines to depict the two figures and he set them off with a background of vertical lines. Expression has been erased from their faces. The whole scene is bathed in an orange light which sharpens the outlines of the figures. The woman dominates. She sinks her lips into the man's neck, her hair tumbles around him, and he is passively situated. She is as if claiming him, appropriating him for herself. Arne Eggum observed that "active love is a dimension that the woman is fulfilling, while the man is characterized by pain in the relationship" (42). A sexual scene becomes a potentially harmful incident as the man seems helpless before the woman who is about to devour him. Is her aim the pleasure or the destruction of her lover?

The vampire is one manner of aggressor; the woman in "Death of Marat" is another. This painting, an eroticized portrayal of a failed love, depicts Munch's break with his mistress Tulla Larsen. A real event carried him across a new threshold and changed the content of his work. Love was fraught with danger, and Munch has loved, been loved, and is now the victim. Physical pleasure has ended in a psychological disaster. Combining realist disillusion with romantic excess, Munch has made himself the central figure in a melodrama a genre where suffering, is exploited for its dramatic

potential. The gun lying by the man shows a failed love and the bed has become a battlefield. The fantasized woman, hair falling on her shoulders in disarray, presents an image of grim potency. As Ragna Stan noted:

The composition within the almost square picture surface is strict. The tension between the horizontal plane and the taut, vertical pose of the woman is underscored by the painting style. She stands paralyzed before the corpse in a collected, statuelike, and self-righteous pose. (83)

She stands, staring defiantly, as the incarnation of erotic violence.

Haunting and macabre, "Madonna" was another painting that caused raised eyebrows. Gerd Woll sees "Madonna" as "the woman in love who, by conception, takes part in the creation of new life and contributes to the continued existence of mankind" (237). Dominant and impassive, this woman seems to materialize out of nowhere; her unnatural gaze indicates a hypnotic power. She looks out and upwards, barely acknowledging the viewer. With wavy lines surrounding her head, she seems to loom out of the picture, giving life and depth to the work, and commanding attention effortlessly. Whereas other frontal portraits appear immobile, her image promises activity.

The paradox of the painting is that "Madonna" becomes an active, independent subject. Munch, like Stoker, drew on the idea of the fatal woman, who often appears as a larger-than-life goddess, less an object for viewing than a subject instigating the action for the work. She rises with a noble pride in the thick softness of her form, allowing herself a celebration of her own erotic powers. Munch's use of the raised and stressed torso is similar to Michelangelo's images of the naked male body. "Madonna" entices, but in an appalling manner; her enigmatic force is somehow fatal. The hallucinatory feel of the painting seduces the viewer into a threatening world. Even here, Munch balances death and sexuality. A skull-like, eerie face, representing the underworld, lurks in the left-hand corner. Bente Torjusen has noted that Munch's "tragic childhood and youth, his frequent encounters with death, became an important factor in the development of his art. Death was to give life to his art" (29).

Stoker's fantasy was excited by sex that was dangerous, forbidden, and divorced from love; it was often fed with violent images. Munch, however, came to terms with pleasure. He often hymned involvement and preferred to have romantic love accompany sex. Munch's sexual imagination operated within the bounds of romantic sexuality; modulating lines between couples, erotically charged, seem to radiate from them.

While Stoker inclined toward the perversely amorous, Munch ultimately strove toward sexual fulfillment, making the shift into loving sexual behavior. Although he did not turn bodies into idealized forms, his women were passionate and capable of sexual abandon without being foul. Heller has noted that he was "extraordinarily compassionate regarding woman's roles" (133). Munch celebrated woman and the female body, and he was able to deal with the intimate relationships between a man and a woman. In sparse interior settings, he brought sexuality into the daylight; he did not emphasize the fantastic at the expense of physical plausibility. He refused to identify sexual power and attractiveness with glamour. It was one thing for Stoker to put sex into the supernatural where it could easily be brushed over; it was another for a painter to openly address sexual misgivings in his art. Munch brought all aspects of sex to his work, providing for richer libidinous possibilities than did Stoker. Men and women are driven to each other out of a profound attraction that is more than simple concupiscence.

"Kiss" is a tender fantasy of a man and woman as a single being.[8] It portrays a longing that is more than physical and dramatizes real intimacy and union. It is both clearly carnal and a vindication of sexuality.[9] Having fallen into an ecstatic state, the couple have lost their self-possession without meeting danger. The two bodies are so fused together they appear almost as one; their faces, what most distinguishes them, cannot be seen; there is a dreamlike timelessness to the work. "Kiss" also eroticizes the male body, the flesh itself, and not the clothing or surroundings. It transgressed physical boundaries in a way Stoker refused to do. Munch did not always struggle with sexuality, but he was able to unite spirit and body in sexual experience.

Munch was able to represent the desiring self as well as desire. "Man and Woman in Bed" (1890) is another paean to unity. Trgve Nergaard called it a "picture of mutual devotion" (*Munch*, 118). The painting conveys the idea of reciprocity in the pursuit of pleasures.[10] It is extraordinarily erotic in its evocative pose and sensuous modeling. The man is seen as desirable by the woman. The subdued colors as well as the cramped and shallow space point to a tragic parting. The figures are emphatically rounded together, the clinging suggesting a lovers' final meeting. He clings with such passion that we are reminded that moments to togetherness are of short duration. The strong emotional bond between the couple is simply expressed. Sad tenderness is often found in Munch's recumbent figures of loving men and women.

Together the couples of "Kiss" and "Man and Woman in Bed" complement each other, forming a whole. They complete each other as clearly as the lost halves of the androgyne myth. The lines surrounding them reflect their flowing energy. Power relations are not brought into focus. Reconciling the ideal and the carnal, the fleeting and the permanent, love is a form of personal pleasure. Munch explored an emotional frontier as well as techniques of linear composition and color. In neither painting is facial expression key to the sensibility the images seek to convey. In both it is the male body that is seen, the body that is the object of desire.

Stoker and Munch stand comfortably together. Confronted with sexuality, both felt a mixture of attraction and dread. They longed to lead fully sexual lives, but were ambivalent about their desires and uncertain about what to do about them. Both depicted the anxiety of attempting to free sexuality from a morality-laden culture. Munch saw sexual expression as a happiness- and harmony-producing activity; Stoker wrote of the perverse exercise of sexuality. Stoker believed that men must appear active in some way in order to fall in line with dominant ideas of masculinity; Munch did not believe that unfulfilled desires must be a permanent state. Artists of sexual anxiety as well as erotic pleasure, both, in feminizing sexual desire, agreed that an encounter with a woman had an absolute transforming power. Stoker's and Munch's visions of sexuality combined the marvelous and dreadful, where fantasy was the passport to a more liberated life.

NOTES

1. Munch incorporating explicit sexuality into his work, tended to be controversial, while Stoker, overshadowed by his friend the actor Henry Irving, tended to be inconspicuous.

2. Perhaps the symbiosis of the supernatural and sexual saved Stoker's works, and Stoker, from the fate of Oscar Wilde. Although Stoker's works offer an erotic reading to the modern mind, Farson and other critics believe Stoker would have disavowed it. In an article in *Nineteenth-Century Magazine*, Stoker wrote that

A close analysis will show that the only emotions which in the long run harm are those arising from sex impulses, and when we have realized this we have put a finger on the actual point of danger. (Farson 209)

In the same article, Stoker called for censorship

There is perhaps no branch of work among the arts so free at the present time as that of writing fiction . . . if no other adequate way can be formed and if the plague spot continues to enlarge, a censorship there must be. (Farson 207–208)

3. Theweleit writes in *Male Fantasies* that

in the narrative literature of the nineteenth-century, there is a remarkable proliferation of characters whose "inner" (true) and "outer" (social) natures are divided. Characteristic of this kind of split is the antagonism between the "inner" and "outer" natures. Dr. Jekyll, the promising young scientist, is about to abandon his risky experiments along with his other youthful sins, in order to enter into a love-marriage with a general's daughter. But after drinking the potion that exposes his inner being to the outside world, he is transformed (the notion of transformation fits this case) into Mr. Hyde. He has to become Mr. Hyde, because otherwise social convention would delay the redeeming union with his beloved too long. In any case, Mr. Hyde abandons himself to the inner stream that will being about his death. (263)

4. Freud, of course, would call this the superego: the experience of anxiety in the experience of pleasure.

5. Merck's essay compares Lucy to Alex Forrest in the movie *Fatal Attraction*: "Like Alex, this vampire steals children and must be punished, dispatched in an orgy of phallic violence" (212).

6. Auerbach reads *Dracula* along with George du Maurier's *Trilby* and Freud's *Studies on Hysteria* and writes that

we are struck by the kinds of powers that are granted to the women: the victim of paralysis possesses seemingly infinite capacities of regenerative being that turn on her triumphant mesmerizer and paralyze him in turn. Dispossessed and seemingly empty, the women reveal an infinitely unfolding magic that is quite different from the formulaic spells of the men. (17)

7. Many critics and psychologists have written on the connection between women and water. See Sandor Ferenczi's *Schriften zur Psychoanalyse*, Volume 1, Frankfurt, 1970, and Elaine Morgan's *The Descent of Woman*, NY: Stein & Day, 1972.

8. Art critic Alicia Craig Faxon writes:

One of the most surprising aspects of Rossetti's influence can be seen in the work of Edvard Munch. This influence has been cited in a number of examples, but the most convincing evidence can be seen in Munch's various versions of "The Kiss," which takes Rossettis' "Paolo and Francesca da Rimini" as a source. (226, 227)

Yet Munch's images do not appear nearly as contrived as Rossetti's.
    9. Heller writes that

Kiss seems to be the first painting to fulfill Munch's intentions as described in Saint-Cloud [Manifesto]: lovers depicted "in that moment when they are not themselves, but only one of the thousands of sexual links tying on generation to another generation." (*Munch*, 78)

    10. Heller writes that

Overtly, the drawing is a demure depiction of a couple engaged in the act of love, and a simple translation into visual terms of the scene Munch described. But the text of the [Saint-Cloud] Manifesto indicates that more was intended. As in "Night," the 'blue haze' represents death; yet at that moment—a moment of grandeur and sanctity—the living couple should be a link in the chain of life granting physiological immortality through the generation of a child, thereby defeating death. (*Munch*, 17)

WORKS CITED

Auerbach, Nina. *Woman and the Demon: The Life of a Victorian Myth*. Cambridge, MA: Harvard UP, 1982.

Belford, Barbara. *Bram Stoker; A Biography of the Author of Dracula*. New York: Alfred A. Knopf, 1996.

Edvard Munch: Symbols and Images. Washington, DC.: National Gallery of Art, 1978.

Farson, Daniel. *The Man Who Wrote Dracula: A Biography of Bram Stoker*. London: Michael Joseph. 1975.

Faxon, Alicia Craig. *Dante Gabriel Rossetti*. New York: Abbeville Press, 1989.

Glover, David. *Vampires, Mummies, and Liberals: Bram Stoker and the Politics of Popular Fiction*. Durham, NC: Duke University Press. 1996.

Merck, Mandy. *Perversions: Deviant Readings*. New York: Routledge, Inc., 1993.

Northern Light: Realism and Symbolism in Scandinavian Painting 1880–1910. NY: The Brooklyn Museum 1983.

Selz, Jean. *Edvard Munch*. New York: Crown Publishers, Inc., 1974.

Stoker, Bram. *Dracula*. New York: Scholastic Book Services, 1971.

———. *Midnight Tales*. Ed. Peter Haining. London: Peter Owen, 1990.

———. *The Lair of the White Worm*. London: Peter Owen, 1991.

Theweleit, Klaus. *Male Fantasies*. Volume I: *Women, Floods, Bodies, Histories*. Trans. Stephen Convay. Minneapolis: U of Minneapolis

Torjusen, Bente. *Words and Images of Edvard Munch*. Chelsea, VT: Chelsea Green Publishing Co. 1986.

Tropp, Martin. *Images of Fear: How Horror Stories Helped Shape Modern Culture (1818–1918)*. Jefferson, NC: McFarland & Co., Inc., 1990.

Varnedoe, Kirk, ed. *Northern Light: Realism and Symbolism in Scandinavian Painting 1880-1910*. New York: The Brooklyn Museum, 1983.

Part Two

The Vampire in Film
and Popular Culture

Chapter 7

Bela Lugosi's Dead, but Vampire Music Stalks the Airwaves

Tony Fonseca

When Lestat de Lioncourt first got together with Satan's Nite Out to form the band, The Vampire Lestat in Anne Rice's *Vampire Chronicles*, he popularized an old relationship shared between vampires and music. This marriage of the "dark gift" and guitar riffs was long in the making: the idea of vampire theme music entered the popular imagination in 1931. Tod Browning's Universal Studio-backed *Dracula* juxtaposed Bela Lugosi's thick Romanian accent and hypnotic fixed stare (achieved by Browning's shining a small light through holes in cardboard to create the illusion of glowing pupils) with Tchaikovsky's romantic masterpiece *Swan Lake*. Tchaikovsky's score became Count Dracula's theme music, for in the minds of Browning's American audience, it embodied the exotic and untamed Transylvanian homeland of Lugosi's suave and seductive vampire.

Nearly fifty years later, director Tony Scott modernized Browning's formula when he discovered that a solid beat, combined with MTV-influenced quick moving, carefully edited camera shots would lead to the mass marketing of musical vampirism. No viewer of *The Hunger* can erase from his or her mind the image of the gaunt, pale-skinned, red-lipped with blackened eyes—in essence vampiric—lead singer of Bauhaus, Peter Murphy, who in his characteristic husky baritone reminded Scott's 1983 audience that Bela Lugosi's dead—or rather "undead" as the song's chorus taunts—thus ushering in a new generation of highly stylized, esoteric vampire films.[1] Moreover, Scott and Murphy infected their American and British viewers with gothic fervor, as they introduced a generation to "vampire nightclubbing" and the goth scene.

J. Gordon Melton, in *The Vampire Book*, marks this scene from *The Hunger* as the birth into darkness of three sister movements: the gothic subculture, gothic music/nightclubs, and vampire music (264–67). As I shall explain, the three movements were originally interdependent, but with time they became separable and were ultimately mainstreamed: "Norms" are no longer shunned in many goth clubs, goth bands such as Siouxsie and the Banshees and The Cure regularly hit the top forty, and vampire music has ventured out of the darkness of the goth scene and onto the airwaves (yes even in daylight). First, I must digress here and define goth music and vampire music, which is not an easy task by any means. My intention is to dispel the myths often associated with the two, which will lead to a better understanding of the current surging popularity of vampire music.

Let me begin by differentiating what is usually meant by goth music from what has been tagged as vampire music. Goth music, like a gothic literary work, is best defined by its atmosphere (musical style) and by its thematic concerns (lyrics). In other words, if Elizabeth MacAndrew were to define goth music, she would pretty much use the same terminology she uses to define the gothic novel. In her seminal 1979 study of gothicism, *The Gothic Tradition in Fiction*, she defined gothic literature as the literature of nightmare, one that explores and often revels in the darker human emotions and one that tests the limits of society (1, 7–8). Likewise, goth music could be defined as the music of surrealism and decadence. It pushes musical boundaries to test what is acceptable in melody, instrument choice, chord progressions, and subject matter. To this end, the music revels in the power of raw experience, and often in the dark side of human nature, which sometimes finds its expression in the monstrous or grotesque. It is the musical equivalent of Ursula K. LeGuin's fiction dragon, which the capitalistic, Puritan-influenced American hegemony fears (34–37).

Goth music is not, however, as it is often mistaken to be, art school music (a term usually associated with the post-punk[2] techno band Depeche Mode). In fact, goth music is more closely associated with punk and metal than it is with techno-pop. In this respect, goth music conforms to Jack Sullivan's view of the gothic: it possesses "a fascination with darkness and irrationality, . . . the projection of apocalypse and chaos . . . with a peaked interest in violence" (2, 4). Being the dark cousin, as it were, of early punk, goth is highly emotional and energetic. Indeed, early Bauhaus and early Joy Division,[3] two ground breaking goth bands of the late 1970s, would be best classified as punk rather than goth. And the musical similarities between these two genres are evident even today. Take, for example, "Wiccaman," a high-energy, guitar driven song by gothic mainstay Nosferatu. It sounds eerily similar to "The Handshake," one of the more political tracks from the blockbuster CD *Stranger than Fiction*, the 1994 release by the quintessential 90s punk band Bad Religion (five physics Ph.D. students who satirize anything and everything, including over-dependence on technology, as in "21st Century Digital Boy"). Despite their musical similarities, goth does differ from punk because goth is less political, less satiric, and, usually, less overtly optimistic. Goth is more concerned with the personal, especially with each individual's darker side. It often does, however, share punk's sense of humor, sometimes pushing the envelope, as seen in some of the more absurdist and sarcastically cruel lyrics of various songs by two very different goth bands, Bauhaus[4] and The Smiths.[5]

Aside from its lacking a sense of humor, the most prevalent misleading myth about goth music is that it is slow, ethereal, melancholic, overly-pensive—in short, unmusical. This perhaps stems from the fact that most analysts of the gothic subculture claim as the origin of goth music the sounds of Black Sabbath; or perhaps it is because most people have heard what many call vampire music solely through Hollywood films such as *The Hunger* or *Nadja* (i.e., one Bauhaus song or some of

Portishead's more downbeat tracks). And based on these few unrepresentative musical examples and those literarily created by major goth writers like Poppy Z. Brite,[6] analysts of goth music often overgeneralize the entire musical genre. Suffice it to say that such a generalization is no more true than it would be to state that all music of the 1970s resembled Barry Manilow's commercial ballads, or that all alternative music sounds like The Violent Femmes or REM.

All of this leads to the most dangerous myth of all, that those who count themselves among goth music's fans, be they goths or just connoisseurs of the musical style, must somehow be demented. This argument is obviously no more true than the claim that those of us who read or (the gods forbid!) even teach horror or vampire courses cruise the university recreation centers looking for young, healthy victims. On the contrary, the truth is that even a careful study of goth music, even of the "cult of suicide" bands, such as Joy Division, Siouxsie and the Banshees, The Cure, The Sisters of Mercy, and Bauhaus, will not warp one's mind (irrevocably that is). Contrary to popular misconception, the music of these bands is energetic, more often than not danceable; it is multi-layered, sometimes to the point of being musically decadent. The crucial point to remember here is that goth music is closely tied with the night club scene, so the nature of the beast would dictate that it must be energetic to survive. In other words, more experimental modern goth works like Nick Cave's *Murder Ballads* may do well among the absinthe drinking crowd (or for the less adventurous goth, the Pernot drinking crowd), but the absurdly funny goth dance hit by My Life with the Thrill Kill Kult (TKK), "Days of Swine and Roses," which has as its chorus the chanted lines "Christian zombie vampire /I am the father, the father of nothing," will go over much better in the clubs.[7] The point I am leading up to here is that if goth music were as unmusical as it is too often perceived to be, then it would have died out in the United Kingdom by the 1990s; however, what did happen was this: Goth music crossed the Atlantic (one has to wonder why no goth-oriented record company has named itself Demeter Productions here) and found an ever-growing legion of loyal followers in the United States. Even today, the musical movement continues to flourish—in fact by some accounts to strengthen—in large American cities such as San Francisco and New Orleans.

One of the results of the Americanization of goth has been the resurrection of the supposedly dead sub-genre vampire music, which has won over legions of followers among mainstream fans. Because of its potential for being mainstreamed, vampire music is not dependent on the gothic subculture nor the club scene. Both Rosemary Ellen Guilery and J. Gordon Melton define vampire music variously, but both agree on a few hard-and-fast definitions of its classes. Vampire music can be defined as (1) music starring famous vampires, or (2) music containing generic vampires (either literally or symbolically), or (3) music from soundtracks of vampire films (162–71, 417–24). The focus of my study is on only the first and second of these categories.

Let me begin, however, by doing a little historical backtracking. Following Bauhaus's release, others have recorded songs about vampires. The most notable of these musicians is Sting, with his tribute to Anne Rice's vampires. "Moon over Bourbon Street." This ballad, from *Dream of the Blue Turtles*, seems to be an attempt to recreate one of Rice's vampires (Louis or Lestat—it's hard to tell) as the narrator of a song about being a reluctant and philosophical hunter of humans. Despite the fact that the production values of the song are excellent and that Sting is a big name act, "Moon over Bourbon Street" never became as popular as *Dream of the Blue Turtles*, the more political track "Russians" or the bubble-gum pop-sounding "Love Is the Seventh Wave." Literal vampires apparently don't sell. In fact, to this day, the most famous song with a literal vampire in it is the 1950s cartoonish track "Monster Mash," which sporadically mentions "Drac."[8]

Perhaps it is the lack of a mainstream market for literal vampires, or perhaps it is because of the movement in modern, often metafictional vampire texts to re-create vampires as obvious personifications (or should I say vampirsonifications) of human atrocity, but in the past seven years, more and more vampire-as-metaphor music has been recorded. Easily the best known and probably the most artistic of these attempts come from one collection, *Bloodletting*, by Concrete Blonde. The title song of the CD, which has the variant title "The Vampire Song," is perhaps one of the best examples of the use of metaphorical vampirism in music. The song tells the all-too-familiar tale of the deadbeat dad vampire, who briefly comes into the life of the narrator and creates a zombie who will never be able to go back into the light of day.[9] When one examines "Bloodletting" in context with all the songs on the collection, especially with "The Beast," it becomes apparent that "The Vampire Song" can be read as the song of the spurned lover, one who is left to join "the walking dead." The CD includes three vampire/spurned lover songs: "Bloodletting," "The Sky Is a Poisonous Garden," and "The Beast." "The Beast," an overtly vampiric song, identifies Love with a capital "L" as the ultimate vampires.[10]

About the same time, the experimental thrash/metal band Faith No More released its monstrously popular CD *Epic*, which contained similar "love sucks" vampire songs. Whereas Faith No More's more typical "The Morning After" is sung from the perspective of the drained and then "turned" victim of vampiric love," as are Concrete Blonde's vampire songs, the more atypical and diabolical "Surprise, You're Dead" is related from the point of view of the vampire/lover, who revels in his causing pain, torment, torture, nausea, suffering, perversion, and calamity, from which the victim cannot escape.[11]

What Sting, Concrete Blonde, and Faith No More realized is that vampire music wasn't just for goth clubs anymore; but unlike Sting, songwriters Johnette Napolitano of Concrete Blonde and the band members of Faith No More[12] discovered that a song with vampirism as its controlling metaphor could be much more marketable than one chronicling the life of an identifiable vampire. As the demand for vampire music increased in the early 1990s, so did the supply. Guilery notes that artists as diverse as The J. Geils Band (rock), Blue Oyster Cult (metal), Grace Jones (rock), Oingo Boingo (pop alternative), and Wire (experimental alternative) were quick to sink their teeth into this market (162). The trend continued throughout the 1990s and reached its apex in 1996, as four of the best known mainstream alternative artists (i.e., singers and bands that were once heard solely on college radio but have since been mainstreamed), namely Sinead O'Connor, The Smashing Pumpkins, The Chemical Brothers, and Rasputina, have recently released songs in which vampirism is the controlling metaphor. Because metaphorical vampirism is so malleable, each artist is able to adapt vampirism to his or her unique musical concerns.

O'Connor, as a guest vocalist on Bomb the Bass's CD *Clear* also adds her political leanings to chart topper "Empire," which she co-wrote with drummer/sample programmer/band conceptualizer Tim Simenon. Here, O'Connor and Simenon equate vampirism with British imperialism—quite an ironic twist considering the xenophobic leanings of the Van Helsing's British army of fearless vampire killers in Stoker's *Dracula*. The metamorphosis of the British "empire" into the imperialist "vampire" is certainly not new, but O'Connor readily appropriates it because it works well with her usual controversial political style (who can forget her ripping apart a picture of Pope John Paul on *Saturday Night Live*, a feat for which she still pays dearly as she is to this day banned from playing certain cities in Ireland). Perhaps it is this ostracization by her own people that leads O'Connor to berate not only the British for their exploitation of Ireland (one of the recurring lines aimed at the Empire of the song's title is "you've got to know your theft") but also those Irish who would allow their country to be colonialized. The song therefore opens not with castigation, but introspection, as O'Connor repeats lines that chronicle the narrator's peering into the soul, the future, and the eyes (each repeated thrice) of her countrymen, and finding there a spy. Throughout "Empire," O'Connor and Simenon hold this tension, attacking both the British imperialist mind-set and Irish complicity. The lesson taught is one that is all too common in vampire folklore and literature—the vampire cannot enter the threshold without the complicity of the victim.

The Smashing Pumpkins, on the other hand, use vampirism to make a highly personal statement.[13] In "Bullet with Butterfly Wings," from *Mellon Collie and the Infinite Sadness*, lead singer and guitarist Billy Corgan uses vampirism metaphorically to express the plight of the modern individual to act with integrity when faced with insurmountable social hurdles." In other words, the vampire is not the self, but the world outside—the entire world, according to Corgan. Given the human-to-vampire ratio expressed in the song's opening line, it should come as no surprise that the singer/narrator of "Bullet," in other words Corgan's Everyman, is ultimately unsalvageable. Just as literary vampirism often infects entire societies, as Dracula attempted to do in his namesake novel and succeeded in doing in Kim Newman's *Anno Dracula*, musical vampirism in this case drains an entire society of its dignity, its passion, and its freedoms. At the song's end, Corgan/the narrator is left standing alone—the Omega man against corporate America's vampirism—realizing that he is nothing more than a rat in a cage. Through this terribly mixed metaphor, "Bullet" reads like a manual for anti-establishment angst-ridden young urban professionals who fear being sucked dry by social and corporate vampirism.

The Chemical Brothers, a new funk-industrial-techno-dance duo out of Manchester, appropriate a more sensual vampirism in their number one dance club hit "Setting Sun."[14] Although "Setting Sun" never mentions vampirism per se, the lyrics refer to a tempting figure who has a young mind but an aged body, one who is the singer/narrator's inner demon; and when these images are combined with the highly charged emotion of the sound samples and driving drum beat (the two defining traits of The Chemical Brothers) the resulting music leads the listener to imagine that the lust object of the lyrics is not entirely human. Not unlike in much of the horror literature, the "monster" seems to radiate from within, perhaps from the singer/narrator's dark side. Given the title and lyrics, "Setting Sun" implies that the desirous supernatural qualities of the object of lust is a type of vampirism, which is interdependent with desire. The relationship between gothicism and eroticism, especially the idea of gothicism's relationship to sexual identity, is nothing new. Maurice Richardson first posited the theory in 1959, and Christopher Craft and William Patrick Day popularized and clarified it in the mid-1980s. Where The Chemical Brothers challenge the usual pattern is in the narrator's/singer's acceptance of this relationship rather than a repression of it. Desire in "Setting Sun" is not grotesque; it simply exists and must be dealt with. As do literary vampires, such as J. F. Le Fanu's Carmilla, this musical vampire fills a hole in its victim's life, one that could be filled only by psychic projection manifested through supernatural means.

Perhaps the most interesting and clever use of vampire music by a mainstream alternative band in 1996 is "Transylvanian Concubine," by the female punk cello trio Rasputina.[15] This Victoria-goth-meets-Gershwin trio, the creation of lead singer/cellist/songwriter Melora Creager, is best known for its remake of Melanie's "Brand New Key," a song described by Creager as being sung through fangs dripping honey. The same could be said of most of the songs on Rasputina's debut CD *Thanks for the Ether*, songs which fall into one of two categories: very strange spoken word tracks, such as "The Donner Party"—in which Creager logically examines two different phenomena and concludes that the founding fathers of America often engaged in ritual cannibalism; and pseudo-historical musical renderings of atrocities committed against women, such as "My Little Shirtwaist Fire." "Transylvanian Concubine" falls into the latter of these two categories, for it is based on the fictional history of the Dracula myth. The song does not, however, focus on the male vampire; rather it takes as its subject Dracula's three wives/concubines. Interestingly, the three women of Rasputina, Melora Creager, Julia Kent, and Carpella Parvo, often appear dressed as three vampiric women, and the band has adopted this image as its logo.

In "Transylvanian Concubine," Creager uses enjambment at the end of each lyrical unit, established as three lines early on, to write a song that vacillates between relating the tale of the vampiric women of the title and satirizing the post-feminist male-identified women of the 1990s," the latter being treated none too kindly in this metageneric work. (The song is so self-conscious that its final line reminds listeners that they should have been listening for a message.) Indeed, the message does come through loud and clear, especially seen in the larger context of the entire CD. First, there's the CD liner artwork, which is a collection of feminine images (teddy bears, sheep, Victorian cut-out dolls) set against a background of various quilt patterns. Then there's the title of the CD itself, *Thanks for the Ether*, alluding to two possible Victorian beliefs/practices—the belief that ether leads to inspiration and the controversy over allowing women to have ether during childbirth. Then there's the fact that the title of the CD is framed by a cutoff length of braided hair, molded into the shape of a heart. And if the listener still doesn't get the visual and verbal sarcasm, he or she is confronted with the three members of the band, dressed in corsets and hoop skirts and scowling, on the inside of the jewel case. Examined as a part of the whole product, "Transylvanian Concubine" can be read as another of Creager's strong feminist statements. Here we see the ultimate irony expressed in vampire music, in that Rasputina satirizes one of the most patriarchal of all images, Dracula, by appropriating, as Dracula himself would have termed them in Stoker's novel had they not been merely props, his women.

One year brought four immensely popular vampire songs. Perhaps this is because vampires are often faddish, as literary history has shown us. Or maybe this sudden popularity of the musical bloodsucker occurred because vampires and music have so much in common, both being used quite often as outlets for human desire. I think, however, that the success formula of these particular songs is strictly economic. As writers like Anne Rice, Chelsea Quinn Yarbro, Suzy McKee Charnes, Dan Simmions, Brian Lumley, and Poppy Z. Brite and directors like William Crain, George Romero, Tony Scott, Francis Ford Coppola, Guillermo Del Toro, and Michael Almereyda have discovered, vampires are an extremely malleable and therefore marketable commodity.

NOTES

1. Vampire films prior to Tony Scott's *The Hunger* tended to be more linear and plot-driven than stylized and image-driven. These pre-1983 vampire films, such as Tod Browning's *Dracula* (1931) or its Universal Studio-backed sequels, the Hammer Dracula films starring Christopher Lee and John Badham's 1979 *Dracula* starring Frank Langella, not to mention the vampire as innocent victim films such as William Crain's *Blacula* (1972) and Dan Curtis's made-for-TV *Dracula* starring Jack Palance (1974), all relied on the basic plot line of find the vampire, chase the vampire, kill the vampire. The only notable exception to this is George Romero's anti-vampire B flick *Martin* (1978), which is character-driven. After the 1979 debut of MTV and the 1983 production of *The Hunger*, there is a marked change in vampire films as they become more metageneric and esoteric. The mark of *The Hunger* can be seen on Francis Ford Coppola's *Bram Stoker's Dracula* (1992). Michael Almereyda's David Lynch-backed production *Nadja* (1994), and Abel Ferrara's vampire film noir *The Addiction* (1995). Of course, there are always exceptions (John Landis' *Innocent Blood* for example, or the little known Cronenberg-esque Canadian film by Holly Dale, unfortunately titled *Blood and Doughnuts*), but the trend is toward experimentation with image.

2. Punk music supposedly died out in the 1980s, but the emergence of bands in the United States such as Green Day, Bad Religion, Social Distortion, Babes in Toyland, and Hole, and the emergence in the United Kingdom of Elastica, The Happy Mondays, Black Grape and Rancid in the last five years indicates a resurgence of the punk sound. The most noticeable difference between early punk (1970s–1980s) and the post-punk bands mentioned above is the move towards a more self-effacing satire.

3. After the suicide of lead singer/song writer Ian Curtis in 1980, Joy Division renamed itself, becoming the more dance-oriented New Order. Guitarist Bernard Sumne, now of Electronic, became the new lead singer/songwriter Bauhaus broke up in 1983 and spawned the experimental neo-hippie punk trio Love and Rockets and Peter Murphy's solo career. Both Love and Rockets and Murphy went on to record more dance-oriented music.

4. Most see Bauhaus as the epitome of gothic music, probably because of Murphy's *Hunger* performance of "Bela Lugosi's Dead," a song that many do not realize is actually tongue-in-cheek. I believe this misunderstanding occurs because Bauhaus was relatively unknown in the United States before *The Hunger*, so their American listeners assumed the song was written for the film. It was actually released in 1979 and removed from the film and is a much more irreverent and absurd song. Other early Bauhaus tracks show this same sense of absurdity and attest to the band's iconoclastic nature. For example, "Dancing" has its dancers

dancing on hot tiles, on tender hooks, and in church isles. Another early song, "St. Vitus Dance," is almost cruel in its humor.

5. Few analysts of goth music ever think to include The Smiths in their discussions of the movement. However, this Morrissey/Johnny Marr-driven band meets all criteria for goth bands, except the band members do not use makeup as part of their performances. Their songs are filled with images of decay, death, the "grayness" of everyday life, isolation, existentialism, a preoccupation with violence, and the horrors of love. Perhaps it is the perky, upbeat characteristic Marr guitar chords that have led music critics to their misconception of the band, or perhaps it is the misguided notion that goth music is always serious. The Smiths are appreciated when one is aware of both Morrissey's love of the dark side of human nature and his sardonic wit, as in "The Queen Is Dead," where he attacks the British royalty and defends his homosexuality: or in "Vicar in a TuTu," another song about cross-dressing. One of the more gothic Smiths' songs is "Cemetery Gates," in which Morrissey sings of a dreaded sunny day. Many Smiths' songs are also rife with cruel and iconoclastic imagery, as is "Bigmouth Strikes Again," which treats Joan D'Arc with absurdity. Finally, there are Smiths' songs filled with death imagery, usually associated with love, such as the ending of "Ask Me," which celebrates the threat of nuclear holocaust, which will bring coy lovers together.

6. In a lecture at Louisiana State University on April 7, 1997, Poppy Brite classified the music that Steve and Ghost, the main characters and band members of Lost Souls?, perform as not goth music but shitkicker music," more akin to The Eagles than Bauhaus, Joy Division, or any of the other 1970s goth/punk bands.

7. "Days of Swine and Roses" can be found on the CD *Confessions of a Knife*.

8. "Monster Mash" was recorded in 1962 (and released on Carfax records!) by Bobby "Boris" Pickett and the Crypt Kickers. It reached the top spot on the Billboard charts and stayed there two weeks. The song was released a third time in 1973, and it sold 2 million copies. It reached number ten on the charts that year. Since then "Monster Mash" has become the unofficial anthem of Halloween.

9. "Bloodletting," from Concrete Blonde's CD of the same name (1990), is also named "The Vampire Song." Its lyrics clearly allude to Rice's New Orleans vampire scene.

10. "The lyrics to Faith No More's "The Morning After" (1989) show the band's more subtle use of vampirism and is similar to "Bloodletting" in its themes and imagery.

11. *Epic*, Faith No More's 1989 release, contains not only "Surprise. You're Dead!" but also "Zombie Eaters," a song which illustrates the vampire/victim relationship between infant and mother.

12. The CD liner notes identify all five band members—Mike Bordin, Roddy Boltum, Bill Gould, Jim Martin, and Michael Patton—as the writers of "Surprise. You're Dead!"

13. The lyrics to The Smashing Pumpkins' "Bullet with Butterfly Wings" are rife with mixed metaphors, yet the song manages to hold together because of the opening vampire image and the movement toward the image of Christ, not as a redeemer but as an innocent and betrayed victim.

14. The lyrics of "Setting Sun" never mention vampirism, but the chanted opening lines call attention to the image of dusk, when vampires come to life, and the remainder of the lyrics (what there are of them: the song is mostly instrumental) imply a supernatural, ageless being associated with desire.

15. Rasputina's "Transylvanian Concubine" is an extremely clever appropriation of vampirism. It contains the marvelous image of fangs ruining pouting lips. One final note: the ellipses at the end of each third line evident in the published lyrics included in the liner notes, mark the enjambment that Creager uses to switch thoughts at will and, thereby, freely to associate vampirism with feminism.

WORKS CITED

Craft, Christopher. "'Kiss Me With Those Red Lips': Gender and Inversion in Bram Stoker's
Dracula." *Representations* 8 (1984): 107–33.

Day, William Patrick. *In the Circles of Fear and Desire. A Study of Gothic Fantasy.* Chicago:
U of Chicago P, 1985.

Guilery, Rosemary Ellen. *The Complete Vampire Companion.* New York: Simon &
Schuster/Macmillan, 1994.

Le Guin, Ursula K. *The Language of the Night: Essays on Fantasy, and Science Fiction* Ed.
Susan Wood. New York: Harper Collins. 1994.

MacAndrew, Elizabeth. *The Gothic Tradition in Fiction.* New York: Columbia UP, 1979.

Melton, J. Gordon. *The Vampire Book: The Encyclopedia of the Undead.* Detroit: Visible Ink
Press, 1994.

Richardson, Maurice. "The Psychoanalysis of Ghost Stories." *Twentieth Century* 166 (July–
Dec., 1959): 419–31.

Sullivan, Jack. *Elegant Nightmares* Athens, OH: Ohio UP, 1978.

Chapter 8

Policing Eddie Murphy: The Unstable Black Body in *Vampire in Brooklyn*

Leslie Tannenbaum

In recent critical conversations about race, it is has become a commonplace that the politics of race involves the politics of reading bodies. For, as Amitai Avi-Ram observes,

The working of sexual and racial prejudices is based upon an attitude toward the body: that the body has meaning, that it possesses a certain transparency as a sign, just like an ordinary word ("good" or "bad"). The infinite variety of human beings is thus at the most basic level organized according to what appear to be visible and patent signs, bodily signs that can easily be "read" according to a code so standard and so universal that its rules hardly enter consciousness. Yet it is those very unconscious codes that are oppressive. (32)

While it has been the work of feminist, African-American, postcolonial and gay/lesbian studies to challenge this notion of the body's self-evident readability, artists of both high culture and popular culture to varying degrees—and often unconsciously—have also participated in this project of disrupting established notions of a "readable" sexual or racial body. A case in point is the 1995 film *Vampire in Brooklyn*, whose use of a shape-shifting black vampire not only establishes an unstable—and therefore unreadable—black body, but also entertains a backlash against this instability both on screen and off. As comedian-turned- villain, Beverly Hills Cop turned criminal, Eddie Murphy, the elusive vampire-actor, instigates a "cops and robbers" game within the plot of the movie but also instigates similar policing—on the part of his reviewers.

The plot of *Vampire in Brooklyn* foregrounds this policing activity because the movie's main action is the vampire Maximilian's attempted courtship and seduction of a police officer. As a rookie cop whose status as a "good cop" is at stake in this film, Rita Veder, played by Angela Bassett, must face and overcome the disruptive powers that Maximilian represents. Her task is complicated, however, by the fact that the destabilizing forces that Max represents are not simply out there: they are inside her as well, as it is revealed early in the film that Rita herself is really half vampire. Max is the last of his race who has come from the Caribbean to seek his own kind, and Rita is Max's target because her body is quite literally marked by vampirism before he even seduces her. In other words, Rita must not only deal with bodily instabilities that Max represents, but must also confront her own unstable body—and she performs this within the context of her social duties as a police officer.

In order to understand more fully what is at stake in Rita's mission and ordeal, we need to outline more precisely the social and personal threat that Max represents. Throughout the movie, the vampire's threat to the body politic is represented by the various ways in which he disrupts the body, most particularly the black body. When he arrives in Brooklyn, Max's first act is to remove the heart of a white mafioso and to dismember that man's partner. These acts of bodily fragmentation precede an equally dramatic operation on a black man. When Max turns a numbers runner named Julius Jones (played by Kadeem Hardison) into his ghoul, Julius starts dropping body parts, a process that continues throughout the film. From leaving his ear in Max's ship to be discovered by Rita and her partner, to his having an eyeball roll across the floor in the final scene, Julius's predicament, besides providing a source of comic relief, also foregrounds other forms of bodily instability, some of which are somewhat more subtle.

Besides destabilizing the bodies of others, the vampire's body itself becomes a source of instability in a number of ways. Because he has to kill humans in order to feed, the vampire is most obviously disruptive of the social fabric and foregrounds the ability of the vampire's body to contain the bodies of others. This absorption of others is both literal and metonymic. In response to an invitation to dinner from Julius, Max spits out a body part of a mafioso and says, "No thanks, I've already had Italian." The mention of eating Italian is repeated a few times in the film, and eating others in general is an ongoing verbal motif, as in Max's telling Rita that he would love to have her for dinner and in Max's telling Julius's uncle Silas that he's on the menu. Throughout the movie, then, vampirism is represented mostly as a form of cannibalism, which threatens the idea of personal possession of one's body by representing the body as a commodity available for consumption by others.

This literal containment of others by a black body also functions metonymically as a mimicking of similar attempts by the body politic to contain its citizens. Because most of Max's victims are white, Max reverses the social order. While the white body politic seeks to contain unruly black bodies, we have here an unruly black body that literally contains whites by eating them and symbolically contains them by disarming two of its most powerful "organs"—the police and the mafia.

Max's body is also disruptive in that it quite literally illustrates the adage that "you are what you eat," as Max sucks the blood of two of his human victims in order to assume their shapes. It is here, of course, that the vampire appears to be most obviously unstable and threatening: his shape-shifting keeps others from apprehending any truths about his body and, hence, truths about his identity. This disruptive instability is given comic emphasis from the very beginning, when Silas describes the vampire's shape-shifting as "flip-flopping" and relates it to a gender-bending experience in which a prostitute that he picked up in Bushwick flip-flopped on him by turning into a man. This example of the disruption of socially established body codes could hardly be more apt.

Like the "flip-flopping" of the transvestite, the vampire's choice of bodily shapes in this film has political overtones, as Max takes the shape of an Al Sharpton-style preacher named Reverend Pauley and a Tarantino-style mafia punk named Guido. And each of these moves is politically subversive. The character of Reverend Pauley questions the power of religion in the African-American community. Disguised as Reverend Pauley, Max is able to con a gullible crowd of churchgoers into thinking that evil is good. And the transformation into Guido is a move that mocks the whole idea of a black man seriously wanting to pass as white, in that the highly cultivated Max makes a socially downward move by taking on the character of a two-bit white street punk, In this case, Guido's white body immediately gains status and power by being taken over by Max's black soul. Here the performative-native nature of white identity is proclaimed through the spectacle of a dark African American very effectively passing as white. Max or Murphy's performative expertise is emphasized by Julius telling Max that he should win an academy award. In both of these cases of bodily transformation, Max is indicating that the body itself cannot be "read" for any important or essential truths.

This ability to read bodies, however, is part and parcel of a police officer's trade and an important part of the larger social project of using the law to regulate bodies— or using bodies to enforce the law. An orderly body politic is dependent upon orderly bodies, and an orderly body is one that is readable. This is underscored when Rita's police partner, Justice, on hearing that a vampire could be among them without their knowing, replies, "I would know." But it's clear that Justice doesn't know, as it takes a while for him to figure out that Max, whom he has just met, is a vampire. Rita, too, is already a bad reader, and she is accused of being a bad cop because she herself is in danger of becoming unreadable. Her sense of identity is thus tied up with her sense of profession, as she is struggling to police herself as well as others. Before she even learns that she is half vampire, she is haunted by fears of being marked as different from others. Part of this is the result of social circumstances, as her mother—an anthropologist who married Rita's vampire father—was incarcerated in an asylum after Rita was born, and Rita was raised in a foster home. Besides having to deal with all of this, and her mother's recent death in the asylum, Rita also has to deal with terrifying dreams and premonitions that haunt her, all of which are connected to her vampire inheritance which ties her to her dead father and to Maximilian. The more she comes into contact with Max, the more Rita comes to realize that the destabilizing forces that make her feel she is going crazy are all from within her own body, from her genetic inheritance rather than her social background. This vampiric body is quite literally represented in the opening of the film, when Rita goes down into the hull of the ship that brings Max to Brooklyn and discovers her own vampire body lying in Max's coffin—an image repeated in a dream sequence that occurs soon thereafter.

The more Rita comes into contact with this knowledge of her own vampiric body, the more her terror is increased by the fact that this body is driving a wedge between her and her profession, as well as the orderly social body that this profession represents. It is no accident that Rita is at her most vulnerable to Max and allows herself to be seduced by him immediately after she is suspended from the police force and thus deprived of any external support that might help her police the vampire without and the vampire within. This point is underscored by her invoking, half-flirtatiously, her position as a police officer when Max asks her to dinner:

Max: I would love to have you for dinner.
Rita: (Moving Slowly toward Max) Look here, I'm a cop.
Max: The police?
Rita: Uh huh . . . the Law. which means. If you try anything funny, I'll shoot you.
Max: Do I look like I'd bite you?
Rita: You'd better not . . . not after the day I've had [alluding to her suspension].

It is at this point that Rita's major trial takes place, in that she must make her "human" side victorious by really proving that she is, indeed, the police, the law—that she is a good cop in every sense of the word. After her seduction by Max, she must police her own unruly body by refusing to feed on the blood of others and by driving a stake through Maximilian's heart.

This pattern of struggle to earn a stable body and thus a stable social identity is highlighted by the familiar horror-story triangle in which a woman must choose between two men, one who is "normal" and one who is "monstrous," who represent, respectively, the angelic and demonic self. In this case the angel is Rita's police partner, unsubtly named "Justice" in symbolic/linguistic antithesis to the unsatiable desires represented by the name of his rival, Maximilian. This conflict between the two suitors and the identity issues at stake are established when Rita first meets Max while on duty with Justice and is almost seduced by Max, which initiates an immediate conflict between the two men. In response to Max's commenting to Justice that Rita is "one of a kind," Justice quickly responds, "But not your kind." In choosing between Justice and Max, Rita is not just choosing between her supposedly human and vampire side, but is also choosing between the cop and the criminal within herself. She must try to prove, in Justice's words, that "she is not a killer."

Of course, Rita proves in the end that she is a killer but that she is capable of killing the right person, Maximilian. And there is a certain amount of irony in Justice's statement during a reconciliation scene that "We're only human," as we know that this is clearly not true for Rita. Because Rita cannot really erase her vampire inheritance; the stakes, then, don't involve any essentialist issues so much as Rita's ability to produce visible signs that she is "only human," that her body is within the pale of the body politic. Her victory in the end merely shows her ability to demonstrate a mastery of body policing, and, thus, of body politics. In other words, she has to prove her body's own readability and her ability correctly to read the body of others, especially unruly bodies.

This drama of body literacy is enacted not only within the film's story but within the press reception of the story as well. Just as Rita and others are engaged in policing unruly bodies on the screen, the movie itself incites the critics to perform an equally strong policing action off screen. Just as Maximilian "flip-flops" within the film, Eddie Murphy performs an equally disquieting transformation by playing a part that his audience and critics are not accustomed to; and the film's playing with genre codes becomes equally unsettling to viewers. In other words, Eddie Murphy's physical body and his metonymic body, the film itself or the artist's, as we call it, become in their instability a source of anxiety and, hence, of policing on the part of the critics.

Most of the reviews of *Vampire in Brooklyn* focus on three central issues: establishing the film's position within a narrative of Eddie Murphy's career, judging the ability—or even the right—of Eddie Murphy to represent a vampire, and identifying the film's genre. All three cases involve attempts at reading the man and his film, and the two frequently become conflated. All told, the negative reviews of *Vampire in Brooklyn* contain some of the most mean-spirited critiques that one could find anywhere, and most of them are *ad hominem*. Because Murphy is here departing from his traditional comic image in order to play it straight, as it were, and because he relegates a lot of the comedy in the film to the "low comic" figures of Julius Jones and his uncle Silas (played respectively by Kadeem Hardison and John Witherspoon), in a style of comedy that we usually don't associate with Murphy, most of the critics were outraged or confused about this (e.g., Ramirez). Instead of focusing on the film itself, they became more concerned with using it to mark Murphy as a success or failure. In other words, a disturbing change in his role in the cultural script is a transgression on Murphy's part, which the critics feel they must punish by enacting the failure that they desire. Murphy's performance as criminal leads to the critics' performance as police.

Many of the critics who did engage with Murphy's performance in the film had a difficult time deciding how to take this performance. Missing a lot of the self-reflexive ironies in the film (many of which were voiced through the choric figures of Silas and Julius), most of the critics took Murphy's performance at face value, claiming that he was trying too hard to mimic Nick Ashford, Billy Dee Williams, Barry White, or Superfly (critics Wloszczyna, Gleiberman, and Drayton). They also had a hard time deciding whether he was appropriately seductive or appropriately frightening— affective criteria that would be difficult for anyone really to prove (critics Tremblay, Stack, R. N., Ramirez, Collin, Ranch, and Rathke). In other words, the body on the screen, like the social body that they felt they could punish or reward, was unreadable to a lot of the critics.

Equally unreadable is the film's genre. Billed as "a comic tale of horror and seduction," *Vampire in Brooklyn* would probably even give Northrop Frye some pause. Some critics claimed that the film—especially since it was directed by horror master Wes Craven—did not satisfy the generic demands of a horror film, while other critics—looking for the familiar Eddie Murphy comedy—were disappointed to find that Murphy's humor was essentially in the form of wry one-liners, such as his responding to Julius saying that the way to a woman's heart is through the church, by saying, "Actually, it's through the rib cage, but that's a bit messy."

As I have already noted, most of the comedy has been taken over by Julius and Silas, whose low-comic presence serves to make Murphy's vamping look more suave and ironic. Many critics saw this as a disappointing division of labor (Stark; Vincent; Braun). And a few critics polarized the odd coupling of Murphy, the comic actor, and Craven, the horror-film director (Vincent; Drayton), to explain what they saw as the generic conflicts within the film. Indeed, the critics seemed to have a good time indulging in as many vampire puns as possible to proclaim the film's failure to meet generic expectations; examples include the following two review titles: "Murphy Loses Comic Bite in 'Vampire'" (Wloszczyna) and "Tired Blood: Humor-Starved

'Vampire in Brooklyn' Bites Off More than It Can Chew" (Stark). And at least two critics couldn't pass up the more obvious temptation to say that either Murphy's performance or the film sucks (Rathke; Wloszczyna).

Closer to the mark were those critics who saw the film as a deliberate genre-bending work, comparing *Vampire in Brooklyn* to the similarly titled revisionist horror film *An American Werewolf in London* (DeLapp; Ranch) or to *Love at First Bite* and *The Fearless Vampire Killers* (Vincent), only to find the Murphy film to be lacking. Two reviewers sensed that the film was attempting to make an ironic move similar to that of *An American Werewolf* (DeLapp; Ranch), but they neglected one important difference: the issue of race. In fact, very few of the reviews even begin to touch the issue of an African-American appropriation of a traditionally white genre.

Here the most obvious cultural predecessor is *Blacula*, which Murphy's film both invokes and refuses from the very beginning: Julius Jones, when he first encounters Max, says, "You ain't gonna pull that Blacula shit on me, are you?" Several critics of *Vampire in Brooklyn* drew parallels with the earlier blaxploitation film, but only to make superficial comparisons in favor of *Blacula* (Wloszczyna; Ebert; Drayton). These critics did not notice that while the earlier African-American vampire film, made in 1972, does contain a social critique, it is imbued with an optimism about racial progress that Murphy's film denies. The heroes in *Blacula* are young African-American professionals whose triumph over the seductive African vampire-prince can easily be read as an assimilationist narrative. There is little overt reference to racial conflict in *Blacula*, most of which is displaced as homophobia, and almost all of Blacula's victims are black. Murphy's film, on the other hand, foregrounds problems of race relations and racial identity in its very generic transgressions.

I have found only one critic who noticed that almost all of Maximilian's victims are white (Tremblay), and he did not take this observation very far. Not only are Max's victims white, but also, prior to being attacked by Max, they make racially denigrating remarks. The mafioso whom Max first attacks calls him "eggplant," Guido calls him "Sambo," and a white, liberal, rich lady first makes nasty remarks about the black "servant problem" to her friend before she tries to save herself from Max with a lame attempt at political correctness: "I understand the plight of the Negro in white capitalist society." In one of his best puns, Max says that this woman richly deserves to be victimized by him. It's clear, then, that Murphy's vampire is really being provoked, and that—unlike Blacula—the vampire in this movie is being invoked as a hero figure, as one who lashes out at modern racism, whether blatant or more subtly liberal.

In case we miss the point about Max's heroic status, this formula-driven film gives a very nonformulaic view of the vampire's death. While Blacula and other vampires usually disintegrate completely at the end of the movie in the obligatory decaying body scene, Max's body is restored to its original handsome state and then undergoes what is clearly an apotheosis, being transformed into a dove that flies out the window surrounded by a saintly aureole. This heroic vision, like any other definitive reading of Max, is undercut by a final scene in which Max is reincarnated as Julius, but the image still remains as an important facet of Max's character.

Like this elusive vampire, then, the discourse of race in the film is one that seems to elude the policing of the critics, probably because it is too complicated for them to comprehend or deal with. Again, this problem is tied to the issue of African Americans appropriating a predominantly white genre. If, in white discourse about race, the vampire stands in as a racial "other," what does it mean when a film establishes vampires as a race within a race that is already marked as "other"? And what does this say to black as well as white audiences? In the postmodern nineties, it's clear that Murphy's film, intentionally or not, is disrupting any idea of a unified and stable black identity, and this idea is emphasized by the reappearance of Maximilian as Julius at the end of the film, which suggests that the vampire within Rita Veder may not lie still either, despite her successful policing. In this strong invocation of unstable, unreadable, and elusive black bodies, then, *Vampire in Brooklyn* is questioning the ability of anyone, black or white, to claim any authority as the police or the law over the body of Eddie Murphy, the body of his work and the black body politic.

WORKS CITED

Avi-Ram, Amitai. "The Unreadable Black Body: 'Conventional' Poetic Form in the Harlem Renaissance." *Genders*, 7 (Spring 1990): 32–46.

Braun, Liz. Rev. of *Vampire in Brooklyn*. *Toronto Sun* 1996, (online).

Collin, Juliette. Rev. of *Vampire in Brooklyn*. The Best Video Guide (online). DeLapp, Bill. Rev. of *Vampire in Brooklyn*. *Syracuse New Times* Net News, 1995. http://www.rwa.com/films/vampbkly.htm.

Drayton, David. Rev. of *Vampire in Brooklyn*. *eyeweekly* (Toronto), Nov. 2, 1995(online).

Ebert, Roger. Rev. of *Vampire in Brooklyn*. *Chicago Sun Times*, (Oct. 27, 1995) (online).

Gleiberman, Owen. "Biting the Dust: Eddie Murphy Is Down for the Count in 'Vampire.'" Entertainment Weekly Online.

R. N. "*Vampire in Brooklyn*." in "Picks and Pans" Section of *People* (online).

Ramirez, Daniel. Rev. of *Vampire in Brooklyn*. *The Tech* (MIT), 115.52 (Oct. 27. 1995): 6.

Ranch, S. Rev. of Vampire in Brooklyn. http//www.Leland.Stanford.edu/-srenshaw Vampireinbrooklyn.htm

Rathke, Susan. "Vampires May Never Die, But Murphy's Career Has." http://www.film.com/film/reviews/V/vampire.brooklyn.stranger.html.

Stack, Peter. "Murphy's 'Vampire' Is All Grin, No Bite." *San Francisco Chronicle*, April 12, 1996, D12.

Stark, Susan. "Tired Blood: Humor-Starved 'Vampire in Brooklyn' Bites Off More than It Can Chew." *Detroit News*, Oct. 22, 1995.

Tremblay, Bob. "'Vampire in Brooklyn' Is Down for the Count." *Middlesex News*.

Vincent, Mal. Rev. of *Vampire in Brooklyn*. *Virginia Pilot*, Oct. 27, 1995 (Pilotonline).

Wloszczyna, Susan. "Murphy Loses Comic Bite in 'Vampire.'" *USA Today* Movies http://www.usatodaycom/life/enter/movieslef206.htm.

Chapter 9

Resurrection in Britain: Christopher Lee and Hammer *Draculas*

James Craig Holte

After World War Two, film producers and audiences turned away from traditional horror films, best exemplified by the Universal monster movies. As Stephen King has pointed out in his analysis of the horror genre, *Danse Macabre*, pulp magazines and comics kept horror alive and well while mainstream fiction and film explored other genres. In the United States, filmmakers interested in exploring the "other," traditionally the subject of horror and fantasy, turned to science fiction, creating such classic films as *The Thing* (1951), *It Came from Outer Space* (1953), *Them!* (1954), *Forbidden Planet* (1956), *The Day the Earth Stood Still* (1951), *The Blob* (1958), *The Incredible Shrinking Man* (1957), and *Invasion of the Body Snatchers* (1955). These, and other science fiction films, positioned terror in space, the atomic age, and the cold war, as these settings appeared far more terrifying to American audiences than Transylvanian castles or Egyptian tombs.

Science and technology, depicted as potential tools for good in *Dracula*, become sources of unease, much as they were in Mary Shelly's *Frankenstein*. In a culture that had recently experienced the double shocks of worldwide genocide and the unleashing of atomic power, the cool, rational scientist was no longer seen as ever on the side of the angels. In England, Hammer Films, an entertainment company established in 1947, entered the science fiction/horror field with such films as *Stolen Face* (1952), *Spaceways* (1953), *The Quartermass Experiment* (1955), and *X- The Unknown* (1956), low-budget films that captured the postwar unease over rapid developments in technology and equally rapid changes in social structures.

In both the United States and Great Britain filmmakers used their films to examine the changing nature of American and British cultures. On both sides of the Atlantic political, social, and economic forces were challenging established orders and relationships, and the science fiction and horror films of the postwar period chronicled the cultural unease felt by many as traditional roles and responsibilities came into question. In 1958, after the success of its popular *The Curse of Frankenstein* (1957), directed by Terence Fisher and starring Peter Cushing as Victor Frankenstein and Christopher Lee as the monster, a film that echoed all of the anti-technological arguments of Mary Shelley's original novel and the Universal Studio's adaptations of the 1930s, Hammer produced *Dracula*, released in the United States as *The Horror of Dracula*, and Stoker's vampire rose from the grave with renewed vigor.

In his intelligent and well-written analysis of British horror films, *Hammer and Beyond*, Peter Hutchings provides both a history of postwar British horror films and an analysis of their function in popular culture, which as John Cawelti, among others, has noted, tends to reinforce the accepted beliefs of political and social ideology. Hutchings observes, for example, that on a fundamental level, "Horror tends to be identified as a means by which an audience comes to terms with certain unpleasant aspects of reality"(17). Hutchings then quotes James Twitchell's useful observation that horror sequences are really formulaic rituals coded with precise social information needed by the adolescent audience. Like fairy tales that prepare the child for the anxieties of separation, modern horror myths prepare the teenager for the anxieties of reproduction (99). Hutchings goes on to examine the particular cultural and aesthetic elements that contributed to the success of Hammer Films' recreation of horror narratives made popular earlier by Universal Pictures: features that focused on Frankenstein, the Mummy, the Wolfman, and Dracula, all creatures who, according to Stephen King, a writer who has had some success in judging the popular culture's desire for horror, represent the fear of transformation into the world of nightmare and the loss of rational control (*Danse Macabre*, 1–15).

Hammer horror films provided viewers with formula narratives for a time of social and cultural transition. As R.W. Dillard noted in "The Pagentry of Death," "The horror film teaches an acceptance of the natural order of things and an affirmation of man's ability to cope with and even prevail over the evil of life which he can never hope to understand" (Hutchings, 23) and, as Ken Gelder asserts in *Reading the Vampire*, gothic horror, a genre that includes vampire narratives, performs this function by presenting texts in which "disequilibrium is inaugurated by violence to the social order, and (an often legally sanctioned) violence is usually the means by which a renewed equilibrium is restored at the end" (93).

People in both Britain and the United States shared serious fears and anxieties. The Second World War and the dawn of the atomic age shattered whatever illusions remained about international cooperation and economic progress, recreating a sense of paranoia familiar to those who experienced the cultural disruptions caused by the First World War and the Depression. Class, gender, and familial relationships were in transition as well. Just as the Universal horror films of the 1930s reflected the unease caused by the Depression—the failure of patriarchal capitalism to provide a stable structure for families or communities—the Hammer horror films of the late 1950s and 1960s reflected the rise of consumerism, the failure of patriarchal structures to reestablish the prewar order, the rise of the middle class, and the changing role of women in society and the family.

A number of factors helped establish Hammer Films as the premier studio for the production of horror films in the 1950s. First, Hammer had produced several successful thrillers for the BBC; and, as a result the company had learned to target specific narratives for specific audiences, especially the emerging teen audience of the postwar period. On both sides of the Atlantic film producers recognized that an increasing percentage of film audiences was composed of young viewers, whose values and expectations were different front those of their parents. Second, Hammer had acquired a stable of actors, technicians, writers, and directors who worked together on a variety of projects establishing a "Hammer style," a formula that stressed physical action, sexuality, the use color photography, and gothic settings. Finally, Hammer Films worked in close cooperation with an American distributor, ensuring both financing and a large potential audience. This permitted the studio to retain its talented cast and crew as well as its first-rate studio.

In his study of Hammer Films, Peter Hutchings suggests that the setting for the Hammer color horror films is a major factor in their success. He writes:

While Hammer horror films need to be seen very much as addressing the social context within which they were fashioned, account also must be taken of the fact that, despite their "modernity," they were set in the past. Clearly the films' engagement with present-day matters was, at the very least, veiled or coded. . . .

The period setting, and the historical space thereby opened up between film and audience, enables a more fantastic, stylised acting out of events, unencumbered as it is with the suggestions of realism carried by modern locations. This displacement ensured that Hammer was never as disturbing to audiences, most critics and the censors, as were more realistic horrors. It might also be the case, and as I have already suggested, that the period setting permitted a conservative nostalgia for a fixed social order, one in which those who were powerless were legitimate prey. (65)

The use of period settings with color photography alone would not have made the Hammer horror films successful. Perhaps the most important element, aside from the adaptation and readaptation of such familiar works of horror as *Frankenstein* and *Dracula*, was the collaboration of such talented professionals as director Terence Fisher and actors Peter Cushing and Christopher Lee.

Terence Fisher had worked as a film editor in England during the 1930s and directed his first film, *A Song for Tomorrow*, in 1948. In 1953 Fisher began working for Hammer films, first creating science fiction films and finally directing Hammer's breakthrough film *The Curse of Frankenstein*. Fisher continued to work in the horror genre until his retirement in 1973. Peter Cushing began his work in the theater as an assistant stage manager and started acting in 1935. Cushing performed on the stage and in films in the late 1940s and early 1950s, eventually landing the role of Victor Frankenstein in Hammer films famous 1957 film, *The Curse of Frankenstein*. He was then cast in his signature role, Professor Van Helsing, in Hammer's *Dracula*.

Perhaps the most famous of the three collaborators is Christopher Lee, who, along with Bela Lugosi, has become identified in the popular imagination with the character of Dracula. Lee had a successful career prior to *Dracula*, performing in such films as *Scott of the Antarctic* (1948), *They Were Not Divided* (1950), *Captain Horatio Hornblower* (1951), *The Crimson Pirate* (1952), *Moulin Rouge* (1952), and *Bitter Victory* (1957). Because of his success at portraying villains, executives at Hammer Films cast Lee as the monster in *The Curse of Frankenstein* and, in 1958, as

Dracula. Despite a long and illustrious career after playing the Count numerous times, Lee is still remembered primarily for his depiction of Count Dracula.

Although the three men did not work together on all of the Hammer horror films, or even all of the *Dracula* series, their work in *The Curse of Frankenstein* (1957), *Dracula* (1958), and *The Mummy* (1959) established a recognizable Hammer style of sexuality, physicality, and clear delineation between good and evil that appeared in many of the studio's productions. Hammer borrowed the monster movie formula from Universal Films, but replaced Universal as the premier producer of horror by a skillful updating of Universal's formulas. Terence Fisher has long been recognized as an efficient craftsman who mastered the art of horror, but David Pirie, in *A Heritage of Horror*, argues that Fisher is a major film director whose body of work transcends the commercial constraints of the period and establishes a coherent world view. Cushing and Lee are now also being appreciated for their work. At one time actors who worked in genre films, especially horror films, received little critical attention. This attitude, however, is changing, and actors such as Peter Cushing and Christopher Lee, as well as Vincent Price, Basil Rathbone, and Boris Karloff, are seen as talented professionals who successfully created and defined genre characters. Cushing and Lee both served their apprenticeships in a variety of supporting roles but became famous playing leads, and antagonists, in Hammer horror films.

Their first famous collaboration was in *The Curse of Frankenstein*, a financial success for Hammer that established the color gothic horror film as a significant genre of its own. Cushing played Baron Victor Frankenstein, and Lee the Monster. Their most famous collaboration was in *Dracula*, in which Cushing's professional Van Helsing confronts Lee's physical Dracula. Many critics now maintain that Lee's Dracula and Cushing's Van Helsing are the definitive film performances in those roles.

Hammer Films recycled its successes, creating series of *Mummy, Frankenstein*, and, of course, *Dracula* films. The *Dracula* series consists of eight films made between 1958 and 1974: *Dracula* (1958), *Brides of Dracula* (1960), *Dracula, Prince of Darkness* (1965), *Dracula Has Risen from His Grave* (1968), *Taste the Blood of Dracula* (1969), *Scars of Dracula* (1970), *Dracula A.D. 1972* (1972), and *The Satanic Rites of Dracula* (1973). In addition Lee played Dracula in *El Conde Dracula* (1972), an ambitious, but under funded, non-Hammer production. Although few of these films are careful adaptations of Stoker's novel, they borrow characters, settings, themes, language, and conflicts from the source. They also create an extended history of Stoker's central character, and in doing so, embellish the myth of the king vampire.

Hammer's *Dracula* is widely recognized as one of the finest adaptations of Stoker's novel. Writing in *The Vampire Encyclopedia* (New York: Random House, 1993), Mathew Bunson asserts that the film is

The epitome of the Hammer Films style of movie making, this colorful, gory, sexy, and well-paced work began the long line of very popular Dracula and vampire productions for the studio. It introduced Lee as the ultimate Dracula and made fangs, red eyes, great amounts of blood, and an overt sexual component an essential part of subsequent vampire films. (124)

J. Gordon Melton, in his excellent study, *The Vampire Book: The Encyclopedia of the*

Undead, observes that *The Horror of Dracula* is

second only to the Bela Lugosi version of Dracula (1931) in setting the image of Dracula in contemporary popular culture. . . . Two elements contributed to the success of *The Horror of Dracula*. First, the movie presented a new openess to sexuality. There is every reason to believe that the interpretation of the psychological perspectives on vampire mythology, such as that offered by Ernest Jones's now classic study *On the Nightmare* (1931) underlay the movie's presentation. . . . The second element of success of *The Horror of Dracula* was that it was the first *Dracula* movie to be made in Technicolor. . . . Color added a new dimension to the horror movie and undergirded its revival in the 1960s. (302–305)

Like most film adaptations of Stoker's novel, the Hammer *Dracula* is not faithful to the original text. To a large degree it relies on the Hamilton Deane play. In addition, significant changes were made in setting, character, and emphasis. Jonathan Harker is not the young English solicitor, but rather a dedicated disciple of the famous vampire hunter Professor Van Helsing. In addition, he and Arthur Holmwood, Holmwood's wife Mina, and sister Lucy live in an unnamed European town just across an unnamed border from Dracula's castle. As a result, the travel passages that are central to Stoker's novel—and impossible to include in a stage play—are omitted. In addition, such major characters as Renfield and Seward are eliminated, as are the famous sanitarium scenes. More than most film adaptations of *Dracula*, however, Fisher's simplified plot and cast of characters retains the power of Stoker's novel. What is lost in complexity and scope is made up in intensity and character development.

In this adaptation the complex conflict between Dracula and society is again simplified. Harker searches out Dracula in order to kill him, and is, instead, turned into a vampire after killing Dracula's one wife. In revenge, Dracula seeks out and turns Harker's love, Lucy, into a vampire. Both Harker and Lucy are destroyed by Van Helsing, who then confronts Dracula in a dramatic struggle for the life of Mina Holmwood. Van Helsing chases Dracula to his castle, where the two engage in a spectacular physical confrontation, resulting in Dracula's destruction.

The changes to Stoker's narrative are significant. Director Fisher and screenwriter Jimmy Sangster cut the narrative to its most essential elements, and in the process, they created a much larger role for the character of Van Helsing than in either Universal's *Dracula* or Prana's *Nosferatu*. Harker and Holmwood are ineffective vampire hunters; only Van Helsing stands between Dracula and Lucy and Mina. As Peter Hutchings argues persuasively, the film deals with weakened masculinity and the failure of the patriarchy; Harker and Holmwood are impotent, and the confrontation between Dracula and Van Helsing is a confrontation between two hostile patriarchs. Dracula is a representation of the evil Father, who wishes to take all the women; whereas Van Helsing is a representation of the good father, who wants to help his sons protect their women, who are, in this violent, male-dominated world, unable to fend for themselves. Hammer's *The Horror of Dracula* is, in a real sense, a far more conservative narrative than Stoker's novel, as it asserts patriarchal values and depicts women as mere objects of possession. Stoker, on the other hand, created a narrative with more complex possibilities, as modern scholars and critics have discovered.

A successful film is more than its ideology, however, and the performances of

Cushing and Lee are the main reasons for the success of *The Horror of Dracula*. Peter Cushing's Van Helsing is, as a number of critics have pointed out, a thoroughly middle-class professional vampire hunter. Unlike Stoker's Van Helsing, who speaks badly-accented English, who somewhat incongruently combines the modern scientific spirit with a belief in medieval Christian mysticism, and who, at times, appears confused and foolish, Cushing portrays the vampire hunter who exudes competency and control. In addition, Cushing's Van Helsing is physically powerful and young, a dramatically different interpretation of the role than Edward Van Sloan's aging vampire hunter in the Universal *Dracula*.

Likewise, Christopher Lee's Dracula is a powerful authoritarian figure. Unlike Stoker's Dracula, who was white haired and dirty, or Bela Lugosi's Dracula, who was sensual and foreign, Lee's Dracula is British, aristocratic, powerful, threatening, violent, and sexual. The confrontation between Van Helsing's controlled, authoritarian professionalism and Lee's violent, sexual domination provides the defining structure for the film. Unlike Stoker's novel, in which various characters are foregrounded at different times, in Hammer's Dracula all the characters except Van Helsing and Dracula are thrust into the background. The result is an exciting personal confrontation between good and evil, which has always been the primary subject matter of good drama.

Both contemporary reviewers and later critics have praised *Dracula* highly. Jesse Zunser in *Cue* called the film "Quite possibly the most horrendous and fearful of all the Dracula tales"(Pohle and Hart, 64), and Dorothy Masters, in the *New York Daily News*, noted that "Unlike most Hollywood quickies, *Horror of Dracula* has allocated time, thought, and talent to an enterprise that successfully recaptures the aura and patina of yesteryear's Middle Europe (Pohle and Hart, 64). Lane Roth, in "Film, Society and Ideas: *Nosferatu* and *Horror of Dracula*," argues that the character of Dracula is closer to being human than in any of the earlier adaptations of *Dracula* and that the emphasis on sexuality and revenge make the film successful. Gregory Waller, in *The Living and the Undead*, praises the film's presentation of vampirism as a superior mode of existence (an innovation that was to be developed by numerous later creators of vampire narratives, most spectacularly by Anne Rice) and the focus on Van Helsing and Dracula as superior beings whose struggles take on a mythic character. Peter Hutchings, in *Hammer and Beyond*, draws attention to the depiction of the uneasiness of the women characters within the bourgeoise family and the projection of male anxiety over the changing role of women as a reason for the film's success. Nina Auerbach, in discussing the Hammer adaptations in *Our Vampires, Ourselves*, observes:

The heart and the horror of *Horror of Dracula* is the family. . . . In this family-bound environment, women rise. Lucy and Mina are under the control of a slew of interchangeable paternalistic men—until Dracula comes. But as Terence Fisher directs these scenes, Dracula is scarcely there. The vampire is too elusive to be another overbearing male; he is the emanation of the anger, pride, and sexuality that lie dormant in the women themselves. Stoker's nightmare of violation becomes a dream of female self-possession. (124)

Fisher, Cushing, and Lee had brought Dracula back to the screen in spectacular fashion. As experienced professionals working within a modern studio environment that was both profitable and creative, they were not about to let Count Dracula remain in the grave, even though little if any of Stoker's narrative material would remain in the later Hammer resurrections of Dracula. The second Hammer Dracula film, *The Brides of Dracula* (1960), however, although directed by Fisher with Cushing playing Van Helsing, did not have Lee as the vampire, and suggested but the most tenuous connection with the source novel.

In his recent insightful study of vampire fictions, *Reading the Vampire*, Ken Gelder argues that *The Brides of Dracula* is one of the most significant films of the vampire genre, and Robert Marrero, in *Vampire Movies*, calls the film a "sensational vampire epic" (51). This is high praise for a film most critics have dismissed as a poorly constructed sequel to *The Horror of Dracula* and one that is scarcely mentioned in surveys of vampire films.

Hammer Films originally intended to have Lee and Cushing recreate their original roles in this film, but Lee argued that he did not want to become known only as a "monster" actor, fearing to be typecast as had Bela Lugosi after his dramatic portrayal of Dracula; and as a result, the film was designed to focus on a disciple of Dracula, a Baron Meinster, played by David Peel.

The film opens with a voice-over by Peter Cushing providing a plot summary of the previous Hammer film and then moves to the main narrative, which depicts an imprisoned young vampire, Baron Meinster, whose mother must bring him beautiful young girls to keep him undead. As Marrero notes, *The Brides of Dracula* contains an interesting incestuous subplot—Meinster, late in the film, turns his own mother into a vampire—as well as several dramatic confrontations between Peel's vampire and Cushing's Van Helsing. And as Gelder observes, the film presents a drama centered about law and order and the breakdown of the family, elements central to Stoker's source and to most of the successful film adaptations as well.

Although not an adaptation, *The Brides of Dracula* does develop these central themes of Stoker's work, as well as appropriating the name of Stoker's central character. Gelder finds Cushing's Van Helsing the most interesting character in the film, observing that *The Brides of Dracula* solves its family crisis through him. In *The Brides of Dracula*, Van Helsing's role is to disillusion the young about vampires—their cult is not as appealing as it may seem. He mediates between the strictness of parents (which doesn't work) and the loose morals of youth (which gets them into trouble); his role, symptomatic perhaps of Hammer's vampire films ongoing recovery of the "Victorian values" of vampire narratives, is one of management (101). *The Brides of Dracula* is, like the more faithful adaptations of Stoker's novel, a cautionary morality tale that employs the basic conventions established by Stoker to examine the issues of authority, sexuality, and control facing the culture at the time of the film's release.

Because of the success of its horror films, Hammer continued to create cinema vampires. In 1963 the company released *The Kiss of the Vampire*, directed by Don Sharpe and starring Noel Willman as Count Ravna. Again, the basic situation owes something to Stoker: a young couple is threatened by an aristocratic vampire, or the world of the ordinary—English middle-class heterosexuality—is confronted with

Continental decadence. The film was not a popular success, although later critics have come to appreciate the film's dream-like qualities.

In an attempt to appeal to a larger audience Hammer convinced Lee to reprise his role as Dracula and in 1965 released *Dracula, Prince of Darkness*. Directed by Terrence Fisher, *Dracula, Prince of Darkness* draws on Stoker's title character and setting but little else. The film opens with a replay of the final scene of *The Horror of Dracula*. After the depiction of Van Helsing's dramatic destruction of Dracula, the credits roll, and the film picks up the events, none from Stoker of course, ten years later. Two traveling couples, sightseeing in exotic Transylvania, arrive at Castle Dracula. One couple easily is entrapped by Dracula's faithful servant, Klove, well acted by Philip Latham, and the husband's blood is used to animate the Count while the wife is transformed into a vampire. The second couple is haunted by Dracula and his new wife until both are destroyed by a wise and courageous vampire-destroying monk of the Van Helsing tradition, played with enthusiasm by Andrew Keir.

The most unusual aspect of this adaptation is the complete absence of dialogue for Lee: he plays a vampire as mute as Max Schreck's 1922 Count Orloc, and the result is a similar monster of menace. In this film Dracula, although dressed in evening clothes, is no aristocrat; rather he is an inarticulate animalistic vengeful horror, a conception close to some of Stoker's depictions. This radical transformation of Lee's character bothered contemporary moviegoers and critics. Lee himself was displeased with the film, observing:

This was the only Dracula film in which I didn't say word. I make sounds, but I don't speak. The reason? May have been that they had no idea of what to give me to say. There was a great deal of dialogue originally, but it was so bad, that I refused to deliver it. I finally said, 'For God's sake, give me some of Stoker's lines.' (quoted in Pohle and Hart, 107)

Another possible explanation for Lee's lack of dialogue is suggested by Robert Marrero, who argues that because of financial difficulties Hammer Films could afford neither Lee's larger salary, now that he was a major international star commanding a major salary, nor screenwriter Jim Sangster's elaborate original script. For whatever reason, the monster in this movie is mute; and despite the objections by both Lee and Sangster the result is not altogether unsatisfactory, because Lee's mute vampire emphasizes the animalistic elements of the character of Dracula that were a crucial part of Stoker's vampire and the source for Murnau's *Nosferatu*.

For the next several years Hammer continued to release Dracula sequels starring Christopher Lee. These films take Stoker's vampire farther and farther away from the setting and source of the original novel but continue to serve as popular vehicles for the examination of cultural concerns and the dramatization of popular fears. The 1968 *Dracula Has Risen from His Grave*, directed by Freddie Francis, was the most financially successful of all the Hammer *Dracula* films and gave Lee his largest role as the legendary vampire. In this film Dracula is once again resurrected from the grave into which he fell at the conclusion of the previous film, by now a convention of the genre, this time by the accidentally spilled blood of a priest. Again undead, Dracula seeks vengeance on the family of the Monsignor who destroyed him in the previous film. In the end, Dracula is impaled on a crucifix, and the priest who inadvertently resurrected Dracula regains his belief, reaffirming faith in religion that was questioned throughout the film. In this film, the focus on religion and the protagonist's questions about his faith reflect the concerns over traditional Christianity that were widespread in the late 1960s.

In *Taste the Blood of Dracula* (1969), Lee's Dracula is revived by three businessmen in a Satanic ritual, who, in the process, destroy his faithful servant. Once again undead, Dracula seeks to destroy the families of those responsible for the death. After much blood and gore, Dracula is destroyed by a young couple, who lock him in a church as the sun rises, thus reaffirming both love and religion as forces to combat evil, represented here as acquisitive capitalism.

In *Scars of Dracula* (1970), director Roy Ward Baker continued to employ Lee and the resurrection formula. This time a vampire bat drops blood on the Count's body and Dracula rises to terrorize local villagers and innocent travelers. In this film, Dracula's violence is more random than in previous ones, and his destruction, a bolt of lightening hitting an iron spike in the vampire's side, suggests divine intervention in Dracula's doom.

The final two films in Hammer's *Dracula* series are *Dracula A.D. 1972* (1972) and *The Satanic Rites of Dracula* (1974). *Dracula A.D. 1972* was an attempt to combine Lee's Victorian Dracula with the hip London of the early 1970s. The result was a complete failure. Both filmgoers and critics were disappointed, and Lee himself observes critically, "My scenes were probably the strongest part of the picture, because I stay in context" (Pohle and Hart, 153). Lee also admits that he never saw the completed film. Few others have either.

The Satanic Rites of Dracula is the final film in the *Dracula* series, and Lee and Cushing are reunited as vampire and vampire hunter. Again Dracula is resurrected and again he hunts and is hunted. Beyond the reunion of Lee and Cushing, there is little of interest in this film except that the director, Alan Gibson, has Lee play Dracula as a modern evil businessman, based somewhat on the character of Howard Hughes. Again Lee provides an appropriate commentary on the film's virtues: "If you will forgive the pun, I think the vein is played out" (Pohle and Hart, 162). Lee did, however, play Dracula in another film, an interesting adaptation of Stoker's novel known as *El Conde Dracula (Count Dracula)* directed by Jesus Franco in 1970.

El Conde Dracula was intended as a major international film production. The original plan was to make the first "true" adaptation of Stoker's novel, a project that has haunted many producers and directors. Producer Harry Allen Towers announced his intentions to cast Christopher Lee as Dracula and Vincent Price as Van Helsing, and Lee was finally to be given Stoker's dialogue. In addition, Terence Fisher was to direct the film. Unfortunately the promised budget failed to appear; consequently, Herbert Lom was cast as Van Helsing and Jesus Franco, director of a series of low-cost Spanish and Italian movies, was chosen to direct the film. The result is an interesting film: the first modern attempt at an accurate adaptation of Bram Stoker's *Dracula*. Unfortunately it doesn't work, despite the best of attentions.

For a number of years Christopher Lee had argued for the creation of a film that would use Stoker's material, and when offered this role he quickly accepted. The film captures a good deal of Stoker's novel. Lee recalls:

"This was the only time in my life that I was able to pay some sort of tribute to Stoker and try— the only actor who has ever done so—[until that time] to show his character on the screen almost entirely as he described, physically—with the exception of hair growing out of the palm of the hands, pointed ears, pointed fingernails. . . . The script was based to a great extent on Stoker's book, but it was only a shadow of what it should have been. (quoted in Pohle and Hart, 147)

In addition to Lee's portrayal of Dracula as Stoker had created him, *El Conde Dracula* follows the basic plot of *Dracula* more closely than most other adaptations, omitting the innovations introduced by the Deane/Balderston play. The problems with the film are its low budget and inconsistent direction. Insufficient funding precluded building appropriate sets or creating effective special effects. As a result, the film lacks the visual dimension of horror necessary for a successful gothic horror film. In addition, Franco's direction draws attention to the camera rather than to the narrative: Franco pans and zooms in almost every scene, creating a swirling vision of Stoker that might reflect Jonathan Harker's nightmares but distorts the narrative for the audience.

Despite the differences in theme, cast, director, and aesthetic achievement, the Hammer *Dracula* films produced between 1958 and 1974 transformed the popular conception of the Transylvanian vampire. Although working together in relatively few of the films, Terence Fisher, Christopher Lee, and Peter Cushing created an image of the Dracula story that had a greater impact than any of the individual films. For a generation of filmgoers, Christopher Lee is Dracula and Peter Cushing is Professor Van Helsing, and in the minds of that generation the struggle of the two takes place in the colorized gothic setting filmed by Terence Fisher. Through the work of the professionals at Hammer Films the image of Dracula was transformed from the stylized black-and-white menace of Universal Picture's Bela Lugosi to the energetic terror of Christopher Lee.

Hammer created a vampire to suit the times, but it was not the only terror in town. Numerous other filmmakers created vampire stories, most of them dreadful, but several of the non-Hammer productions of the 1950s and 1960s deserve mention even though they have little direct connection with Stoker's *Dracula*: Paul Landres's *The Return of Dracula* (1958), Mario Bava's *Black Sunday* (1960), and Roman Polanski's *The Fearless Vampire Killers* (1967).

The Return of Dracula, starring Francis Lederer as Count Dracula, like most of the more popular Hammer films of the period, borrows Stoker's character but not much else. In this film Dracula moves to America after attacking a relative of a family that has recently emigrated from the old country. Lederer is an effective Dracula, and the film suggests some of the tensions between European and American cultures and customs that would become a standard feature of many later Hollywood vampire films. In *Black Sunday*, released in England as *Revenge of the Vampire*, Mario Bava created a visually exciting gothic tale of violence, eroticism, and vengeance, the sub-themes of Stoker's novel. Although the film has several references to a Dracula-like figure, its relationship to the main Stoker tradition is primarily atmospheric.

The most famous, and perhaps most misunderstood non-Hammer vampire film of the period is Roman Polanski's *The Fearless Vampire Killers*, also known as *Dance of the Vampires* and *The Fearless Vampire Killers*, or *Pardon Me but Your Teeth Are in My Neck*. Polanski's film adapts its basic situation from Stoker—a noble Transylvanian vampire terrorizes the peasant countryside and is confronted by a learned vampire hunter and disciple—but borrows its tone from the Marx Brothers. Polanski's film is an effective parody of both the Universal vampire films of the 1930s and, more specifically, the successful Hammer films of the late 1950s and 1960s. Polanski, who, in addition to directing, plays the faithful assistant to Jack MacGowan's absent-minded Van Helsing figure, Professor Abronsius, manages to create a narrative that is at times both comic and horrific.

The Fearless Vampire Killers is, perhaps, the perfect vampire film for the end of the 1960s; it recognizes that vampire films have become a sub-genre their own and as such deserve both homage and parody. Once other filmmakers and audiences recognized the same fact, the result was an explosion in vampire films in general and a serious return to Stoker's *Dracula* as source material for a number of major adaptations.

WORKS CITED

Auerbach, Nina. *Our Vampires, Ourselves*. Chicago: U of Chicago P, 1995.

Berenstein, Rhona. *Attack of the Leading Ladies: Gender, Sexuality and Spectatorship in Classic Horror Cinema*. New York: Columbia UP, 1996.

Bunson, Mathew. The *Vampire Encyclopedia*. New York: Crown, 1993.

Gelder, Ken. *Reading the Vampire*. London and New York: Routledge, 1994.

Hutchings, Peter. *Hammer and Beyond & The British Horror Film*. Manchester and New York: Manchester UP, 1993.

King, Stephen. *Danse Macabre*. New York: Everest House, 1981.

———. *Salem's Lot*. New York: Doubleday, 1975.

Marrero, Robert. *Vampires Hammer Style*. Key West, FL: RGM Publications, 1974. Melton, J. Gordon. *The Vampire Book: The Encyclopedia of the Undead*. Detroit: Visible Ink Press, 1994.

Pohle, Robert W., and Douglas C. Hart. *The Films of Christopher Lee*. Metuchen, NJ: Scarecrow Press, 1983.

Stoker, Bram. *Dracula*. Westminster, UK: Constable, 1897.

Waller, Gregory. *The Living and the Undead: From Stoker's "Dracula" to Romero's "Dawn of the Dead"* Cranberry, NJ: Associated Univ Presses, 1987.

Chapter 10

I, Strahd: Narrative Voice and Variations on a Non-Player Character in TSR's "Ravenloft" Universe

Margaret Carter

In a fantasy role-playing game, the referee and the players collaborate in creating a narrative. Commercially printed materials, if used, serve as guidelines for this creation. A published "module" or "dungeon" functions as more than an instruction manual, for a narrative line is sketched in; yet the module as printed constitutes less than a complete story. The author of the module leaves gaps to be filled by the referee's embellishments and the players' choices. Thus, a "dungeon," though a written composition, differs from other types of literature.

This view of a role-playing game as a narrative collaboration brings to mind C. S. Lewis's comment on the fact that modern poetry often has no fixed "meaning" and lays itself open to a variety of interpretations:

> We can no longer assume all but one of these readings, or else all, to be "wrong." The poem, clearly, is like a score and the readings like performances. Different renderings are admissible... The explicators are more like conductors of an orchestra than members of an audience" (Lewis, 98).

Fantasy role-playing invites a similar analogy. In a gaming session, the referee-in the TSR universe to be discussed here, known as a "dungeon master"—acts as conductor, while the players serve as the orchestra. The printed "dungeon" functions as the "score" for the ongoing composition.

The cooperative construction of a work in progress applies not only to gaps in the narrative line, left for dungeon master and players to bridge, but also to the non-player characters outlined by the writer of the dungeon. A non-player character exists on the page as a set of statistics and a few paragraphs of description. The dungeon master must bring this villain or potential ally to "life" in interactions with player characters, fleshing out the traits prescribed in print. Thus, just as two different gaming sessions result in two distinct narrative lines, so various dungeon master-player collaborations may produce different characterizations of the same non-player character.

The gaming universe created by TSR, Incorporated, consists not only of rule books, modules, and boxed sets, but also of novels and short story collections based on various game worlds. This fiction naturally features non-player characters who have proved commercially successful among role-playing aficionados. TSR has published a significant amount of fiction set in the "Ravenloft" continuum, a "demiplane" of existence dedicated to dark fantasy, a realm where horror reigns, comprising an indefinite number of "domains."

Count Strahd von Zarovich, the vampire lord of Barovia, the original Ravenloft domain, has appeared in several gaming supplements and at least three novels. The concept of Ravenloft, in fact, began with a module of that name (1983) starring Count Strahd. Strahd, as a character, was elaborated in the Ravenloft boxed set (1990) and developed in various directions in the novels to be discussed below. His evolution illustrates the protean nature of non-player characters in role-playing games and the variety of personae that can be produced from a single set of character statistics.

Under the rules of TSR's handbook *Advanced Dungeons and Dragons*, of which the Ravenloft game world is a subset, characters are delineated by six ability scores, each generated by a roll of three six-sided dice and therefore ordinarily having a maximum score of eighteen. These are strength, dexterity, constitution, intelligence, wisdom, and charisma. "Levels" or "hit dice" designate a character or monster's experience and power, controlling such factors as his or her prowess in combat, capacity to learn magic spells, specialized skills, and how much damage (measured in "hit points") he or she can absorb without dying. "Alignment," vital to understanding a non-player character such as the vampire Strahd, is an essential part of endowing him or her with personality. The *Player's Handbook* defines a creature's alignment as "a guide to his basic moral and ethical attitudes toward others, society, good, evil, and the forces of the universe in general" (*Advanced Dungeons and Dragons*, 46). All possible alignment orientations are organized around the four poles of good, evil, law, and chaos. (Only intelligent beings possess alignment; non-sentient monsters and ordinary animals and plants are always neutral.)

While "good" and "evil" hold roughly the meanings familiar to us from the standards of our own culture, "law" and "chaos" require some explanation. Lawful characters "maintain that order, organization, and society are important, indeed vital, forces of the universe" (*Advanced Dungeons and Dragons*, 46). A lawful individual, even if evil, tends to obey rules. A lawful evil person, for instance, rather than breaking his word, will instead manipulate promises so that he can achieve his selfish goals within the boundaries of the agreement. Chaotic individuals, on the other hand, "see the universe as a collection of things and events, some related to each other and others completely independent" (46). Tending, to disdain fixed rules, such people "believe in the power of the individual over his own destiny" (46). Therefore, not surprisingly, the chaotic evil opponent is most feared and loathed by player characters. "Chaotic evil characters are motivated by the desire for personal gain and pleasure" and "see absolutely nothing wrong with taking whatever they want by any means possible" (47). While a player character may arrive at a truce with a lawful evil enemy and expect the agreement to be honored, no such possibility exists with a chaotic evil foe.

The *Advanced Dungeons and Dragons* system defines vampires as chaotic evil monsters. Strahd, accordingly, is assigned that alignment. The 1983 *Ravenloft* module characterizes the Count as slightly more powerful than the average vampire. In addition to standard vampiric powers, such as regeneration, shape-changing, and charming victims, he has attained 10th-level magic-user status. In that capacity, he can cast potent spells such as fireball and animate dead. His intelligence is listed as "genius" (the module does not provide a numerical value). This module narrates Strahd's history, which remains constant, with various elaborations, through all the publications in which he appears: In life, Strahd was a noble warlord and stern ruler. He reached middle age without any chance to relax and enjoy the fruits of his conquests. When at last relative peace descended upon his realm, his younger brother, Sergei, joined him. Sergei fell in love with a local maiden, Tatyana. Strahd also became enamored of the girl, who looked upon him only as a venerable elder brother. Finally driven to desperation, Strahd murdered Sergei as part of a pact with Death itself. As a result, Strahd became a vampire. Rather than turning to him for comfort in the loss of her betrothed, Tatyana killed herself. Strahd's realm, Barovia, was drawn into an alternate dimension and became the first domain of Ravenloft. Ever since, Strahd has obsessively sought to win Tatyana, reincarnated in a succession of women.

In the original module, Strahd, though unusually powerful, is a relatively straightforward villain. The character description emphasizes his hatred for all living creatures. This personality trait springs from his pre-vampire existence, when he hated his pious, rather naive brother, Sergei (from whom he had been separated for many years), on sight. The Ravenloft boxed set (1990) expands the world of the original module into a multifaceted "demiplane," with Strahd's domain only the first of many. This publication expands the Count's powers and further details his personality. Like the module, the later manual characterizes him as "a warrior noble who was once good and just" (Lowder, *Ravenloft: Realm of Terror*, 116). Harsh years of constant warfare led to his bitterness in later life. After becoming a vampire, he developed his skills in magic, becoming a powerful necromancer. He also made a nonaggression pact with the Vistani, the gypsies of Ravenloft, who often act as his allies. His bond with the land itself gives him special powers; for instance, unlike standard vampires, he needs no invitation to enter a dwelling within his realm. The later manual gives him higher statistics than the original version; he now ranks as a 16th-level necromancer with eleven hit dice instead of ten (though he still has the same number of hit points, 55). He ranks above average on all six ability scores, with an intelligence of 18 (maximum). Originally he could be hit in combat by plus-one magical weapons, but now he can be wounded only by weapons of plus two or higher. He remains, however, the "ruthless, cold, calculating genius" (*Ravenloft: Realm of Terror*, 117) of the earlier version. He has only two weaknesses, his egoism and his obsession with Tatyana.

From this description, the novelists who have written about Strahd have developed him into a fully rounded fictional character. He plays a central role in the first Ravenloft novel, *Vampire of the Mists*, by Christie Golden (1991). The novel, of course, does not use the impersonal, omniscient narrative voice of the module and the boxed set. In *Vampire of the Mists* we view Strahd through the eyes of Jander Sunstar, an elven vampire drawn into Ravenloft through the lethal mists that separate the demiplane from the mundane world. In an article for the magazine *Dead of Night*, Christie Golden explains that TSR enlisted her to write a story "set in Strahd's younger days, as a new vampire in the demiplane of Ravenloft" (Golden, "Birth of a Vampire," 42).

Jander, by contrast, is an older vampire with considerable experience in the ways of undeath; yet, unlike Strahd, he has not become irredeemably evil. Golden mentions her difficulty in creating a cruel, vicious vampire who is still capable of falling in love. She decided, instead, to make Jander atypical of his kind. "My vampire didn't love pain and cruelty. He didn't delight in draining, or enslaving his victims. Jander loved beauty, grace, and music. . . . He loathed his undead state" (Golden, "Birth of a Vampire," 43). Entering Ravenloft and becoming a guest in Strahd's castle, Jander must fight the Count's attempts to lure him into an existence of callous bloodshed.

In Golden's treatment, Strahd clearly remains chaotic evil. He "disciplines" his subjects by killing those who disobey. He torments both human beings and animals for pleasure. He feeds by killing and tries to induce Jander to do the same. Jander, who lived on the blood of animals in his former home, finds that he cannot drink from animals in Ravenloft; however, he strives to prey on human victims without harming them. His love for the mysterious madwoman Anna, whose spirit he has pursued into Ravenloft, remains a guiding force behind his actions. He attempts to live honorably within the constraints of his cursed existence. Strahd, on the other hand, has no qualms about betraying allies for his own advantage. When decades of precarious "friendship" between Strahd and Jander end in open conflict, Jander, with the help of a priest, attempts to destroy the evil vampire. Thanks to his bond with the land, Strahd, though at the point of death, escapes. In contrast to Strahd's single-minded devotion to his own continued existence, Jander voluntarily exposes himself to death in sunlight to keep from becoming further corrupted by the potential evil of his nature. Jander provides a case study of a vampire who resists the descent into a chaotic evil mind-set (a possibility to be discussed below in relation to Findley's *Van Richten's Guide to Vampires*, another Ravenloft publication).

Strahd, however, although unquestionably evil, displays a human dimension in Golden's novel not seen in the gaming materials where he first appears. Jander, a lover of beauty and music, finds a hint of the same emotion within Strahd. The Count shows his guest an organ, a musical instrument previously unknown to the elf. "Jander could tell that part of him [Strahd] longed to caress the instrument once again, make it sing after all this time. Yet there was also apparently pain in the performing" (Golden, *Vampire of the Mists*, 110). After Strahd plays for Jander, the elf brings forth his wooden flute, and the two of them play a duet. At the sound of Jander's flute, Strahd "looked up, and something like delight mingled with surprise on his pale face" (111). After the duet, "Jander could read his own pain in Strahd's dark eyes" (111). Making music causes them anguish because it reminds them of their alienation from mortal life. In this interlude, Strahd is moved "by something other than murder, power, rage, or grief. He had been moved by beauty" (112). The vampire lord of the Ravenloft module and boxed set would not succumb to the lure of music or feel regret for his inhuman condition.

Golden makes other changes in Strahd's personality. In contradiction to the original module's statement that the Count hated his brother, Sergei, at first sight, the novel portrays, through Strahd's own memories, a more complicated situation. Sergei idolizes his older brother with "brotherly love at first sight" (Golden, *Vampire of the Mists*, 250) and Strahd responds warmly: "As much as the aging warrior could, Strahd loved Sergei" (250). He admires Sergei but sometimes despairs at the youth's naiveté. At first his envy of the handsome, warm-hearted young man remains under control. Hatred takes over only when Tatyana comes between them. Similarly, Strahd's obsessive desire for Tatyana becomes genuine, if corrupted, love in this novel. When he mentions her to Jander, Strahd's voice becomes "soft" and the elf senses "a tenderness that Jander would never have expected from him"; the Count's face "relaxed in reverence (115–16). Perhaps Jander is able to perceive these human emotions in Strahd because Jander himself resists evil and remains capable of unselfish feelings. Nevertheless, Jander is not blind to Strahd's essential evil; he recognizes that Strahd does not tell the whole truth about Tatyana's death. When Jander discovers the truth—that Strahd seeks Tatyana in a succession of doomed women who seem to reincarnate her—the elf realizes that Strahd's love has become an "eternal dance of mutual torment" (268).

Strahd also appears as an important secondary character in *Knight of the Black Rose*, by James Lowder (1991). Again an undead being from another world—in this case, Lord Soth, the undead knight from TSR's Dragonlance series—enters Ravenloft and becomes acquainted with Barovia's lord. Lowder's portrayal of the Count more closely resembles the unadulterated villain of the original module. This vision of Strahd makes him an appropriate companion and antagonist for the thoroughly damned Lord Soth. As in Golden's novel, Lowder's Strahd is known to most of his subjects only as a powerful necromancer who has extended his life span by magic. Soth seeks Castle Ravenloft to learn the scope of Strahd's power and find a means of escape from Barovia. Strahd, in turn, wishes only to manipulate Soth and the ghost of Caradoc, Soth's seneschal, who has followed the Death Knight into Barovia. Lowder portrays Strahd as coldly evil, calculatingly cruel, and motivated only by self-interest, a textbook chaotic evil figure. This Strahd displays no softer emotions. He feels excitement at the arrival of Soth in his domain because "it had been a long time since a problem worthy of his serpentine intellect had presented itself" (Lowder, 62). Recalling his murdered brother, Sergei, Strahd feels only amusement at the memory of Sergei's naive, sentimental nature. In this version, Strahd does not "love" Tatyana. His feeling for her is described as "all-consuming desire" (101), "unrequited desire" (102). He shows no sign of regret for his transformation into a vampire, but instead values his immortal existence and invulnerability to sickness and infirmity. When he casts a spell to transfer a gypsy prisoner's life force to Soth, Strahd displays a cruel ecstasy from which Soth perceives that for "a creature . . . who sustained himself on the life force of others, serving as a conduit for the transfer of such energy was a tantalizing, invigorating experience" (215). In short, the Strahd of *Knight of the Black Rose* is utterly selfish, unscrupulous, and power-hungry. Just as the narrative viewpoint of the gentle vampire, Jander, shows us a Strahd capable of appreciating beauty and regretting the loss of his humanity, so the narrative viewpoint of the evil

Lord Soth shows us an unambiguously evil Strahd.

Though Golden's Strahd is more complex than Lowder's and retains more of his humanity, both clearly conform to the profile of "chaotic evil" as outlined above. P. N. Elrod's *I, Strahd* (1993), the first-person autobiography of the vampire lord, deviates from the chaotic evil alignment prescribed in both the *Advanced Dungeons and Dragons* characterization of vampires and the specific character statistics outlined for Strahd in the Ravenloft module and boxed set. Elrod's subtly different portrait of Strahd raises the question of whether a vampire must always be chaotic evil. As a vampire is a highly intelligent being, cannot he or she exercise free will in choosing some other alignment?

The TSR manual *Van Richten's Guide to Vampires* by Nigel Findley (1991) addresses this question in the chapter entitled "The Mind of the Vampire." The narrative persona, Dr. Rudolph Van Richten, is an erudite foe of supernatural evil whose own son was destroyed by a vampire. Therefore, Van Richten shows the bias expected from an implacable enemy of the undead. Nevertheless, he gives the question of vampiric alignment a balanced treatment. He maintains that in most cases "the transition to undeath itself works this grim change," exacerbated, in the case of a voluntary vampire such as Strahd, by the fact that he was already evil in life (Findley, 77). Van Richten, however, allows for exceptions in instances where the new vampire pursued goodness in life and retains enough strength of will to resist the pull of his or her changed nature. (Jander Sunstar, Golden's elven vampire, clearly falls into this category.)

Van Richten cites a good man who was transformed by an evil vampire and later attained his freedom when the master vampire was destroyed. At first the young vampire acted as an anonymous benefactor to the people of the nearby village. As years passed, however, he became bitter about the villagers' lack of appreciation for his generosity. His demands upon them became more severe, until finally his benevolence turned into hatred. Van Richten theorizes that over time, every vampire inevitably loses "his sense of kinship with the living" and comes to "believe that their very fates [are] petty things, unworthy of his consideration" (79). This insidious progression may explain why Golden's elven vampire feels he must destroy himself before the remnants of his devotion to life fade irretrievably. The principle also explains why Strahd, in Golden's and Lowder's versions, has become chaotic as well as evil.

Elrod, however, treats the vampire lord's post mortem development differently. She points out (in an interview for the Vampire Information Exchange) that in writing about someone else's creation, she "could not discard the history that had already been written about the character" ("Interview with P. N. Elrod," 11). Yet the details she invents to flesh out the established history slant the vampire's personality in a new direction. She developed an immediate fondness for Strahd, "because as everyone knows, it's a LOT more fun playing the villain" (11). Unlike her own vampire protagonist, Jack Fleming, Strahd does not operate under the constraints of goodness. Elrod remarks that Strahd is "not a nice person by any stretch, but I understand him;" readers "may not like him but they know why he is the way he is" (12). Although the gaming materials prescribe a chaotic evil alignment for the Count, Elrod remarks that he "has a strong sense of law and order" (11). Examination of her treatment Strahd reveals that she does indeed metamorphose him from a chaotic into a lawful character.

Elrod's *I, Strahd: The Memories of a Vampire* (1993) covers the Count's last years of human life, his transformation, and the early stages of his vampire existence. The novel includes a third-person frame narrative from the viewpoint of Dr. Van Richten, herbalist and occult investigator, who explores Castle Ravenloft in the (mistaken) belief that Strahd lies helpless in hibernation. It is Van Richten who discovers the first-person journal that comprises the body of the book. The investigator enters Strahd's home with the conviction that the vampire lord is evil, a belief unshaken by reading the autobiography. This bias is strengthened by his realization that Strahd's journal appears to be bound in leather made from human skin. "Damn the thing that was capable of such an obscenity," Van Richten reflects (Elrod, *I, Strahd*, 8). He does, however, recognize Strahd as a unique individual and a dangerously intelligent enemy. Surveying the contents of the Count's private rooms, Van Richten observes that, "though Strahd was a monster, he valued his comfort" and "had excellent taste" (6). The investigator is keenly aware of and cautious about Strahd's magical defenses. The introductory frame, therefore, prepares the reader to meet a diabolically clever "monster" responsible for a terrible "cost in lives and misery and agony of spirit for those hapless souls he'd touched" (3).

The shift to Strahd's first-person account introduces us to quite a different individual. In the opening chapter of his autobiography, Strahd appears as a military strategist who has just won a long, bitter war and become master of a magnificent (though neglected) castle. Though a stern man with no real friends and no room in his life for the softer emotions, he seems just and not given to gratuitous cruelty. The first chapter deals with an assassination attempt, which Strahd of course survives. His one passion is revealed when he allows blood from his superficial wound to soak into the ground, with the vow, "Draw near and witness. I, Strahd, am the land" (49). Unlike the Strahd portrayed by Golden and Lowder, Elrod's Strahd also has a capacity for humor. On his tax-collecting tour of his new realm, he endures with distaste the custom of having children present him with flowers at each village. He remarks, "If the mothers expected me to reward their offspring with a kiss or a copper, then they would just have to live with the disappointment. I'd been forced to do many terrible things in the name of duty, but one must draw the line somewhere" (52–53). On this tour he also demonstrates the kind of justice his subjects are to expect. Taxes are computed severely but, to all appearances, fairly (for example, allowing for poor crop yields and the ravages of war). A burgomaster who has enriched himself rather than conveying the accumulated money through the proper channels is stripped of his possessions and executed. Strahd inflicts no penalty on the common villagers, only ordering them to choose a new burgomaster and make up the missing revenues from the dead one's extorted wealth.

Further insight into Strahd's character is conveyed by his reaction to his first meeting with his younger brother, Sergei, handsome, warm-hearted—"everything that I was not" (63). The contrast reminds Strahd of the harshness of his own life, ruled by "passion for war and obedience to duty" (64). He has spent his entire adult life away from home, deprived of the family environment Sergei has enjoyed. Strahd's affectionate memory of his late mother is demonstrated by his naming the castle after her, "Ravenloft for Ravenia"(65). He sees in Sergei "myself as I should have been. Not that I begrudged Sergei his own life, but that mine had been all but used up, sacrificed to the demands of duty and obligation" (67). His ambivalence toward his brother is clear: "I looked at Sergei and felt a hot surge of anger for my lost years and envy for all those that lay before him. Yet, I could not hate him. He was bound by tradition as well" (67). The contrast between fresh youth and embittered middle age reinforces hints given in earlier chapters, when Strahd notices the gray in his beard and later angrily rejects his subjects' proposal to celebrate his birthday. Thus Elrod lays the groundwork for Strahd's obsession with his own aging and his latent jealousy of Sergei (at first kept in check by Sergei's open admiration for his warlord brother), while maintaining the reader's sympathy for the Count.

The next section of the novel further develops the contrast between the brothers. Despite their mutual affection, Strahd grows impatient with Sergei's spontaneous generosity to the common people, which Strahd thinks can lead only to trouble. Any gesture of beneficence Strahd makes is carefully designed for political advantage. Strahd is annoyed by what he sees as Sergei's naive behavior. His impatience turns to fury when Sergei falls in love with a penniless orphan, Tatyana. The critical juncture of the story occurs when Strahd meets Tatyana—and falls in love with her at first sight. The imagery he applies to her suggests the renewal of his lost youth and love for life: "She was sky and earth, air and music, sunlight without shadow" (103). Her adoration of Sergei, contrasted with her reverential awe toward Strahd, whom she treats as an elder brother, soon poisons Strahd's emotions, but his initial reaction makes it clear that his love began as a sincere desire for her happiness. We see a different person from the battle-hardened warrior when he remarks, "I had years of laughter stored up inside me, it seemed, and without the least effort this lovely girl was bringing it forth" (104).

Along with Sergei's hero-worship of Strahd, Tatyana's opinion of him hints at latent goodness. She surprises him by saying, "When your armies came, we were in fear of what might happen to us, even as we rejoiced in our freedom. But the years of your rule have been peaceful. You've taken away our fears, and we are grateful" (104). Admiring the magnificence of his castle, she says, "I've seen some of the beauty you've made here, which means that I've seen some of your soul as well, and this is a good place. You may be a fierce warrior, but there is much warmth in you" (104). We may assume either that Tatyana does, in fact, see positive qualities in Strahd unknown even to himself, or that her innocence leads her to project her own virtues onto him.

Whatever possibility for good exists within Strahd, it is overwhelmed by darkness when his magical research unearths a spell for the winning of one's heart's desire. Up to that point, he has resisted the notion of killing his brother. He dreams only of winning Tatyana's love; the "malignant thought" of doing something worse he rejects as "beyond dishonor, something so shattering it was beyond evil itself" (107). These scruples vanish when, on the eve of Sergei's wedding, "black despair" takes possession of Strahd (123). Yielding to the lure of the evil spell he has found, he murders his closest survivor, his only friend, and drinks the dying man's blood to seal a compact with Death. Killing and drinking from Sergei completes Strahd's transformation; when he looks into the mirror immediately afterward, he sees no reflection. As established in earlier TSR materials, Tatyana leaps to her death, her body vanishing in the magical mist that springs up around the castle. In that moment Strahd describes himself as "a man like any other. A man who has lost everything, who has nothing left. Nothing. A man broken by unspeakable pain" (165). He quickly learns, though, that he is no longer "a man like any other." When he allows the arrows of the traitors besieging his castle to penetrate his body, he finds that he cannot die.

Elrod makes it clear that Strahd becomes truly evil only when he embraces the pact with Death. Even after his transformation, his ruthlessness has direction and discipline. While venting his rage on the traitors who have poisoned his servants and taken over the castle, he protects those who remain loyal to him. He even makes a point of releasing his surviving henchmen from his service and sending them out of harm's way. Terrible as his vengeance is, over the next year, he treats his obedient subjects justly. Mildly surprised when his officers, unaware of the disaster that has overtaken Castle Ravenloft, arrive on the scene to pay taxes as usual, he reflects, "I came to realize I was yet ruler of Barovia, with responsibilities and duties to perform" (197). He restrains himself from feeding on the tax collectors, for "they were sworn into my service, and I, in turn, was sworn to protect them. My change from life to unlife had not negated that pledge" (198). His sense of duty extends to destroying a gang of bandits who have stolen part of the tax monies gathered by one community. Nearly fifty years after the attack on the castle, he finally tracks down the traitor, whom he manages to kill (with some difficulty, as the villain has also become adept in magic). Strahd's revenge is ghastly—he transforms the traitor into a vampire and imprisons him in a sealed crypt—but the vampire lord's sense of honor does not allow him to harm Lady Lovina, whose family has remained loyal to him.

Throughout the novel Elrod similarly slants events in Strahd's favor. Aside from Sergei and others caught in Strahd's obsession with Tatyana (for instance, the foster father of Tatyana's first reincarnation, killed by Strahd after the old man stakes the girl, whom Strahd has vampirized), his victims invite their fates by their own misdeeds. Unlike Strahd as envisioned by Golden and Lowder, Elrod's vampire remains a person of honor. Elrod's Count Strahd evolves from lawful neutral (perhaps with good tendencies) to lawful evil, rather than the conventional vampiric alignment of chaotic evil. The *Player's Handbook* cites an "iron-fisted tyrant" as an example of a lawful evil figure (*Advanced Dungeons and Dragons*, 47), a description that certainly fits Elrod's Count Strahd.

Strahd also retains the dry humor that characterizes him in life. He rests in a coffin by day, not only for protection from the sun, but also to keep "roaming insects and curious rodents" from crawling on him; he notes, "it is a rare craftsman who likes to sleep with his tools" (Elrod, *I, Strahd* 195). As a side issue to his revenge for the death of the maiden he believes to be a reincarnation of Tatyana, he uses his hypnotic power to send a fanatical priest on a pilgrimage and simultaneously commands the cleric to bathe every day for the rest of his life. "It was the least I could do for his congregation," the Count maintains (292)—an act of sardonic benevolence not usually expected of a vampire. Another humanizing touch Elrod's Strahd displays is his fondness for bats and wolves, which he treats like pets or companions. His despair never quite leaves him, though; he arouses our sympathy by his yearning to "sleep for more than just a single day, sleep away all my sorrows" (306). By the time Van Richten arrives, however, Strahd has, unknown to the outside world, awakened from his hibernation. The third-person Epilogue, returning to the frame narrative, shows him sparing the oblivious Van Richten's life, not out of mercy but out of indifferent overconfidence. Amused by Van Richten's headlong flight from the gathering darkness, Strahd decides to deal with the occultist if and when he returns. Elrod's final paragraphs show Strahd more concerned about resuming his memoirs than pursuing yet another vampire-hunter.

The vampire lord reappears in Elrod's short story "Caretaker" (1994). He travels incognito as "Lord Vasili," Count Strahd's envoy, to avoid meeting people who "either were terrified or overwhelmed me with ceremony, or both" (Elrod, "Caretaker" 364). The reader gets the impression that Strahd enjoys his forays into society, for more than the "distraction" he mentions and the exercise provided for his horses (304). In this story he behaves like a harsh but fair ruler who simply happens to be a vampire. He risks his undead "life" to combat a fire raging out of control, which he discovers to have been started by robbers. In the midst of invoking a rain-making spell to quench the fire, he rescues a girl whose family and neighbors have been slaughtered by the bandits. Strahd ignores "the temptation of her blood," wraps her in his cloak for warmth, and sends her to safety before hunting down the marauders (310). He contemplates the robbers with disgust: "A predator myself, I well knew the joy of the hunt, but also the responsibility, and to wantonly kill all your prey means your own death as well" (310). He particularly condemns these "predators" because "Barovia was mine, the land, the peoples. . . . I would tolerate no interlopers despoiling my property. Strahd von Zarovich looks after his own" (310–11). This statement makes his protective behavior sound like prudence rather than honor, but in this story, at least, he unleashes his vampiric rage only upon the guilty. When he feasts on the robbers' blood, he reflects that "I was well rewarded for holding my hunger in check against the girl" (311), again suggesting self-centered motives for his restraint. He later reminds himself, though, to stop at the village and "see how the girl was being treated," implying that he feels a lord's responsibility for this insignificant subject (316). The very title of the story suggests that Strahd "looks after his own" from duty as well as prudence. Where we might expect an evil tyrant to boast of his benevolence while revealing his true nature through his actions, Strahd's behavior shows the reverse pattern. While he explains his choices in self-interested terms, the vampire lord's actions hint at disinterested concern for the land and the people he rules.

Thus, Elrod, though adhering to the official history of Strahd's career, as far as earlier texts have established it, structures her original contributions to his biography so as to create a character widely at variance from the chaotic evil antagonist of the 1983 *Ravenloft* dungeon module. That module and the more powerful variant character profile for Strahd in *Ravenloft: Realm of Terror* (the manual in the boxed game set) establish the vampire lord's basic traits and outline a past for him. Golden, in *Vampire of the Mists*, presents Strahd through the viewpoint of a reluctant vampire, Jander, clinging to remnants of goodness. Therefore, Golden's narrative emphasizes Strahd's few surviving traces of humanity, while still framing him as a chaotic evil antagonist for her elven hero. Lowder, in *Knight of the Black Rose* portraying Strahd as the evil opponent of a protagonist equally evil, allows the vampire lord no quality that might inspire the reader's sympathy. Lowder's Strahd, seen through his interaction with the cynical, self-centered, ruthless Lord Soth, is simply a cruel, rapacious, and capricious tyrant. Elrod's creative misreading (in the Bloomian sense) of the texts presented to her as background sources produces a harsh ruler who, though evil, "has a strong sense of law and order" and retains human quirks such as humor.

The evolution of Strahd thus illustrates the elastic nature of characters in role-playing games and the freedom of a dungeon master or fiction writer to "orchestrate" or "choreograph," based on a set of statistics and a few descriptive phrases, an individualized persona for a character whom other interpreters might develop in entirely different directions.

WORKS CITED

Advanced Dungeons and Dragons 2nd Edition Player's Handbook. Lake Geneva, WI: TSR, 1989.

Elrod, P. N. "Caretaker" in *Tales of Ravenloft* Ed. Brian Thomsen. Lake Geneva, WI: TSR, 1994.

———. *I, Strahd: The Memoirs of a Vampire*. Lake Geneva, WI: TSR, 1993.

Findley, Nigel. *Van Richten's Guide to Vampires*. Lake Geneva, WI: TSR, 1991.

Golden, Christie. "The Birth of a Vampire." *Dead of Night*, 9 (April 1994): 42–44.

———. *Vampire of the Mists*. Lake Geneva, WI: TSR, 1991.

Hickman, Tracy, and Laura Hickman. *Ravenloft*. Lake Geneva, WI: TSR, AD&D Module 16,1983.

"An Interview with P. N. Elrod." *The Vampire Information Exchange Newsletter*, 65 (December 1993): 10–14.

Lewis, C. S. *An Experiment in Criticism*. Cambridge, England: Cambridge UP, 1961.

Lowder, James. *Knight of the Black Rose*. Lake Geneva, WI: TSR, 1991.

———. *Ravenloft: Realm of Terror*. Lake Geneva, WI: TSR, 1990.

Part Three

Modern Vampire Fictions

Chapter 11

The Mother Goddess in H. Rider Haggard's *She* and Anne Rice's *The Queen of the Damned*

Bette Roberts

Anne Rice acknowledges to her biographer, Katherine Ramsland, that the concept of a great family that could be traced back to ancient times in *The Queen of the Damned* was inspired by "a man at the beginning of the novel" *She*, written by H. Rider Haggard (quoted in Ramsland, *Vampire Companion*, 164). In *The Mummy*, written in 1989, one year after *The Queen of the Damned*, Rice also pays tribute to Haggard's *She*, along with other works by writers "who have brought 'the mummy' to life in stories, novels and film." Indeed, readers recognize many variations of mummy plot conventions in Rice's *Mummy*: the curse on archeologists who disturb the tomb of a resting pharaoh, the accident that brings the dead back to life, the revenge and violence that ensue, the greed of those hoping to exploit the situation, and the efforts finally to destroy the unleashed horror or return it to its tomb. Vestiges more specific to Haggard are also apparent, such as the desire for eternal life represented in Rice's elixir and the unfulfilled love and vengeance plot in the relationship between Ramses and Cleopatra, who is a less powerful version of Haggard's Ayesha.

Rice clearly, then, invites readers to enjoy Haggard's motifs in *The Mummy*; however, when Ramsland asked her to identify the origin of Akasha's name in *The Vampire Chronicles*, Rice curiously mentioned the name of a place on a map in *Lost Cities of Africa* (Ramsland, *Vampire Companion*, 8) instead of Ayesha in Haggard's *She*. Of course we cannot make too much of Rice's comment; as she talks often and freely about her life and work, she may, if asked another time, recall Ayesha as a source. Yet the similarity of Haggard's Ayesha and Rice's Akasha, along with Haggard's full title "She-Who-Must-Be-Obeyed" and Rice's reference to Akasha and Enkil as "Those-Who-Must-Be-Kept,"[1] in addition to the 1988 composition of *The Queen of the Damned* with her 1989 dedication to Haggard in *The Mummy*, suggest that we take a closer look at Haggard's novel for a fuller understanding of *The Queen of the Damned*.

Indeed, this study proves to be especially fruitful in identifying Rice's treatment of the Mother Goddess, a mythic figure central to her novel, and the full implications of Lestat's rejection of Akasha in favor of Maharet in the end. Unlike the light-hearted *Mummy, The Queen of the Damned* shows that Rice is deeply engaged with the complex cultural, psychological, and feminist issues raised by confrontations with the Mother (perhaps too deeply to discuss casually in an interview) and that she constructs her own version of the myths to legitimize her vampires and address a late-twentieth-century audience rather than a late Victorian one.

Despite important differences in character configurations and specific circumstances, the mainsprings of the plots in both novels are the same: the protagonists' quests for truth leading to self-identity and the revenge prophesied for crimes thousands of years before. Both plots end in the defeat of powerful goddess figures, Ayesha in Haggard's novel and Akisha in *The Queen of the Damned*. *She* details the adventures of Leo Vincey and his narrator-guardian L. Horace Holly, who set out to answer provocative questions raised in mysterious, ancient manuscripts left by Vincey's dying father to be opened on Leo's twenty-fifth birthday. Financed by money left to pay for their expedition, Holly and Leo search for the "beautiful white woman" who rules over a savage race somewhere deep in the heart of Africa and who possesses eternal youth. It is she who murdered Leo's Greek descendant Kallikrates some 6,000 years before in a fit of jealousy; it is his murder that remains unavenged. Accompanied by their servant Job, Holly and Leo journey into the African jungles, where they go through the perils of insects, wild animals, swamps, and Amahagger tribespeople to find Ayesha in the volcanic mountains of Kor. Because Leo so closely resembles Kallikrates, the dead love of Ayesha's life, she believes that he is, indeed, the reincarnated Kallikrates returned to fulfill her destiny and redemption.

Both men, fascinated by her unparalleled beauty yet horrified by her cruelty and malevolence, are unable to resist her power and fall obsessively in love with her. (Like Rice's Akasha, Ayesha can "blast" or incinerate people for sport; she also wears a snake-like belt.) As Leo agrees to become her consort with whom she intends to establish absolute rule over the world, Holly speculates:

What was there to stop her? In the end she would, I had little doubt, assume absolute rule over the British dominions, and probably over the whole earth, and, though I was sure that she would speedily make ours the most glorious and prosperous empire that the world has ever seen, it would be at the cost of a terrible sacrifice of life" (Haggard, *She*, 170).

Fortunately for the world, Ayesha is mysteriously destroyed by the pillar of fire that she identifies as the source of her immortality, which she intends to share with Leo. When she stands in its path to show Leo the way and reassure him by her example, she is grotesquely transformed into a corpse the size of a monkey, with millions of wrinkles (194). Holly and Leo, both preferring mortality to the risk of achieving eternal life, manage to get themselves back to civilization after suffering through more life-threatening adventures in the jungle.

Rice's handling of settings and time is more complicated than Haggard's single-plot chronology: her vampires range from the frozen depths of the arctic to San Francisco, to the Himalayan mountains to Haiti, ending in the Sonoma mountains of California, and through inset narrations of the past, from the present to pre-civilized times and back to the present. The quest here is Lestat's coming to terms with his vampire nature, which means discovering the origins of vampirism and his connection with the community of vampires. In his rebellion against the apparent insignificance of his condition, he becomes a rock star and boldly reveals in his music too much about the vampires, thereby endangering their survival among humans.

In the "Proem" to the novel, the ancient vampire Marius reads a declaration that all vampires go to Lestat's rock concert in San Francisco to destroy him. Within the simultaneous plots involving many separate groups of human and vampiric characters en route to San Francisco recurs the inexplicable dream of red-haired twins that unites the strands of the action and sets up an unresolved fate or prophecy yet to be fulfilled. During the climactic concert, it is clear that Lestat has not only aroused many vampires intent upon destroying him but awakened the original mother of vampires, Akasha, who values his bravado, saves him from the others, and takes him away. Like Ayesha, Akasha has plans for establishing a new world with herself as a new god and Lestat as her consort. Seeing males as the source of violence and evil, she orders that "All males save one in a hundred" be destroyed (Rice, *Queen*, 62) so that women will rule. Lestat, suffering from the same weakness of will as Leo, carries out her edict in grisly scenes of violence.

Meanwhile, the narrative of Lestat and Akasha's violence alternates with Maharet's explanation of vampire history to the vampires gathered at her home. Originally a good witch from a pre-civilized culture near Akasha's and now a vampire, Maharet recounts the brutal torture she and her twin sister, Mekare, suffered at the hands of Akasha, Mekare's vow of revenge, the sisters' separation, and Maharet's efforts to preserve the great family she has traced through twenty centuries. To ensure the independent survival of both humans and vampires, the group wonders how they can destroy Akasha without ending their own lives, as whatever happens to their mother, Akasha, in turn happens to them because her blood runs in theirs. In the second major climax of the novel, the dreaded Akasha arrives with Lestat, and the vampires, including Lestat, try to dissuade her from her egomaniacal scheme. Unseen for two centuries, Mekare returns from the jungle to accomplish her revenge by decapitating Akasha and then ingesting her heart and brain so that the vampires may live. The dreams of the red-haired twins thus fulfilled, the vampire group breaks up, and Lestat returns to his vampire friend Louis in New Orleans and his human friend David Talbot in London.

Clearly Ayesha in *She* and Akasha in Rice's novel play very similar goddess roles involving female power. Ayesha herself has no challenges to her unlimited rule over the Amahagger people and believes that her ends justify any means. She argues that as good often comes from evil and evil from good, moral concerns are completely irrelevant. In a scene similar to Lestat's and the other vampires' debate with Akasha, Holly is unable to argue against her casuistry and rightly fears the potential of "a being who, unconstrained by human law, is also absolutely unshackled by a moral sense of right and wrong" that he sees as separating humans from beasts (Haggard, *She*, 136). Ayesha represents the Terrible Mother archetype that jeopardizes civilized society represented in the male figures of Holly and Leo.

In *No Man's Land*, Sandra Gilbert and Susan Gubar devote some forty pages to

Haggard's novel, which they see as summarizing and transforming the legend and history of the femme fatale (21). Arguing that Ayesha represents the New Woman and that her power reveals male anxieties over the threat of New Women to patriarchal values and social structures (6), they note that the "erotic apocalypse" that destroys the femme fatale is "a crucial revision of earlier depictions," where the Circean woman triumphed (22). According to Gilbert and Gubar, Ayesha is destroyed because the threat to patriarchy only earlier imagined is now real in the late-nineteenth century. Nina Auerbach, too, sees Haggard's novel as appealing to fears "that the learned and crusading 'New Woman' may incarnate as well the awakened powers of the old, adored woman" (37).

Akasha, too, has "no true morality, no true system of ethics to govern" her actions (Rice, *Queen*, 361); when Lestat tries to show her the worth of the human world, she sees it as "paltry" compared with her own vision (362). Like Holly, Maharet's vampires fear the outcome of Akasha: "We know now what evils the Mother has already begun to do. Can the world stop this thing if the world understands nothing of it?" (385). Yet Rice, who recently said that she tries to avoid "gender cliches" (quoted in Riley, 49), complicates the rather transparent gender issues of Haggard's novel by setting up an alternative within the Mother archetype, an invention that prevents the reader from seeing a victory of one set of values assigned to one gender over another. Maharet also represents the maternal in her nurturing of the great family and her willingness to let the human race take its own course.

While Ken Gelder sees matriarchal values still prevailing over the patriarchal because of Akasha's rationalism and Maharet's emotionalism (116), Janice Doane and Devon Hodges argue that "sexual difference is a dead issue," because the battle is between "versions of the maternal" instead of between women and men (433). Ramsland adopts this view, also, in stating that Rice "does not move back and forth between the male and female. Instead the female has emerged and divided into two perspectives: one associated with pain and death and the other with life" (*Prism*, 306). Mekare's decapitation of Akasha does, indeed, strike out at the seat of rationalism; yet the ingestion of Akasha's heart and head suggest that what she represents becomes part of Mekare, an option that Rice leaves open when Lestat writes, "Had any of her survived in Mekare? . . . Or had her soul been released at last when the brain was torn loose?" (Rice, *Queen*, 425).

Comparing Ayesha's destruction by the clearly masculine pillar of fire with the blending of masculine and feminine values in Akasha's death helps to clarify Rice's appeal to the more androgynous, less sexist values of a contemporary audience and calls attention to what Rice herself sees as the real source of evil, the purely intellectual that manifests itself in rulers, governments, or individuals who justify their inhumane policies (like war) and inflict them upon others (quoted in Riley, 157).

Considering the impact of the Mothers upon the male protagonists also reveals Rice's adaptations of the myth for a more contemporary audience. Technically, Lestat's counterpart is Leo. Both blond-haired, they are the consorts chosen to share absolute rule with the goddess figure; they are the lovers who become torn by their helpless passion for what they know to be evil. In having the older Holly accompany Leo on the journey, however, Haggard aggrandizes the threat of the Mother and the emasculation of the males. Holly's being a college professor and even somewhat of a misogynist (*She*, 61) does not protect him from becoming obsessed with her beauty and jealous of her love for Leo. While Holly speculates on the impact of their experience with Ayesha and the "next act" of this fated drama, the less analytical Leo remains devoted to the goddess and the idea of some future reunion through reincarnation or other means.

With the dead Ayesha resembling a monkey, anxieties about the New Woman appear to be linked with those of evolution shared by a late-Victorian audience. Ayesha's survival-of-the-fittest notions of power end in her going back down the evolutionary scale rather than forward. This interpretation is complicated, however, by Holly's own simian appearance mentioned throughout the novel and in his nickname, "Baboon." Critics of Haggard's Darwinian motifs tend to agree that his philosophy is confused and contradictory, as his heroes confront nothingness yet cling to the hope of evolving into higher forms (Etherington, xxix).

Instead of a triangular confrontation of two men versus the Mother, Rice sets up a triangle that involves Lestat achieving his self-identity as a vampire through the opposition of two Mothers, Maharet and Akasha, and the values they represent. This configuration illustrates Northrop Frye's point years ago on how "allegory is constantly creeping in around" the "fringes" of the Romantic novel, where "we find Jung's libido, anima, and shadow reflected in the hero, heroine, and villain respectively" (304). Here the parts are played by Lestat, Maharet, and Akasha, with Maharet and Akasha suggesting' the psychological conflicts or choices in Lestat.

In her efforts to "transform horror formula into mythology" (Hoppenstand and Browne, 5), Rice's narrative symbolizes Lestat's internal journey that leads toward his abandonment of his own schemes that have ignored his relationship to other vampires to satisfy his need for significance and finally his renewal of mischievous pranks when he recovers his resilient nature. As Barbara Waxman explains, Lestat learns to recognize his limitations as a vampire; he cannot exercise the absolute moral freedom that he feels in killing men for Akasha (Rice, *Queen*, 269). Instead of a sexist message, Waxman sees Rice's plot as post-existential in its recognition of contingencies that limit individual choice and freedom (88). The dialectic of Rice's novel and its allegorical pattern of conflict may, in fact, account for her "viewing it as the only one of her novels that she dislikes," where, according to Ramsland, she felt that philosophy rather than fantasy carried the plot (Rice quoted in Ramsland,"Lived World," 25).

Despite the different implications of these confrontations with the Mother, the worlds imaged in both novels are decidedly female with curious similarities. Etherington, along with other Haggard critics, calls attention to the female topography of *She* (xxv), as Holly and Leo's journey deep into the "dreadful womb of the volcano" (199) takes them through a canal, a cup-shaped hill, and a tunnel to the fertile crater of Kor where Ayesha resides. Rice does not limit herself to one setting, but does have Akasha (and Enkil) protected in a subterranean arctic tomb and Maharet living in a home hidden deep within the Sonoma mountains, with the back of the house "dug out of the mountain, as if by enormous machines" (Rice, *Queen*, 74).

Ayesha and Akasha both envision societies where females are equal or dominant;

Ayesha's is already established in the Amahagger tribe that serves her. Holly notes that "While individuals are as proud of a long and superior female ancestry as we are of our families in Europe, they never pay attention to, or even acknowledge, any man as their father, even when their male parentage is perfectly well known" (Haggard, *She*, 57). Women "are not only upon terms of perfect equality with the men, but are not held to them by any binding ties" (57). This is a world where "women do that they please," according to tribesman Billali, who says, "We worship them, and give them their way, because without them the world could not go on; they are the source of life" (78). However, almost as if Haggard were intent upon giving men the last word and showing the perversity of female power, Billali explains that when women become "unbearable," in every second generation the men "kill the old ones as an example to the young ones, and to show them that we are the strongest" (78).

As described earlier, Rice's Akasha envisions a world of female domination after she carries out her annihilation of 99 percent of the male population. Yet in Rice's novel the idea of matrilineal descent is transformed into the family nurtured by Maharet and originating with her human daughter, Miriam. Maharet traces information on "women who had gone back to The Time Before the Moon" and writes of "which daughters had been born and the names of those daughters born to them" (Rice, *Queen*, 387). As it is impossible for her to know if the children of the men were "truly" of her blood, she keeps the "thread" matrilineal (389). Instead of a lost African tribe, Maharet's Great Family now has members in every people, race, and country, so it symbolizes the human family threatened by Akasha. Therefore, it is fully integrated into the larger dialectic of the novel, the polar values represented by Maharet and Akasha.

Considering Haggard's Ayesha alongside Rice's Akasha and analyzing the transformations of the Mother Goddess into Rice's novel shows the timelessness of archetypes and the extent to which they may be modified to represent cultural values. Indeed, Rice's reaching into the world of myths and adapting them to fit the vampire revitalizes the whole tradition for a contemporary audience. *The Queen of the Damned* is a good example of what one critic sees as a major reason for Rice's appeal. Attributing the popularity of the Indiana Jones movies to their being "modernizations" of Haggard traditions, Garyn G. Roberts argues that "Such re-introduction, recontextualizing, and reworking explain much of the critical, cult, and popular success and acclaim of Anne Rice" (69).

NOTE

1. Noting influences from Haggard's childhood in *She*, Norman Etherington writes that the full title of the novel came from "a rag doll used by the family nursemaid to frighten the children into obedience" (xxvi). Unlikely to be purely coincidental, Rice refers to rag dolls twice in *The Queen of the Damned*, with the dreams of the twins, Maharet and Mekare, that Jesse links to the tapestry quilt at Maharet's: "Each little rag-doll being had a tiny pair of green buttons for its eyes, a carefully sewn nose and red mouth" (Rice, *Queen*, 132), and with Jesse herself, whose body feels "floppy like that of a rag doll" when she is mortally wounded (*Queen*, 218).

WORKS CITED

Auerbach, Nina. *Woman and the Demon: The Life of a Victorian Myth*. Cambridge, MA: Harvard UP, 1982.

Doane, Janice, and Devon Hodges. "Undoing Feminism: From the Preodipal to Post-feminism in Anne Rice's Vampire Chronicles." *American Literary History* 2.3 (Fall 1990): 422–42.

Etherington, Norman, ed. Critical Introduction. *The Annotated She: A Critical Edition of H. Rider Haggard's Victorian Romance, with Introduction and Notes*. By H. Rider Haggard. 1887. Bloomington, IN: Indiana UP, 1991, xv–xliii.

Frye, Northrop. "Theories of Genres." *Anatomy of Criticism: Four Essays*. New York: Atheneum, 1969. 243–337.

Gelder, Ken. *Reading the Vampire*. New York: Routledge, 1994.

Gilbert, Sandra M., and Susan Gubar. *No Man's Land; The Place of the Woman Writer in the Twentieth Century*. Vol. 2: *Sexchanges*. New Haven, CT: Yale UP, 1989.

Haggard, H. Rider. *She*. 1887. *The Annotated She: A Critical Edition of H. Rider Haggard's Victorian Romance with Introduction and Notes*. Ed. Norman Etherington. Bloomington, IN: Indiana UP, 1991, 3–209.

Hoppenstand, Gary, and Ray B. Browne. "Introduction: Vampires, Witches, Mummies, and Other Charismatic Personalities: Exploring the Anne Rice Phenomenon." In *The Gothic World of Anne Rice*. Bowling Green, OH: Bowling Green State Univ Popular Press, 1996, 1–12.

Ramsland, Katherine. "The Lived World of Anne Rice's Novels." In *The Gothic World of Anne Rice*. Eds. Gary Hoppenstand and Ray B. Browne, 13–33.

———. *Prism of the Night: A Biography of Anne Rice*. 1991. New York: Plume Books, 1992.

———. *The Vampire Companion: The Official Guide to Anne Rice's "The Vampire Chronicles."* New York: Ballantine Books, 1993.

Rice, Anne. *The Queen of the Damned*. New York: Alfred A. Knopf, 1988.

Riley, Michael. *Conversations with Anne Rice*. New York: Ballantine Books, 1996. Roberts, Garyn G. "Gothicism, Vampirism, and Seduction: Anne Rice's 'The Master of Rampling Gate.'" *The Gothic World Of Anne Rice*. Eds. Gary Hoppenstand and Ray B. Browne. 55–70.

Waxman, Barbara Frey. "Postexistentialism in the Neo-Gothic Mode: Anne Rice's *Interview with the Vampire*." Mosaic, 25.3 (Summer 1992): 79–97.

Chapter 12

Blood Spirit/Blood Bodies:
The Viral in the Vampire Chronicles of
Anne Rice and Chelsea Quinn Yarbro

Heidi L. Nordberg

I

> What resists reflection is the idea of a quasi-material something that infects
> as a sort of filth, that harms by invisible properties, and that nevertheless
> works in the manner of a force in the field of our undividedly psychic and
> corporeal existence.
>
> —Paul Ricoeur,
> *The Symbolism of Evil*[1]

Infection, contagion, mutation, a blurring of material and psychical definition—these characteristics appear with increasing frequency in our discourses, whether in relation to vampires, AIDS, or media networks. Not only are these no longer archaic notions, but we increasingly rely on these viral characteristics to indicate fragmentary degrees of sameness and difference. Viral forms that cluster, separate, replicate, and reconfigure themselves complicate, and often replace, outmoded and destabilized absolutes and dualities. Texts that specifically thematize the construction, crossing, and dissolution of dualities and boundaries are particularly open to a viral reading. Vampire fictions, in particular, blur and complicate the boundaries between life and death (the undead), spirit and body, health and illness, and good and evil. These viral complications focus, first of all, on blood. From the Hebrew Scriptures to our late-twentieth century vampire novels, "the blood is the life," but what this statement signifies differs from narrative to narrative. Beliefs and anxieties regarding the changing conceptions of blood form a central matrix of possibilities for vampiric fictions. Like Paul Ricoeur's notion of the archaic sense of "stain" or "defilement" that resists reflection, what I am calling the "viral" is a way of clustering the recombinant shards of possibility that vampire fictions explore: invisible properties of contamination and infection, mixtures of the psychical (emotional, intellectual, spiritual) and the corporeal (material, bodily, chemical), power and sexuality, parasite and host.

When narrated from the point of view of the "other," as in the vampire "chronicles" of Anne Rice and Chelsea Quinn Yarbro, the traditional villainous qualities of the vampire subside somewhat, replaced by the vampires' own, often complicated existential questions. Their vampires express a range of personalities and possibilities for undead existence, placing the essential "what if" question in a context both historically detailed and, by dint of the vampires' near immortality, transhistorical.

II

> Think on the nature of this great invisible thing which animates each one of us, and every blood drinker who has ever walked. We are as receptors for the energy of this being; as radios are receptors for the invisible waves that bring sound. Our bodies are no more than shells for this energy.
>
> —Anne Rice,
> *The Queen of the Damned*, 385

What is invoked by "the blood is the life" in Anne Rice's vampire chronicles depends in large part on a type of viral cyborg structure that encompasses all the vampires as a whole, although most of the vampires are never fully aware of this. If one can provisionally rely on a somewhat unreliable set of narrators, vampires result from a fusion of the Egyptian Queen Akasha and the evil spirit Amel, who is greedy for physical "pleasures and powers."[2] Having already learned to draw small quantities of blood into himself and finding the taste to his liking, Amel enters into the wounds of the betrayed and fatally stabbed Queen. The tiny material center of the spirit merges with her body, while its spirit energy merges with her soul. Amel's individual subjectivity is lost in this fusion, but certain characteristics—most importantly the possibility of material immortality, an insatiable thirst for blood and a greed for sensuality of all kinds—are transmitted to all vampires when they are made. Queen Akasha is the first vampire, from Queen of Egypt to the "Queen of the Damned."

Amel's spiritual part, into which Akasha has been incorporated as the center, is organized as an almost unimaginably immense web, or vine, of light in which the souls of subsequent vampires are trapped. In this story of origins, the viral is projected outwards onto gigantic invisible proportions and comes into life with the merging of itself with the host, Akasha. The blood becomes the transmission site and the material source of energy for this spiritual (i.e., non-material) web.[3]

When the vampire Marius becomes aware that the Druidic cult within which he was made a vampire came down from this source, his reaction is to compare this structure to a kind of vine:

It made sense that something was in my blood impelling me to drink more blood. It made sense that it heightened all sensations, that it kept my body—a mere imitation now of a human body—functioning when it should have come to a stop. And it made sense that this thing had no mind of its own but was nevertheless a power, an organization of force with a desire to live all its own. And then it even made sense that we could all be connected to the Mother and the Father because this thing was spiritual, and had no bodily limits except the limits of the individual bodies in which it had gained control. It was the vine, this thing, and we were the flowers, scattered over great distances, but connected by the twining tendrils that could reach all over the world. (Rice, *The Vampire Lestat*, 445)

Significantly, Marius's description of the network as a vine replicates and inverts the metaphor of the vine in John 15:5 that Jesus uses to describe the spiritual connection of believers to each other and to him, the source of their power.[4] Rice's vampire network is a dark materialization of the kingdom of heaven.

A more twentieth-century description of this structure is transmitted to Lestat through Akasha as she picks up the thoughts of the dying young vampire named Baby Jenks, who is freed from the network by the spiritual efforts of the mother she had herself murdered.

It was the white figure that amazed her. It looked just like a statue, like the Blessed Virgin Mary in the Catholic church. She stared at the sparkling silver threads made out of some kind of dancing light. And as she moved higher, she saw that the silver threads stretched out, tangling with other threads, to make a giant net over the whole world. All through the net were Dead guys, caught like helpless flies in a web. Tiny pinpoints of light, pulsing, and connected to the white figure. Oh, poor souls of all the Dead guys locked in indestructible matter unable to grow old or die. But she was free. The net was way far away from her now. (Rice, *Queen*, 54)

With each infection, the vampire becomes part of this immense structure, but without losing a sense of his or her individual subjectivity. The infection is, however, two-tiered. At one level, the vampires are part of and host to the mutation created by Amel's fusion with Akasha. The mutated blood connects them physically and psychically with each other. At the same time, they become part of the feeding mechanism that, in an erotic manner, preys on human blood, both for individual survival and in order to feed the greater appetites of the whole. The youngest vampires are in need of more human blood, partly because it provides energy for the mutated blood to "work endlessly on all the soft human tissue . . . not merely to animate the tissue, but to convert it slowly into something else" (Rice, *Queen*, 117). Additionally, beginning with the transformation of the dying King Enkil, the burden of the blood thirst can be shared.[5] In a kind of pyramid scheme, the older vampires rely on what I think of as the "worker vampires" to satisfy the greater share of necessity; like most workers, they are expendable if flawed—or if they wander into someone else's territory.

The oldest vampires, Akasha, Enkil, Khayman, Mekare, and Maharet, being closest to the source of power, have heightened abilities and strengths, which can reinfuse younger ones if the older ones are inclined to share their blood—a rare occurrence.

When Lestat exchanges blood with Akasha for the second time, for example, they form a "shimmering circuit" (Rice, *Vampire Lestat*, 486), which strengthens Lestat and gives him even more power and new abilities. However, because Akasha's body, specifically her heart and/or mind, is the point of origin, other vampires are affected by attacks upon her. When she and Enkil are left in the sun to burn, they are strong and ancient enough already that they get only a good bronze tan, while younger and weaker vampires the world over explode or are badly burned and deformed.

With the eventual destruction of Akasha, the annihilation of all other vampires is narrowly avoided only because the twin witches Mekare and Maharet symbolically resume the funeral feast of their mother that had ironically been interrupted by Akasha centuries before. Mekare consumes the heart and the brain and thus becomes the new "Queen of the Damned." By this time, the network of blood has been mirrored by a computerized image that looks remarkably like the larger vampiric body and represents another form of immortality, "The Great Family," the diagram of all of Maharet's mortal descendants.

Given the religious inversions and complications Rice introduces, the Christian economy of suffering, sacrifice, and love differs very little from the vampiric itself. The vampires, like Lestat and Marius, who do not require systems of religious thought, or even of ethics, to sustain and justify them, are the obvious protagonists. Systemization and rigid logical thought too often serves as rationalization for epic violence, as with Akasha's manipulation of human religious beliefs or her grand scheme to murder most males on earth. Rice's vampires are mutating beings, on a monstrous border beyond the human and partaking of both the demonic and the divine. The spiritual world in Rice's novels is not at odds with the physical; they form a continuum of merging and emerging possibilities.

Although ideas about religion, God, and the devil are formative of the psyches of some of the vampires—their existence is even witnessed by Lestat—theological ideas are destructive to most of her characters. What emerges from the various quests of the vampires is a theology of particularity, where aesthetics is the ultimate value-judgment. However "damned" Lestat may feel, he does not take the chance to be cured of this vampiric infection. In *The Tale of the Body Thief*, Lestat has the opportunity to escape the vampiric "family" by trading bodies with a gifted human, but in the end, he chooses to return to himself as he is. It also remains unclear from the narrative of *Memnoch the Devil* whether Lestat's (invited) drink of blood from the dying Christ has removed him from the previous structure, combined the two very different "vines" into a new mutation, or finally, whether the whole experience was an illusion perpetuated by Memnoch to his own ends. What is clear from that part of the chronicles is that Lestat does not approve of the aesthetics of the game that is "revealed" to him; both sides, that of God and of Memnoch (the devil), are ultimately more offensive than fascinating to Lestat.

The phantasmatic "life" of these vampires serves to configure modes of addiction, aesthetics, gender roles, and, most importantly, power. Their position of being preyed upon as an extension of the Amel/Akasha spirit body and preying upon the blood of humans puts them in the ideal position for Rice to play with erotic power relations, which is after all, the primary theme of her writing, however existential. The sexuality of Rice's vampires centers on enhanced, even hallucinatory aesthetic appreciation (most importantly, the appreciation of the ecstasy of the blood swoon itself). Although they sometimes have strong feelings for their victims, it is very difficult in that drunkenness of power for the vampires not to kill the humans they embrace in this manner.

Rice claims that her vampires, freed from conventional sexuality, are transgendered, but what she really charts are the possible hybrids, mutations, and inversions, as well as the simple replications of stereotypes. They are not without or above gender despite the fact that they are unable to copulate; their eroticism is personative, polymorphous. Despite all the excitement and the occasional obsessions they have with one another, and despite the covens and the attempted pseudo-family structures, they are primarily narcissistic and Machiavellian, and, as such, separated from one another. As Marius explains to Lestat:

Most vampires are distrustful and solitary beings and they do not love others. They have no more than one or two well-chosen companions from time to time, and they guard their hunting grounds and their privacy as I do mine. They wouldn't want to come together, and if they did overcome the viciousness and suspicions that divide them, their convocation would end in terrible battles and struggles for supremacy like those revealed to me by Akasha, which happened thousands of years ago. We are evil things finally. We are killers. (Rice, *Vampire Lestat*, 486)

Even their moments of intimacy are too extreme, and can be read in terms of power. For example, Lestat experiences the intrusion of Armand's telepathic, filmic story upon his consciousness as fascinating, ecstatic, and overwhelming, even more so than the kill.

It was a monstrous intimacy with another being, an intimacy that made even the rapt moments of the kill seem dim and under control. He was opened and could no longer contain the dazzling stream of pictures that made his old silent voice seem thin and lyrical and made up. . . . Never, never in all my existence, not mortal or immortal, had I been threatened with an intimacy quite like this. (Rice, *Vampire Lestat*, 290)

The so-called intimacy here is rather more like psychic rape than sharing.

"The blood is the life" in Rice's vampire chronicles refers to the psychical and physical energy that maintains and enlarges a structural mutation that has assimilated all of the vampires into a single whole, a hybrid being, while maintaining the illusion of individual autonomy. While transformative-native possibilities for each individual vampire should not be underrated—in fact her vampires serve also to illustrate the perils of conformity—the system into which they have been incorporated makes of them both victims and villains. They even experience their connectedness as overwhelming, both threatening and fascinating, much in the way of Rudolf Otto's idea of the "holy" or Georges Bataille's notion of the sacred, sacrificial "wound".[6]

III

> Among vampires there is a most abiding love. Think of how the change
> was accomplished, and you will perceive why this is so. But once we come
> into our life, the expression of that love changes, as well. We hunger for
> life, Mister Tree. And that is the one thing we cannot offer one another.
> —Chelsea Quinn Yarbro,
> "Renewal," *The Saint Germain Chronicles*, 70

Chelsea Quinn Yarbro's vampire fiction signifies something quite different by "the blood is the life." In the Yarbro accounts, there is no monstrous silver network. What little is explicated of origins is an individual narrative, not a cosmological one.

Long before he was brought to Egypt, Saint-Germain was initiated into the cult of his god (who was, of course, a vampire) because he was a prince born at the dark of the year. "When I was old enough," he explains to a trusted Egyptian priest,

I was left in the sacred grove, my hands bleeding, waiting to offer myself to the god. He came, of course, and accepted my dedication, for when I grew to manhood, I drank his blood, and became one of his, destined to break free of death. . . . He died, fought at my side, he died and never rose again, for his head was struck from his body. (Yarbro, *Out of the House of Life*, 364)

The vampire, in Yarbro's fiction, is the archetype of the dying and resurrected God made literal and human.

For each vampire there is a kind of choice, since each is aware of the monstrous qualities within themselves and the risks they pose to others. What they are is in itself monstrous, but that does not mean that they have to act out the worst. In *Hotel Transylvania*, where Madeleine de Montalia is threatened by a group of devil-worshippers in the Paris of the Sun King, Saint-Germain seeks to warn her by explaining something of the nature of this choice:

There is a Power, which is only that. It is like the rivers, which nurture us and can destroy us. Whether we are prosperous or drowned in floodwaters, the rivers are the same. So with this Power. And when it lifts us up and opens our eyes to goodness and wonders, so that we are ennobled and inspired to kindness and excellence, we call it God. But when it is used for pain and suffering and degradation, we call it Satan. The Power is both. It is our use alone which makes it one or the other. (Yarbro, *Hotel Transylvania*, 62)

And again in "Advocates," the collaborative "novelet" that Yarbro wrote with Suzy Charnas, Saint-Germain defends a murderous vampire, Weyland, with this argument:

If it were only my need, I would roast him in hot coals. But that is him speaking in me, the beast that we are, the thing that makes people call us creatures of death. . . . But we do not kill. We instill life where death comes, we can banish it. . . . If we accept the bond of blood, we accept the ties of life as well, and we revere it as no mortal human can. And it is for that reason, for our cherished life that I ask you to treat this monster as the ghost of what we have been, that you do not condemn him to execution, either at the hands of his rivals. . . . or his predators; that you free yourselves in freeing him What are we: creatures of death or life? (Charnas and Yarbro, "Advocates," 155)

Yarbro's vampires exist at a much more human level than Rice's "unearthly" vampires. They do not look significantly different from humans, and they have a stronger connection to place, which accounts for the nourishment they absorb from their native earth. This connectedness is what allows their freedom of movement, and even allows them to walk during the day. As creatures of the earth, anything that interferes with their contact with native earth is debilitating, and in the case of water, sunlight, or fire, potentially fatal. One of the more clever and amusing traits of Yarbro's vampires is that they line their shoes with native earth, precisely for this reason. They are also vulnerable to anything that destroys the nervous system—the traditional stake, beheading, and the like. In a more general sense, connectedness to place and life allows them to exist in close proximity to humans, if they can avoid mirrors and make appropriate refusals of food and drink.

"The blood is the life." For Yarbro's vampires, the power that is used to uplift and to love comes back through mortal blood with the passion and love that is life. That is what they feed upon, but it is a reciprocal exchange, more psychical, finally than physical. They must bring pleasure and fulfillment to their mortal lovers through intimate caresses, touching, and conversation. They are (conveniently) freed from the necessity of killing, because they need no more blood than would fill a wineglass. The blood, for Yarbro's vampires, represents not only the fulfillment of necessity and appetite, but the nourishing qualities of affection and love, without which the blood is not much more than bread and water would be to humans.

At its richest, the blood that is taken with love is also taken with the knowledgeable acceptance by the lover of each vampire for what he or she is and the acceptance of the risk of contagion that comes with repeated contact. Being with a vampire several times makes a mortal lover vulnerable to the vampiric infection, which eventually forces the lovers to seek another partner. They thirst for life, and cannot offer that to one another. The passion must come from a living person, from living blood. Unlike Rice's vampires, who revel in druglike, narcissistic pleasure, Yarbro's vampires can have no pleasure of their own without the pleasure of a mortal other.

The limits of the viral infection are given, established with this communion, where the essential part of a unique person is shared with another. A crossing of boundaries and a mingling of subjectivities occurs, and what crosses cannot be simply categorized as either physical or psychical. Mortals that become vampires learn to love other mortals by necessity, although love for their "maker" remains. However, aren't these vampires just a little too ethical, too loving, too charming? Isn't it convenient that their wealth is for the most part produced alchemically by Saint-Germain and not stolen from victims as in Rice's fiction? Above all, isn't this virus just a little too benevolent?

The reason for this is that the truly malignant aspect of the viral is not where one might expect it to be in these narratives. While vampires are conscious of the monstrousness possibilities of their nature and for the most part choose to affirm life, the horror of Yarbro's vampire narratives resides much more fully in the human population. Humans are the killers, parasitical upon each other in much more destructive ways than her vampires could be. The very words of destructive manipulating mortals, like Anastasi in *Darker Jewels*, can seem viral. In that novel, the mortal Xenya does not want to listen to him as he cajoles, orders, and threatens her, for his words seem "slippery and clinging, contaminating" (Yarbro, *Darker Jewels*, 217). Madeline de Montalia, in a letter to Saint-Germain at the end of *Hotel Transylvania*, confirms this idea:

In my reading of history there is war and ruin and pillage and lives snuffed out with such profligacy that my breath is stopped by the senselessness of it. One would think that all humanity had nothing better to do than feed on its own carrion. Think of the destruction you have seen, and the endless foulness. Whole peoples have perished for a few men's greed, or desire, or sport. I have thought as I read these books, how many much worse things there are in this world than vampires. To know your freedom. To live in the blood that is taken with love. (247–48)

It is also the basis of Olivia's response to Falke in *Out of the House of Life*:

A jackal feeds on carrion. Falke That offers nothing to those who are of my blood. The virtue of the blood is in the life; if the life is gone, then the blood can offer nothing. . . . It is life I seek, Egidius Maximilliaan Falk. . . . I take no carrion; I have no victims. Do I? This last question was wistful. Do I?, she repeated, trying not to dread his answer. Not in me, he said. (3, 17)

While the viral is thus contained in Yarbro's fiction, there is still a form of contagion that has to do with maintaining inflexible boundaries of community and with the compulsion to define self against other. In *Crusader's Torch*, Saint-Germain writes to Olivia that

The continued clash of Christianity and Islam has only served to make each side more zealous and unyielding. There is precious little room for reason or moderation now, and you will not convince me that the skirmishes will not continue until once again there is war, presented in the more flattering guise of Crusading. (102)

And again, in *Darker Jewels*, Saint-Germain voices this fear of contamination between groups and their perceived need for boundaries:

For the Rus are wary of foreigners. . . . they take great care to avoid dealing directly with us, for fear that we will contaminate them. . . . These people do not trust any outsiders. They wash their hands and faces after speaking with any of us, to insure that they have no taint of that-which-is-not-Rus. I have done what I may to respect their ways, but I know that what they do rankles the Jesuits. (67)

The behavior of the Rus toward the Jesuits mirrors back to them, in an ethnic or national register, what they themselves practice in a religious register. Rather than make the Jesuits conscious of their own fears and unfairness toward persons of other faiths, this experience "rankles" and, more than that, serves as a kind of catalyst for negative judgments and destructive behaviors toward Saint-Germain.

In Yarbro's fiction, the true viral vampiric is historical and resides in the mortal. Saint-Germain, having been undead for thousands of years, had gone through periods of blood greed, patriotic reveling, and murderous frenzies, but he learned that there is better "nourishment." As he attempts to explain to the destructive Mr. Lorpicar, "Terror, certainly, has a vigor, but it is nothing compared to loving" (Yarbro, "Cabin 33;" *The Saint Germain Chronicles*, 193).

Unlike Rice's vampires, Yarbro's vampires tend not attack one another. When her vampires are attacked, crucified, shot, left unprotected in the sun, drowned, dismembered, and blown up, it is as a result of human actions. (Even the misguided vampire Mr. Lorpicar is destroyed by the intervention of a mortal.) The times and places where the vampires "live" is full of petty acts of destructiveness, intrigue, manipulation, corruption, thievery, and the like. The colonizing Spanish in the Peru of *Mansions of Darkness*, for example, destroy what they can of the Incan population and assimilate the rest whether through intimidation, rape, or conversion.

IV

> It is along the frontier of blood—on the red line between pure and impure—that the inexhaustible drama between the sacred and the profane is played out: between the history of the divine, and the history of the human element that would struggle free of the human.
>
> —Piero Camporesi,
> *Juices of Life*, 121

Rice's vision is a deconstructed or confounded theology, where the vampire is a true "other" to humanity. Her vampires are pastiches of human possibility, and their primary mechanism is a movement from metamorphosis to mutation: an idealized form of delayed metastasis, from dying human to something other than human. The vampire is posthuman in a measure of intensity and not just longevity, a form not bound by social restraints, but by certain kinds of continually expanding metaphysical conditions of possibility. Her vampires are strictly parasitic on humanity, but in the way that humans are parasitic upon animal and plant life: humans are fascinating prey, nothing more.

The rapture of taking blood is eroticizing power because in this moment of transit from human to vampire the blood is transformed from the fluid basis of life to a form of inhuman energy. In this transit or interface, boundary oppositions meld. However, vampires in her works are in complicated power relations with one another—to such an extent that it is almost possible to imagine that humans are unnecessary, and that vampires could feed off of one another, if need be. The blood is a kind of transformation drug, and despite its destructive addictiveness, it offers too many rewards to be denied, once tasted.

Yarbro's vision is a humanistic and utopian one. Her vampires are what humans could or should be, were they not limited by petty rivalries, greed, competition, and the like. They have been freed, at least with one another, from the negative aspect of community. The primary mechanisms working in these narratives are projection and displacement. There is no real "other." Vampires are less parasitic upon humans than they are symbiotic with them. Humans are parasite and host upon each other in much more destructive ways.

The eroticism of taking blood can be interpreted through two different lenses, two possibilities that appear to be working at once. One is to stipulate that her vampires, as ideal humans, offer pleasure and love as a gift, where a higher form of the human gives of itself altruistically, a form of grace without theology. This would explain the relative lack of a myth or narrative of origins and the lack of her characters' interest in one. The other is that her vampires are a form of literalization of the gods, where the psychic material in the blood is simply better "food." Love is presented as nourishment, and valorized over mere appetite. This would mean that the contact with humans has more self-interest than the gifts of pleasure would seem to indicate. In support of this idea, for all of the good that her vampires do, they do warn a human close to being infected (and they have time to do so, as this requires a number of occasions), and they also show some measure of remorse for "infecting" another.

A kind of virus that is transmitted by blood and grants the possibility of eternal life is morally ambiguous and addresses the ambivalence that human beings have toward this possibility and its price. It also resonates against ideas about race, community, and sexuality and even comments on the submerged cannibalistic subtheme of communion. On the other hand, vampires are something more than human, something of otherness that mirrors our anxieties and hopes, our imagined communities and boundaries, our power relations, back to us. Whatever we project outwards comes back to haunt us uncannily, for like Pogo's "enemy," "we have seen the vampire, and it is us."

NOTES

1. In the context of his hermeneutical interpretation of myth and religious consciousness, Ricoeur's description of defilement as a symbol of evil represents only the lowliest, archaic, and "pre-ethical" precursor to progressive symbolizations of sin and guilt. In the latter symbolic structures, the symbolic myth of infection from without reappears as a free choice of the will that transposes it "inward" "to express a freedom that enslaves itself, affects itself and infects itself by its own choice" (152). Only in relation to an idea of the individual servile will, in other words, does the archaic sense of evil become evident as a symbol that informs later types of religious consciousness.

Yet precisely the combination of factors that Ricoeur describes as archaic—contagion, infection, a blurring of materiality and psychical definition, and mysterious and "invisible" powers—characterize the viral, the non-self that threatens to invade, overpower, and change one's being, but that has no agency, intelligence, or capacity for emotion. The viral stands in, not for what one chooses in freedom to be affected by, but rather for what is thought of or experienced as infection and colonization: what intrudes and violates, invades and takes up residence, contaminates and sometimes kills.

2. This idea was elaborated on in *The Queen of the Damned* as follows:

There was also abundant evidence that what we called bad spirits envied us that we were fleshly and also spiritual—that we had the pleasures and powers of the physical while possessing spiritual minds. Very likely, this mixture of flesh and spirit in human beings makes all spirits curious; it is the source of our attraction for them; but it rankles the bad spirits; the bad spirits would know sensuous pleasure, it seems; yet they cannot. The good spirits did not evince such dissatisfaction." (Rice, *Queen*, 280).

See also pp. 3 1 0–1 1.

3. Ibid., pp. 292, 310, 316, 366–72.

4. The text of John 15:3–10 are as follows in *The New English Bible* (Oxford Study Edition):

I am the vine, and you the branches. He who dwells in me, as I dwell in him, bears much fruit; for apart from me you can do nothing. He who does not dwell in me is thrown away like a withered branch. The withered branches are heaped together, thrown on the fire, and burnt. If you dwell in me, and my words dwell in you, ask what you will, and you shall have it. This is my Father's glory, that you may bear fruit in plenty and so be my disciples. As the Father has loved me, so I have loved you. Dwell in my love. If you heed my commands, you will dwell in my love, as I have heeded my Father's commands, and dwell in his love.

5. As Rice explains:

It wants more like you. It wants to go in and make blood drinkers of others as it did with the King; it is too immense to be contained within two small bodies. The thirst will become bearable only when you make others, for they will share the burden of it with you." (Rice, *Queen*, 371)

6. Otto, *The Idea of the Holy*; Bataille, *Theory of Religion*.

WORKS CITED

Bataille, Georges. *Theory of Religion*. Trans. by Robert Hurley. New York: Zone Books, 1989.

Camporesi, Piero. *Juice of Life: Symbolic and Magic Significance of Blood*. Foreword by Umberto Eco. Trans. by Robert R. Barr. New York: Continuum, 1995. Originally published as IL Sugo della Vita: Simbolismoe magia del sangue. Milan: Arnoldo Mondadori Editore SPA, 1988.

Chamas, Suzy McKee, and Chelsea Quinn Yarbro. "Advocates." A novelet featuring Weyland and Saint-Germain. In *Under the Fang*. Ed. Robert R. McCammon, The Horror Writers Association. New York: Pocket Books, Simon and Schuster, 1991.

Otto, Rudolf. *The Idea of the Holy: An Inquiry into the Non-Rational Factor in the Idea of the Divine and Its Relation to the Rational*. Translated by John W. Harvey. 1928. London: Oxford University Press, 1958.

Rice, Anne. *Memnoch the Devil*. New York: Ballantine Books, 1995.

———. *The Queen of the Damned*. New York: Ballantine Books, 1988.

———. *The Vampire Lestat*. New York: Ballantine Books, 1985.

Ricoeur, Paul. *The Symbolism of Evil*. Translated by E. Buchanan. New York: Harper & Row, 1967. pp. 25–6.

Yarbro, Chelsea Quinn. "Art Songs" 1991, from *The 7th World Fantasy Convention Program Book, Eds*. Jack Rems and Jeffrey Frane, 1996. Frane,. 1996.

———. "Cabin 33" 1980, *Shadows 3*, Ed. Charles L. Grant, New York: Doubleday, 1980.

———. *A Candle for d'Artagnan: An Historical Horror Novel*. New York: Tor, 1989.

———. *Crusader's Torch*. New York: Tor, 1988.

———. *Darker Jewels: A Novel of the Count Saint-Germain*. New York: Orb, 1995; Tor Hardcover, 1993.

———. *A Flame in Byzantium*. New York: Tor, 1987.

———. *Hotel Transylvania: A Novel of Forbidden Love*. New York: St. Martin's Press, 1978.

———. *Mansions of Darkness: A Novel of Saint Germain*. New York: Tor, 1996.

———. *Out of the House of Life: A Novel of the Count Saint Germain*. New York: Orb, 1994; Tor Hardcover, 1990.

——— "Renewal" 1982, *Shadows 5*, Ed. Charles L. Grant. New York: Doubleday. 1982.

——— *The Saint Germain Chronicles*. New York: Timescape Pocket, Simon & Schuster, 1983.

Chapter 13

Kelene: The Face in the Mirror

Stephanie Moss

> Brilliance of silvered-backing to suspension. God gazes on nothing (but) the same. Pure being (of the) mirror. In which reflection has no reflection, no obvious replicating effect, no shadow of a doubt as to self-identity, no trace of something having taken place.
>
> —Irigary,
> *Speculum*, 356

The female mysticism that Luce Irigary posits as a site of subversion can be understood through the metaphor of the mirror. In the Lacanian theory that Irigary parodically mimics, the mirror functions as the site of self-duplication and loss, a space in which the subject recognizes itself as separate from the mother who has, hitherto, supplied all instinctual needs. The child must begin the long journey toward self-sufficiency, supplying for itself those needs, now repressed and transformed into desire. Gazing at itself in the mirror, the child appears to itself complete, unfragmented, and unbroken, a vision of wholeness that becomes a misrecognized reflection of a lost infantile union and of gratified animal instincts. Because the self in the mirror is seen as an unruptured exterior reflection rather than the interiorized subjectivity now split by the newborn—forever submerged and therefore inaccessible unconscious—the face in the mirror becomes the object of desire.

This silver-backed image appears at the same developmental moment that the child acquires speech, so that when the child falls in love with its mirror image it enters into a linguistic system that has been constructed by paternal laws. The appearance of the face in the mirror, thus, represents the sociocultural embrace of the child by a paternal society, and, just as the child's psychical development is constructed by the Freudian Oedipal experience formulated from the male child's perspective, so its mirror image is gendered male through the structuring of thought by a patriarchal language. The face in the mirror, therefore, becomes a fragile aggregate of desire for mother, self, and lover, one more space in which woman is not.

However, like woman, God is unrepresentable, outside the paternal linguistic system. Thus, when woman looks into the face of God instead of into the mirror of society she does not see reflected the social codes that tell her she is not; she sees nothing. The blank silver-backed surface of God's ineffable face gives woman an unfilled space in which to construct herself, and it is for this reason that Angora identifies the female mystic as the subject who can disrupt Lacanian theory. It is also a possible reason for the fearful dependency that flourished between God and woman, woman and God during the thirteenth to early sixteenth centuries and provides the impetus behind the medieval phenomenon of feminine ecstatic visions.

Chelsea Quinn Yarbro's *Kelene: The First Bride of Dracula* (1998) interrogates Irigary's theory that the relationship between female and her God subverts the patriarchy. Yarbro first inscribes and then reverses a feminist understanding of mysticism as liberator. The sixteenth-century protopubescent female hero of the narrative, Kelene, is an illiterate mystic. She has heard the voice of her Militant Angel since she has possessed a memory. The chronological setting of the novel is the year 1500, twenty-one years before Martin Luther penned and posted the ninety-five theses that would interrogate and collapse Christian hierarchy by allowing the individual a personal knowledge of God. At this historical moment the Western world teetered on the brink of both a print culture and a Reformation that together would transform scribal texts into books and thereby abrogate Church command of divine and earthly knowledge of God.

Since Kelene's voices by-pass the human/priest communication link established by both the Eastern and Western Catholic churches by dismissing the priest as earth-to-God switchboard operator, her voices function in much the same destablizing way as the vernacular bible by allowing the individual to receive God's word directly without ecclesiastical intervention. This historical moment is carefully selected by Yarbro, not only because it conforms to the dates established in Stoker's novel, but because mysticism will become a rallying point for the Radical Reformation that will wrest control of divine knowledge from the Church, an historical process that will proclaim human liberty through the science and philosophies of Newton, deism, Locke, and democracy, but will continue to leave the female out of the conversation. By using female mysticism as her master metaphor, Yarbro demonstrates the intensity and vigor of Church authority in the very historical moments of its greatest weakness, employing gender politics to unearth the rotting roots of the patriarchy in organized religion.

The narrative develops the brief and astonishing moment of Jonathan Harker's encounter with the female vampires in Dracula's castle into the story of the crossing over of Dracula's first vampire bride into eternal life. Its narrative structure is simple, centering around the journey, a search for home and hearth that backgrounds so many Victorian novels. When Kelene's family home in Salonika, Macedonia, is threatened by the Ottoman incursion, her Militant Angel tells her to flee and take her family, promising to protect them. Kelene leads them on a quest for freedom that becomes an *anti-bildungsroman*, a journey not to adult identity, but into the embrace of the vampire where Kelene will remain eternally protopubescent. There is no epithalamious Victorian ending to Kelene's journey, and if this novel has a wedding song, it is joyless one.

During the journey, Yarbro makes use of carefully chosen rest-stops that mark geographical sites of religious contention, environments in which Eastern Catholicism met Western Catholicism and both in turn confronted the alterity of the Turkish empire. By inscribing locales in which radically different world religions confronted each other, Yarbro extends her interrogation of organized religion beyond the bounds of western culture. One such stop—Sarajevo—becomes a controlling metaphor, acting as a prompt to the reader to compare the war-torn Sarajevo of today with the war-torn Sarajevo of four centuries ago. It is obvious to the reader that not much has changed. The city thus functions as a master trope for religious hatred, a controlling metaphor for death and irrational destruction that establishes a framework through which the rest of the novel may be read.

From Sarajevo, Kelene and her family journey to Belgrade, a city perched on the border of Hungary, Wallachia, and the Ottoman Empire. Belgrade in the sixteenth century was another nodal point of religious contestation, a fact made clear in Yarbro's introduction to the city:

Belgrade was filled with soldiers from all over Europe, some of them blatantly mercenary, some of them religiously motivated to stop the advance of the Ottoman Empire. The streets rang with a cacophony of languages; the markets were hectic with activity. (*Kelene*, 156)

Beneath the clamorous atmosphere of this large city, a terrified environment of hushed struggle prevails, but incipient clashes are felt rather than heard as the transactions of the emerging capitalist and global marketplace muffle the panic of the individual swept up in inexorable geopolitical forces.

As in many of Yarbro's historical texts, these settings function as metatropes, characters that determine the narrative along with the eponymous hero. It is in the prototypical slave market of Belgrade that the family sells Kelene, purchased for a king's ransom by Dracula to become his bride and slave. This material exchange thus mimes the economics of arranged marriages, evincing the fact that despite Kelene's privileged discourse with the divine, she remains an object of barter. The parodic marriage of Kelene to Dracula provides a biting commentary upon the interrelationship between church and gender politics; the female mysticism that Irigary finds subversive is directly responsible for Kelene's enslavement in one of the most patriarchal relationships in fiction, that of Dracula and his female brides. In the Stoker novel that acts as Yarbro's wellspring, Dracula's brides are his children, housed and fed by the vampire, their very lives dependent upon the vampire's continued existence. The arrested physical development that Kelene will experience is thus partnered by the arrested social development inherent in the history of marriage.

Yarbro's ironic examination of religious relations of power does not merely reveal the ahistorical tyranny of the Church; the novel also demonstrates the fluid boundary between saint and sinner that is inherent in church dogma. The fact that the face of God and the Devil perceived in the mirror are one and the same is clearly inscribed on page one, which takes the reader into the heart of an ecstatic vision experienced by Kelene. We know from the novel's subtitle, *The First Bride of Dracula*, that the voices Kelene hears are not from God but from the vampire, and the novel is built upon an ideological grid that establishes this dramatic irony: Kelene's mystical and divine voice is that of the vampire.

The divinity of this voice is ratified by Kelene's father and his validation empowers Kelene within her nuclear family; however, empowerment merely becomes another reflection in the patriarchal mirror, as Diogenes, the nuclear father, collapses his daughter's gifts into his own authorial inner space:

"Our daughter has shown remarkable gifts since she was very young." said Diogenes, his voice hypnotic in its intensity. "There have been other women in my family who have had such gifts, but none so greatly as she." (25)

It does not becomes clear until journey's end when Dracula is manifest in all his malevolency that the women in the family have seen more acutely than Diogenes. Their recurrent question—whose God does this voice represent and why has he chosen Kelene?—surfaces and is repressed, melts and discandies as Diogenes, with Yarbro's tacit approval, credits their response to jealousy: "You would not know if [the angels] lied or not. You will listen to me [your aunt] or you will be ruined by your own folly, and your father's pride"(2). Yarbro thus constructs an alternate Trinity of God, the Vampire, and the nuclear father, insuring that female subjectivity is banished to the margins even while Kelene is celebrated for her gifts.

However, as the narrative progresses, Kelene's visions become familiar: the embrace of the dark angel is strangely erotic and patterns the historical experience of medieval mystics:

Darkly glorious the angel rose before [Kelene], his wings outspread like a cloak, his head refulgently haloed. His mightiness was like a god of the times before salvation, he commanded veneration. In one hand he held a shining sword, in the other there was a chalice. There was majesty in his stance. He embodied the ineffable, his splendor filling Kelene with such wonder that she felt suspended by it, hardly able to breathe, her pulse in her own ears. . . . The angel bent down and pressed his full, hard mouth to her forehead, his kiss burned there as she stared up into his aquiline features. She wondered if she could fall into his eyes, or be transfixed by them. . . . Then he drew back from her, spread his enormous, dark wings and left her, alone and shivering on the crest of the mountain with only his kiss to warn her. (30–31)

Kelene's mystical visions thus recall historical medieval experiences such as those of the thirteenth century Flemish female mystic, Hadewych:

He swallows you into Himself. . . . He will teach you what He is, and how wonderfully the one beloved dwells in the other . . . in mutual enjoyment, mouth in mouth, heart in heart, body in body. (Borchert, 40)

Like the experiences of the fifteenth-century English mystic, Margery Kempe, whose ecstasy was marred by "horybyl syghtys & abhominabyl," Kelene is horrified "that she could so profane a sacred thing" (Beckwith, 211 quoting Kempe; Yarbro, *Kelene,* 31).

It is this likeness of Kelene's visions to the historical record that facilitates Yarbro's brilliant interrogation of religious mysticism. Manipulating the reader, Yarbro keeps affective sympathy with Kelene and her father, Diogenes, and the voices of the women in the family, who clearly intuit the true deception of the mystical visions, take on the whining tone of female complaint. We, as readers, follow Kelene and the seductive call of her Militant Angel into a land of death, torture, rape, and finally into a place of hopelessness and captivity. As the novel darkens and Dracula reveals himself in waking human form, we, like Kelene, slowly awaken to the horrific knowledge that her (and our) psychic bondage will soon become eternal. As we participate with Kelene in this awakening, we realize that heaven and hell, the Lord's Supper and Satanic cannibalism are contingent constructions and that the unreflectable face in the silver-backed Irigaraynian mirror is also that of the vampire.

As Kelene walks into her room in Castle Dracula for the first time we are not surprised that she notes among the quotidian appointments that, "There were no mirrors" (Yarbro 98). This absence of mirrors suggests that the unreflectable face of the vampire is like that of the unreflectable face of God, mutually constructive. The master/slave dialectic that informs the relationship of Dracula and his first bride makes visible the fact that there can be no binary without the mutual participation of both halves. *Kelene: The First Bride of Dracula* thus recalls and rejects Dracula as liberator, a construct that along with the portrait of Dracula as tyrant is inherent in Stoker's master text. Kelene has defied the religious patriarchy only to enslave herself to its double, a satanic punishment due all who challenge the coded laws of religion. As Sarah Beckwith writes of the medieval mystic Margery Kempe:

Margery's hallucination is more the sign of her shame than her subversion. It is sent as a punishment [for] . . . all who do not obey [God's] law. It is a sign, less of her transgression, than the unconscious effects of subjugation to that very law. Coming from the devil, not God, it is juxtaposed with her "gloryows visyonys" from God, Our Lady, and the saints, only to be discarded, appearing in the form it does because of the necessity for its sublimation." (211–12)

However, the vampire as savior, a reading that lurks in the dark recesses of Stoker's novel, informs other Yarbro works. In the Saint-Germain series, the radical realization of the vampire as gender freedom-fighter is embodied by the small dark man who can be seen as an anti-Christ only from the chauvinistic persecutive of the church patriarches. Saint-Germain says to a young woman rebelling against an arranged marriage: "I do not like to see you or any woman make herself seem less than she is in the name of acceptance. It not only belittles you, it belittles me as well. (*Blood Legacy*, 147)

In Yarbro's *Writ in Blood*, Saint-Germain articulates the mutually constructive relationship between vampire and female; this time, however, it reveals that man can only climb as high as woman is allowed to climb with him.

As for the possibility of true mysticism, Yarbro describes the human encounter with the unknown in her *Michael* series. As the planchette of the Wedgie board begins to move and the wind begins to blow, a mystical voice that is the antithesis of Kelene's Militant Angel speaks:

WE ARE AN ANCIENT ENTITY THAT COMES TO ALL WHO ASK. OUR PURPOSE IS TO TEACH SOME UNDERSTANDING OF THE EVOLUTION OF THE PHYSICAL PLANE SO THAT THE STUDENT CAN REACH SOME INSIGHT INTO HUMAN BEHAVIOR WHICH WILL ENABLE HIM THEN TO STOP BROODING OVER INTERPERSONAL RELATIONSHIPS OR THE LACK THEREOF AND CONCENTRATE ON PERSONAL LIFE. (*Messages from Michael*, 21)

These mystical voices, like that of Saint-Germain, recognize the socially based construction of gender and sexual identity:

THERE ARE NO SEXED SOULS. . . . [IT IS THE] BLINDNESS OF THE PHYSICAL PLANE THAT CAUSES MANY TO PERCEIVE ONLY THE BODY, AND NOT THE NATURE OF THE SOUL. (*Messages*, 88, 158)

By juxtaposing *Kelene, The First Bride of Dracula* to both the *Saint-Germain* and *Michael* series, the mirror in which God, the vampire, and the female cast no reflection can be seen, indeed, as a blank surface. It is one that the patriarchy may appropriate in order to write itself, or it may be a blank surface that reveals not only the freedom to write oneself, but, more importantly, the fact that the essence of human nature is ungendered. When the soul sheds its gendered reflection and perceives the fathomless blaze of an unqendered selfhood deep inside, Irigary's ecstatic poetry finds true human liberation:

When I look upon you in the secret of my "Soul," I seek (again) the loss of specularization, and try to bring my "nature" back to its mirroring wholeness. (Irigary, 197)

WORKS CITED

Beckwith, Sarah. "A Very Material Mysticism: The Medieval Mysticism of Margery Kemp." *Gender and Text in the Later Middle Ages.* Ed. Jane Chance. Gainesville: UP of Florida, 1996.

Borchert, Bruno. *Mysticism: Its History and Challenge.* York Beach, Me: Samuel Weiser, 1994.

Irigary, Luce. *Speculum of the Other Woman.* Trans. Gillian G. Gill, 1974. Ithaca: Cornell UP, 1985.

Yarbro, Chelsea Quinn.

———. *Kelene: The First Bride of Dracula.* New York: Avon Book, 1998.

———. *Messages from Michael.* New York: Playboy Press, 1979

Chapter 14

The Construction of the Vampire in Yarbro's *Hotel Transylvania*

Sharon A. Russell

I once had a professor for a Jane Austen seminar who talked about how much he envied someone reading *Pride and Prejudice* for the first time. I wonder what it would have been like to have been one of the first readers of a book with the strange title, *Dracula*. Those of us living at the end of the twentieth century can never recover the experience of approaching that book with the innocence of its original audience. Right now I wish I could recall the experience of my first encounter with *Hotel Transylvania* by Chelsea Quinn Yarbro. I am fascinated by the way an author sets up the first in a projected series and how a reader reacts to a first encounter with a novel that plays with genre expectations: What clues does the author give the reader, and how are character and plot introduced in a novel that builds on audience expectations in order to redefine them? The problems confronting an author who wishes to alter reader expectations are particularly complex in the case of vampire literature. This was especially true in 1978 when those novels that dealt with the figure tended, with few exceptions, to conform to the tradition established by Bram Stoker and reinforced by cinematic versions of *Dracula*.

Yarbro was certainly aware the necessity of working with the expectations of her readers. The inclusion of notes at the end of the book provide the person who has finished the work with further information about its sources and the author's attitude toward vampires. The first novel in the Count Saint-Germain series radically subverts the traditional traits of this horror figure, but the author carefully retains enough elements from the lore to provide a transition from evil to good vampire while still keeping the figure viable within the tradition. A close examination of the opening of *Hotel Transylvania* indicates the various methods Yarbro employs to call on the reader's knowledge of the vampire and alter the reader's attitude towards this figure.

The novel's title both refers to a real place, as explained in the notes that follow the book, and a place associated with Dracula. The description "A Novel of Forbidden Love," which follows the title, suggests a possible shift in genre expectations. This book may focus on love rather than horror, which might place it with other historical romances. The contradictory clues the reader receives are further complicated by the dedication to Christopher Lee and the quotation from *Manon*: "A nous les amours/et les roses," which follow the title page.

The novel seems to proclaim its connection with Dracula's epistolary mode by opening with an excerpt of a letter from la Comtesse d'Argenlac to her niece, Madelaine de Montalla, the love interest. The labeling of the letter as an excerpt and the inclusion of the date, September 13, 1743, immediately give the reader the sense of entering in the middle of a historical event. The reader is led into the world of the novel and its principal forces both good and evil. Count Saint-Germain is first introduced through the letter which mentions both his musical abilities and his resemblance to another man who appeared in 1701. The connection between the two men suggests the possibility of a single, ageless character, but the reader must defer any real conviction about this trait until further information is given. The letter also begins the process of introducing some of the central characters. Yarbro associates names with traits, clothing, and unique events to assist the reader in tracking the various groups of characters whose foreign names might otherwise present difficulties.

Saint-Germain is more formally identified in the opening of the first chapter which follows the letter. The author tells the reader Saint-Germain is only one of his many names and suggests again a long time span and a life in different locations. She often refers to his age at this point in the novel, suggesting connections to the most attractive aspect of the figure. If the traditional vampire's need for a form of human sacrifice and the related threat of contagion through contact are a way of tempering the reader's natural desire for immortality, Yarbro's hero is gradually revealed to have lived a much longer life than the genre model; he is aware of the difficulty of his kind of life and seeks no converts. At this point in the story agelessness does not automatically indicate the nature of the central character, especially when he is associated with magicians.

The Count is on his way to a meeting with the alchemists/sorcerers who will provide a separate plot line that connects to the rest of the novel towards the end. He uses one of his other names in dealing with these people, Prinz Ragoczy. In exchange for helping them with their search for the means of creating diamonds, the Count asks for their help in purchasing the hotel of the title. Just as Count Dracula must deal with agents and asks Harker about ways to make other transactions in a secret manner, Saint-Germain must use fellow alchemists to assist him in a purchase that must remain hidden.

The concept of a house joined to the deeper idea of home—that place where one will truly feel at home—will be repeated in all of the Saint-Germain novels. Rather than the traditional enclosure of the Gothic castle the Count builds house after house attempting to alleviate some of his alienation. He is tied to his native earth, yet ever prevented from feeling at home. Over and over in the novels his homes are destroyed, or he is forced to abandon them. All of the houses in the Saint-Germain novels are described with attention to historical accuracy and filled with art treasures collected during the course of his long life. While the hotel is not built to his specifications, it does acquire the secret room that is essential to his dwellings when later in the novel the alchemists relocate their work to the basement of this building. Contrary to the vault of the traditional vampire, Saint-Germain's hidden room houses alchemical experiments and the athanor that creates the jewels that form a part of his visible wealth and fame. The transformation of ordinary commodities into enduring gems, especially diamonds, the strongest and hardest of the precious stones, can also be seen as a metaphor for the transformation of humans into the enduring life of the vampire.

While the knowledgeable reader might recognize genre implications of the Count's need for home, Yarbro inserts clues throughout this chapter. When the landlord offers him a cup, Saint-Germain responds, "I do not drink wine" (13). By the end of this section he makes a direct reference to Transylvania, which should give a reader with only the most basic information about the genre a clear idea of his true nature and the beginning of an understanding of his connection to Dracula. He explains why he wants to purchase the hotel. There was a faraway look in Saint-Germain's compelling eyes as he said, "I suppose its is because Transylvania is my native land, and I have been Prince of the Blood there." His expression cleared. "It is true, gentlemen, that one's native earth has a pull, no matter how long, or at what distances one lives" (18). These details do not definitively define the Count, and the reader might wonder about how to reconcile the conflicting associations of horror figure with a generous, reasonable, and just central character. Yarbro ensures the positive acceptance of the Count both through her presentation of his character and in her use of other characters as foils for him. At the end of the chapter another letter describes Madelaine's love of "the bizarre and the fantastic" (19), which will predispose her to an appreciation of Saint-Germain.

The next chapter introduces many key characters in a social situation where further additions to the description of the Count affirm both his goodness and his true nature. He does not eat. "'I am not hungry just at present,' he said, thinking that it was not quite the truth" (21). But he is attentive to Mme. Cressie, who is ill. The evil humans who pose the real threat are also gradually introduced in this chapter, with ominous references to strange uses for virgins and rude confrontations with men associated with Saint Sebastien setting up the ultimate confrontation between the two "Saints." The evening ends with the first meeting between the Count and Madelaine, leaving them as they conclude their formal greeting. Yarbro closes the chapter with another excerpt from a letter, this time from Mme. Cressie to her sister. She writes about strange dreams she has which she both likes and distrusts. She also introduces her troubles with her husband and his friends and what will prove to be well-founded fears of them.

The next chapter presents the reader with further information about several characters as Madelaine and her aunt discuss the previous evening. Madelaine's interest in the Count is balanced by her aunt's brief revelations about the Black Masses associated with Saint Sebastien's group and with Madelaine's father. A slight detail brings up thoughts of the vampire. Madelaine's garnet necklace has a problem with a link that has scratched her neck. This same defect will later provide the blood for her first romantic encounter with the Count, where he does indeed drink from her neck but without the negative implications of the traditional vampire. By the point she presents this event, Yarbro has so developed Saint-Germain's character that the reader can accept him as a romantic hero.

The fourth chapter which brings good and evil into a direct confrontation furthers the reader's appreciation of Saint-Germain's humanity as opposed to Saint Sebastien's embodiment of the negative elements of the vampire tradition. Saint Sebastien thinks ahead to the day when he will posses Lucienne Cressie, when "he would plunge his dagger into her neck and catch the hot blood in the Chalice at the very moment of his ecstasy" (39). The details of the Sabbat he dwells on far exceed even the actions of the traditional vampire. The ceremony he anticipates emphasizes an attack on a female that is both sexual and violent. Its perversion of the traditional substitution of blood for sex is essential to the development of Yarbro's version of the genre. Whereas the Count is an example of moderation in that he never drinks deeply and gains his satisfaction from giving pleasure, Saint Sebastien wants sex, blood, and death to satisfy his sadism and lust for power.

The contrast between the two men is heightened by the events that follow Saint Sebastien's musings. When his coachman avoids three beggars in the road, Saint Sebastien becomes so angry he smashes the man's knees and leaves him on the road. "Saint Sebastien licked his lips once as he studied his stricken coachman, his eyes somnambulant with strange pleasure" (11). Roger, the Count's aide, finds the coachman, Hercule, and gets his master. When Hercule meets Saint-Germain, he asks him who he is. "Roger's master heard the question and answered it. 'For the most part, I am le Compte. Saint-Germain, this century'" (42). The chapter ends with Madelaine's idea of vampires as reported by her aunt to Madelaine's father.

Occasionally she quite astounds me with her erudition. When Saint-Germain was regaling us at supper with his droll stories, she rallied him when he had begun a tale of vampires, saying that to fear them was the greatest folly, since any blood would appease them. All one would have to do was to offer them a lamb, or a horse, and the matter was settled. You should have seen the amazement on Saint-Germain's face. He kissed her hand and told her he conceded the match. (43)

This incident economically provides a humorous contrast to the serious presentation of human evil, serves as a counter to the real qualities of vampires that the Count will soon present to the young woman, and gives him the encouragement to speak to her of his true nature.

While further small incidents confirm the positive elements in the Count's character, Yarbro uses a description of Lucienne's dream that deals in some detail with an unusual sexual encounter. The "he" who suddenly appears in her room is not named, but by this time his identity must be clear to most readers. The pleasure associated with a nocturnal encounter with a vampire is violently contrasted with her experiences with the Satanic sect. Lucienne attempts to escape and is captured by Saint Sebastien, who fits the traditional image of the vampire. "She looked up to see a tall, thin man of perhaps sixty years, dressed in the height of fashion. His grey eyes were hooded, almost reptilian, and the smile he wore was more frightening than anger would have been" (53). The ritual he initiates attacks women with a sexual violence not found in vampires. Dracula is, at least, interested in his victims. No one at the Sabbat cares about Lucienne, least of all her husband.

The next chapter completes the pattern of alternation of good and evil. The Hotel Transylvania is the site of the decisive encounter between the Count and Madelaine. At its end she welcomes him as her vampire lover. The conversation that leads them to this point returns to the concern with time that first gave the reader an indication of the Count's true identity. While Dracula also expresses an isolation created by his longevity, Saint-Germain's view of time is shaped by his appreciation of humans. He answers Madelaine's question about why he should be concerned with her. "Your life is so sweet and so dreadfully short, I do not think I could bear to lose one hour of it to them" (64). Yarbro acknowledges the usual view of a vampiric encounter when Madelaine describes how the Sisters taught her that the undead drank the blood of Christians and stole their souls (65). But Saint-Germain has already told her of Lucienne's pleasure. He was not the one who stole her soul. The inversion of Christian ritual is connected to humans rather than vampires. Saint-Germain is finally established as the true romantic center of the novel. He is the perfect gentleman, the courtly and passionate lover, and all of the other men are imperfect, especially when compared to him.

The union of Saint-Germain and Madelaine marks the point in the novel at which the reader has received most of the information concerning the Count's identity and his relationship with the traditional vampire. Much later he reveals yet another area where humans are associated with the evil traits of these genre figures. He has no trouble with any elements of the Christian tradition, but the Devil worshippers in the novel must avoid the symbols of Christianity. Yarbro does not depart from tradition in the methods of killing a vampire. As Saint-Germain says,

To kill me . . . my spine must be severed completely. A sword, a stake, perhaps one of those unpleasant new bullets, anything that breaks the spine will kill me. One of my blood was killed by a collapsing building in Rome. And fire. I can burn, like all living things. (171)

In the epilogue Madelaine joyfully awaits her death and her rebirth into eternal life. She finally clearly voices the lessons she has learned through her understanding of the true nature of the vampire, lessons which Yarbro conveys to the reader.

In my reading of history there is war and ruin and pillage and lives snuffled out with such profligacy that my breath is stopped by the senselessness of it. One would think that all humanity had nothing better to do than feed on its own carrion. Think of all the destruction you have seen, and the endless foolishness. Whole peoples have perished for a few men's greed, or desire, or sport.

I have thought as I read these books, how many much worse things there are in this world than vampires.

To know your freedom. To live in the blood that is taken with love. Saint-Germain, Saint-Germain, I can hardly wait. (248)

Hotel Transylvania deals with the period "before the revolution," but this novel does not concern itself with the larger events of world history. In the first book in the series Yarbro concentrates on her alterations of the genre traditions, alterations that involve the addition of elements of the historical romance to her novel. Once the characters are established she selects historical periods in her subsequent novels that are crucial to the central theses of these works: history is not just the backdrop for her characters and plots. This emphasis on historical events which examine the destructive nature of the human is just as radical a departure from the genre tradition as is her earlier introduction of the Count as a romantic hero. She shifts her concentration from the vampire as the embodiment of a liberating sexuality to an exploration of his relationship with the excesses of history. While his sexuality as a vampire is still important in the story as a counter to the sexual abuses of women so prevalent among mortals, it is his perception of the human in history that is foregrounded.

The sexual undertones in *Dracula* are present, although concealed. Yarbro writes in a different period. *Hotel Transylvania* appeared after the altered views of human sexuality that resulted from the sixties and the women's movement. Yarbro's vampires are as much a product of these changes as Dracula is of the Victorian era. Saint-Germain also follows the vampires presented by such actors and Christopher Lee, whose sexuality is much more explicit, and he reflects recent cultural changes. Unlike Dracula, Saint-Germain does not represent those forces of nature that must be suppressed if bourgeois society is to continue. His sexuality is only feared or despised by those characters who have gone against nature and have perverted sexuality. It is because he does not threaten established society that he does not have to be destroyed. He attempts to preserve the best of the social structure from attack by the forces of evil.

Dracula's role in the novel suggests that the price that must be paid for eternal life is a dissolution of the boundaries that exist in the natural world, a dissolution that can lead to the destruction of society. This threat must be contained, order must be restored. Saint-Germain's role suggests humans may not be able to control the forces of evil because human evil is so powerful and destructive it breaks down the ordinary social structures which have been developed to control it. Saint-Germain represents the superhuman effort that is necessary for good to triumph. He is able to employ a wisdom that comes from a long experience of history. He maintains his eternal life through love, through the fulfilling of women. His most modern attitude toward women is balanced by his stand for a certain conservation of the social order, which seems to be necessary to maintain the genre.

Yet the Count is still a radical figure. His approach to sexuality with its insistence on the fulfillment of the woman alters the iconography of the genre. The vampire still presents a subversion of the cultural norms. Yarbro's insistence on his unselfish love reflects an altered understanding, of the position of women in the world. Dracula may have undermined Victorian society, Saint-Germain forces us to reflect on our own.

WORK CITED

Yarbro, Chelsea Quinn. *Hotel Transylvania: A Novel of Forbidden Love.* New York: St. Martin's Press, 1978.

Part Four

Contemporary Issues
in the World of the Undead

Chapter 15

Deadly Kisses: Vampirism, Colonialism, and the Gendering of Horror

Teri Ann Doerksen

Vampire texts, like so many late Victorian fictions, drew a significant part of their simultaneous popular inspiration of fascination and horror from their portrayal of the Other, the exotic, the mysterious, the unfathomed. Such portrayals were common in the colonialist English literature of the Victorian period; after all, this was a time during which the sun of the English empire was presumed to be illuminating the entire globe—and one by-product, for the English, was that they were able to imagine themselves as the torchbearers of civilization, proudly enlightening and civilizing all the mysterious and dangerous exotica with which they came into contact.

At the same time as the English "poured light," as they saw it, on the darkly exotic lands that they explored, they also spent much time and energy cloaking in darkness some of the most noticeable elements of their own society. While the middle- and upper-class Victorians in England cheerfully explored and critiqued the organization of other cultures from the cozy comfort of their parlor chairs, it never occurred to most of them that their own class structural organization was itself open to investigation. Similarly, there was no continent so dark nor so murkily shrouded, to the minds of most Victorians, as the continent of their own sexual desires. Sheridan Le Fanu's "Carmilla," first published in 1872, and Bram Stoker's *Dracula*, first published in 1897, provide markers against which to map out the links between Victorian portrayals of illicit sexuality through the metaphor of the vampire and other period representations of darkness, Otherness, and the exotic as they connect to representations of gender and sexuality.

As Patrick Brantlinger has noted, English representations of Africa did not describe the continent so much as they created a parallel continent, a Dark Continent, whose existence justified English conquest:

Africa grew "dark" as Victorian explorers, missionaries, and scientists flooded it with light, because the light was refracted through an imperialist ideology that urged the abolition of "savage customs." As a product of that mythology, the Dark Continent developed. . . . For middle- and upperclass Victorians, dominant over a vast working-class majority at home and over increasing millions of "uncivilized" peoples of "inferior" races abroad, power was self-validating. (185)

The English explorers abroad were creating a product much in demand at home: justification of power through representations of others in a way that made it quite necessary for the English to go in and take control. Texts that elaborated on the export of English civilized behavior to exotic lands proliferated. Travel narratives, popular accounts of explorations, and fictional accounts of civilized explorers became increasingly popular. Late in the Victorian period, authors like H. Rider Haggard made literary careers out of such vicarious explorations. And among the social circles in London it was becoming increasingly common to put exotic, dark people—Native Americans, Aborigines, and Africans—on display at the height of fancy parties, in order to coo and titter at their differences, the very existence of which clearly rationalized to the Victorian mind the imperialist process. An important shared element of all of these phenomena, I would argue, was an element of horror, engendered at the moment in which the Other, laden with implications of darkness, inferiority, and illicit sexuality, came into direct contact with the familiar world of the English reader or observer.

A closer look at some of these cultural phenomena illustrates that both gendering and sexuality are implicit in such appropriations of other cultures and that illicit sexuality was never far from other kinds of darkness in the English imagination. In H. Rider Haggard's *She* and *Ayesha: The Return of She*, for example, our intrepid English heroes, the handsome Leo and his older and uglier guardian, Holly, visit first the darkest Africa and then the farthest reaches of Tibet. In each location, the action is spurred by their interactions with exotic locals, black-skinned cannibals in the former case and soft-spoken Tibetan monastics in the latter. In each adventure, the object of their quest is an unlikely white goddess living among her black- or brown-skinned admirers. These adventure quests are shaped by a love triangle, with Leo at the apex: in each case there is a symbolic struggle over his body by a brown-skinned woman, who wants to love and obey him, and the strong-willed white Ayesha, who wants to love him and use him to colonialize and rule all of Europe.

Clearly, there is a complex struggle here between a sexuality that subscribes to English mores but breaks the color barrier and a sexuality that maintains the color line but threatens English colonial supremacy. Ayesha is a monster of a woman by Victorian standards; while Victoria's reign was strengthened by a mythos that made England the strong but gentle mother of the colonial world and Victoria herself a matronly figure, Ayesha wants power for power's sake in a manner that the Victorians would have gendered male. In addition, her incredible beauty gives her a hypnotic-like power over all men, not unlike the power that many vampires, including Carmilla and Dracula, hold over their victims. Though white herself, Ayesha is both exotic and inimical to English life. Each time Leo loses her yet again, it is clearly a victory of sorts over the hidden dangers of the Other.

Texts like Haggard's comprised a part of an elaborate English mythos about Otherness and sexuality that was intensified and accentuated through scientific discourse and first-hand experiences with "real, live" exotic specimens in circulation at home. Sander Gilman points out that the act of representing, whether through literature or through carnival-type exhibition,

serve[s] to focus the viewer's attention on the relationship between the portrayed individual and the general qualities ascribed to the class. Specific individual realities are thus given mythic extension through association with the qualities of the class. These realities manifest as icons representing perceived attributes of the class into which the individual has been placed. The myths associated with the class, the myth of difference from the rest of humanity, is thus, to an extent, composed of fragments of the real world, perceived through the ideological bias of the observer. ("Black Bodies, White Bodies," 223)

One of the ways in which such a mythos was constructed to associate Otherness and darkness with illicit or uncontrolled sexuality in the English mind was through the exhibition of African women, Gilman notes that "by the eighteenth century, the sexuality of the black, both male and female, becomes an icon for deviant sexuality in general" ("Black Bodies, White Bodies," 228). Lengthy pseudo-scientific works were issued with hundreds of medical illustrations of black women's vaginas in order to prove, in the words of J. J. Virey in 1819, that they evinced a "voluptuousness" that was "developed to a degree of lascivity unknown in our climate, for their sexual organs are much more developed than those of the whites" (quoted in Gilman, "Black Bodies, White Bodies," 232).[1] The argument was that if Africans could be proven to have different genitalia than whites, they could be classified as belonging to a lower branch on the evolutionary tree than their European neighbors, and the colonization of their lands could be imagined as a Darwinian necessity rather than a political choice.

Such generalized interpretations were supported by the displays of individuals. For example, when Sarah Bartmann (Saartje Baartman), an African woman, was exhibited in England in the early nineteenth century, she was labeled in explicitly sexualized terms as the "Hottentot Venus." The primary focus when she was displayed were her prominent buttocks, which were imagined to be a sign of her overdeveloped sexuality. Popular prints of her naked body were sold in the public marketplace, ostensibly as mere scientific curiosities. And when she died at the age of 25, she was dissected, and her buttocks and her external genitalia were donated to the Musee de l'homme in Paris, where they are still on display.[2] Autopsies of her body, written up by Henri de Blainville in 1816 and Georges Cuvier in 1817, emphasized "the comparison of a female of the 'lowest' human species with the highest ape (the orangutan)" (Gilman, "Black Bodies, White Bodies," 232).

It is important to note that once the association between Africans, evolutionary inferiority, and illicit or overdeveloped sexuality was adequately made, at least to the Victorian mind, the generalization was rapidly extended to include the lower classes within England. Sander Gilman makes an eloquent argument that both artistic and scientific representations of prostitutes and other lower-class English women rapidly appropriated the tropes of enlarged buttocks and enlarged genitalia familiar from discourse about Africans. In addition, literature of the period strongly suggests that, by late in the century, the connection between poverty and savagery was widely assumed. Contemporary writers often spoke of the poor of London as a savage and wild race and described visits to London's poorer areas as safaris into darkness; such titles included *In the Wilds of London* by James Greenwood (1874) and *In Darkest England and the Way Out* by William Booth (1890).

Clearly, sexuality was imagined as emerging hand-in-hand with the exploration of dark and hidden places, and the tight control that the middle-class English imagined themselves to have over their own sexual desires was brought into high relief by comparison with less civilized, more lustful peoples. Brantlinger connects this phenomenon with Victorian fears about the possible failure of this repression:

Just as the social class fantasies of the Victorians (*Oliver Twist*, for example) often express the fear of failing into the abyss of poverty, so the myth of the Dark Continent contains the submerged fear of falling out of the light, down the long coal chute of social and moral regression. In both cases, the fear of backsliding has a powerful sexual dimension. If, as Freud argued, civilization is based on the repression of instincts and if the demands of repression become excessive, then civilization itself is likely to break down. (215)

Vampire texts, which became increasingly popular as the images of the Dark Continent proliferated, provided an exploration of illicit sexuality shrouded first in the construction of metaphorical "creatures of darkness," to replace the inhabitants of Darkest Africa, and second in the displacement of the kind of penetration involved in literal sexuality into the metaphorical realm of a somewhat different kind of "penetration." Both Victorian writing about Africa and Victorian writing about vampires serve similar cultural functions: they create an almost fairy tale mythos in which the danger of released sexual repression is met and defeated by the civilizing functions of controlled desire and coolly factual objectivity and narration.

Both "Carmilla" and *Dracula* are framed by scientific narrative structures that would not have been out of place in one of Virey's case study reports—or, for that matter, in Kraffl-Ebing's *Psychopathia Sexualis*. "Carmilla," in fact, is prefaced by a short Prologue that proclaims it to be from the collected papers of a learned (and entirely fictional) Doctor Hesselius. *Dracula*, of course, is imagined to be the collected papers associated with the Van Helsing investigation into the events following Jonathan Harker's visit to Transylvania. Most of it is produced in a thoroughly modern manner, as well, by Mina, upon a brand-new office typewriter.

Like earlier studies of Africans, these texts attempt to grant an aura of scientific verisimilitude to their narratives. And both, of course, explore in some depth a series of illicit sexual encounters, thinly disguised by metaphor, which are ultimately resolved through the utter destruction of the sexual initiator (and the more willing of his or her prey) and the re-establishment of a properly controlled sexual structure for those who remain behind. It is noteworthy, too, that just as African woman were much more likely to become the objects of scientific exploration into deviant sexual physiology, in both "Carmilla," which features a female vampire, and *Dracula*, which principally describes a male vampire, those susceptible to contamination with vampiric sexuality are almost exclusively female.

Le Fanu's "Carmilla," which was first published in 1872, is often discussed by scholars because of its remarkably well-articulated account of lesbian sexuality enacted through vampirism. In it the first-person narrator, Laura, recounts her gradual seduction by a visiting friend, a young lady named Carmilla. The language used to describe the romance between the two is quite explicit. Despite Carmilla's cozy footing as Laura's companion, however, she is established as an Other, and the threat of released sexuality that she represents is mitigated by a return to appropriate Victorian morality by the end of the text.

In the first paragraph of the story it is made clear to the reader that despite the remote continental setting, Laura and her father are thoroughly English. They are living in a liminal space, Englishmen taking tea in the depths of a superstition-clouded wilderness. Carmilla, when she appears, makes even this wilderness look like the sheltered confines of civilization. From the beginning, she is shrouded in mystery, in a darkness that Laura cannot penetrate no matter how she tries. Carmilla arrives under mysterious circumstances, and Laura's family is asked never to question her about her circumstances. Laura notes again and again the "ever wakeful reserve" (262) that Carmilla exercises with respect to her past. Aside from admitting that she came from an ancient and noble family somewhere to the west, she is entirely impervious to Laura's tentative explorations. She has odd habits and periodically disappears mysteriously. She seems linked to Laura by an inexplicable series of shared dreams and visions, but her nature remains unfathomable. She is a Dark Continent, but she is the Dark Continent of English nightmares: instead of waiting in one place to be explored and illuminated, she comes in search of civilization in order to corrupt it where it lives.

And the corruption, as has been noted many times, is definitely sexual. Laura's first meeting with this sultry vampire is in bed, when she is still only a child. When both Laura and Carmilla are young ladies, Carmilla's attentions, her raptures about Laura's lips, her protests of love, scenes in which she "presse[s] [Laura] more closely in her trembling embrace, and her lips in soft kisses gently glow upon [Laura's] cheek" (264) spur Laura to wonder if the very feminine Carmilla is a man in disguise:

Was she, notwithstanding her mother's volunteered denial, subject to brief visitations of insanity, or was there here a disguise and a romance? I had read in old story books of such things. What if a boyish lover had found his way into the house, and sought to prosecute his suit in masquerade, with the assistance of a clever old adventuress?. . . But except for these brief periods of mysterious excitement her ways were girlish. (265)

The culmination of the seduction, of course, is as close to orgasmic as popular literature of the time could possibly come. The ultimate proof of the sexual connection, however, comes from the scientific mind of the Baron Vordenborg, who saves the day, and Laura's life, with his knowledge of vampire lore. He explains that:

The vampire is prone to be fascinated with an engrossing vehemence, resembling the passion of love, by particular persons. . . . It will never desist until it has satiated its passion, and drained the life of its coveted victim. But it will, in these cases, husband and protract its murderous enjoyment with the refinement of an epicure, and heighten it by the gradual approach of an artful courtship. In these cases it seems to yearn for something like sympathy and consent. In ordinary ones it goes direct to its object, overpowers with violence, and strangles and exhausts almost at a single feast. (317)

This extremely rich passage ties together several crucial connections. First, this is definitely a lesbian courtship, to be culminated in a feast both literal and sexual—the vampire's passions, after all, are the first to be sated; for hunger, other victims are available. This is reaffirmed by mentions throughout the text of local women who die mysteriously during Carmilla's seduction of Laura. It makes clear another point, too: the corruptive force of this dark, illicit sexuality is focused on the English landed classes. The vampire chooses only the lower classes for her snacks. This meshes with Gilman's suggestion that the landed classes believed the lower classes to be already closer to the primitive and the sexual than the more refined middle and upper classes. The triumph over Carmilla, then, is a triumph over the primitive influences that have never been conquered by foreigners and the lower class and are repressed only imperfectly in the English elite—and it suggests the destructive power should those repressed sexual desires ever be loosed upon the world.

This point is driven home even more firmly, if you will pardon the rather morbid pun, in Stoker's *Dracula*. The sexual imagery in *Dracula* has been well established, as has the fact that Stoker was quite careful to keep his vampires heterosexual. I would like to take a brief look at the scene at Lucy's tomb, however, on the day that would have been her wedding day. Lucy Westenra is an interesting case. She lived, in one sense, a chaste life. Her body, however, was, in metaphorical terms, that of a sexual wanton. Aside from the fact that she was repeatedly penetrated by Dracula, she also shared bodily fluids with all three men who had wanted to marry her and with several who did not. Practically every male character in the text donates blood to her at one point or another. And this donation is clearly sexualized; the other men elect not to reveal their donations to Arthur, Lucy's fiancé, when he reveals that he considers this transfer of blood to constitute consummation of their marriage:

Arthur, poor, fellow, was speaking of his part in the operation where his blood had been transfused into Lucy's veins; I could feel Van Heising's face grow white and then purple by turns. Arthur was saying that he felt since then as if they two had been really married in the sight of God. None of us said a word of the other operations, and none of us ever shall. (174)

Van Helsing even notes that such a situation makes Lucy into a "Polyandrist," and himself into a bigamist.

The result of this animal behavior on Lucy's part is that she, like Sarah Bartmann, is transformed textually from a woman into a half-woman/half-animal. Whereas the "Hottentot Venus" is seen as evidence of a less evolved culture, Lucy represents a devolution, an active movement away from the Victorian concept of civilization—and toward the savage, the primitive, the sexual, the uncontrolled. Clearly the "Darkness" has the potential to infect the "Light." Lucy's metaphorical harlotry, and the savagery it implies, must be brought back into line, in Victorian terms. The colonizer has become the colonized, the natural order has been reversed, and the corresponding threat to English supremacy must be mitigated—in this case through a horrific parody of the sexual act that reasserts the power of the masculine, the English, the "civilized," by means of a ritual sexual act that destroys as it deflowers.

The men all go to Lucy's tomb together to destroy her on the night that would have been her wedding night. Arthur is chosen, fittingly, as "the hand which would restore Lucy to us as a holy, and not an unholy memory" (215). At the moment in which a virginal Lucy would have been penetrated for the first time by Arthur on their wedding night, the vampire Lucy is penetrated through the heart by the stake that Arthur holds. Again, the connection between the sexual and the animal is reasserted: as all the men watch, her body shakes and quivers as if she were in the throes of orgasm, and her teeth champ as if she were a beast. Arthur, we are told:

never faltered. He looked like a figure of Thor as his untrembling arm rose and fell, driving deeper and deeper the mercy-bearing stake, whilst the blood from the pierced heart welled and spurted up around it. His face was set, and high duty seemed to shine through it. . . . And then the writhing and the quivering of the body became less, and the teeth ceased to champ, and the face to quiver. Finally, it lay still. The terrible task was over. (216)

Killing the vampire is sex: it is a condoned variety of sex, associated with marriage, that undoes illicit sex. Lucy, for most of the story the bloodless one, even bleeds, as a virginal bride is supposed to do on her wedding night. Illicit and unbridled sexuality is conquered through the never-ending vigilance of the Englishman. Moreover, the scene confirms the necessity for the colonizing process, no matter how destructive: to beat down the forces of darkness in Africa and to repress the animal nature within the English themselves are parallel processes, equally crucial to the maintenance of civilization.

In both of these classic vampire texts, the vampires are mysterious creatures of darkness, and they actively pursue the English. The gender implications of their particular manner of metaphorizing the colonization of the Dark Continent are particularly intriguing. I have argued that these texts construct horror by making a carefully constructed Other, the vampire, which mirrors English constructions of primitive sexuality, a dangerous aggressor. The vampire illustrates the dangers of releasing Victorian sexual repression, and reifies the notions that exotic foreigners and the lower classes are more primitive than, and therefore ideally ruled by, the English.

English ingenuity, in both cases, aided by scientific resourcefulness, succeeds in destroying the threat. In doing so, however, these texts, taken together, provide an interesting message about gendering and homosexuality. The line between evil/illicit sexuality, as defined by vampire behavior, and condoned behavior is quite clearly marked (Stoker, for instance, in a famous scene, makes clear with Mina that oral sex with someone not your husband is a very serious no-no.) But creatures of darkness and their behaviors are so clearly distinguished from acceptable behavior that, within the compass of darkness, boundaries are neutralized. Extramarital heterosexual liaisons and lesbian romances are conflated, pitched in together with oral sex and other lesser sexual acts. When Le Fanu groups lesbianism with other common sexual acts, lesbianism becomes almost mainstreamed. "Carmilla" and *Dracula* create horror by manipulating gender expectations and cultural preconceptions about proper sexual behavior, but in doing do they open to public discourse acts that previously had been relegated to darkness.

NOTES

1. J. J. Virey, "Negre," *Dictionnaire des sciences medicales*, 41 vols. (Paris, 1819), 35: 398–403.

2. The Saartje Baartman phenomenon has been much discussed in recent criticism. Sander Gilman discusses her history and its implications at length in both "Black Bodies, White Bodies" and *Difference and Pathology: Stereotypes of Sexuality, Race, and Madness* (Ithaca: Cornell UP, 1985). See also Anne Fausto-Sterling, "Gender, Race, and Nation: The Comparative Anatomy of 'Hottentot' Woman in Europe, 1815–1817," in *Deviant Bodies: Critical Perspectives in Science and Popular Culture*, eds. Jennifer Terry and Jacqeline Urla (Bloomington, IN: Indiana UP, 1995) and Bernth Lindfors, "Ethnological Show Business: Footlighting the Dark Continent," in *Freakery: Cultural Spectacles of the Extraordinary Body*, ed. Rosemarie G. Thompson (New York: New York UP, 1996).

WORKS CITED

Booth, William. *In Darkest England and the Way Out*. New York: Funk and Wagnells, 1890.

Brantlinger, Patrick. "Victorians and Africans: The Genealogy and Myth of the Dark Continent" In *"Race," Writing and the Difference It Makes*. Ed. Henry Louis Gates, Jr. Chicago and London: U of Chicago P, 1986.

Fausto-Sterling, Anne. "Gender, Race, and Nation: The Comparative Anatomy of 'Hottentot' Women in Europe, 1815–1817." In *Deviant Bodies: Critical Perspectives on Difference in Science and Popular Culture*. Eds. Jennifer Terry and Jacqueline Urla. Bloomington, IN: Indiana UP, 1995.

Gilman, Sander. "Black Bodies, White Bodies: Toward an Iconography of Female Sexuality in Late Nineteenth-Century Art, Medicine, and Literature." In *"Race," Writing and the Difference It Makes*. Ed. Henry Louis Gates, Jr. Chicago and London: U of Chicago P, 1986.

———. *Difference and Pathology: Stereotypes of Sexuality, Race, and Madness*. Ithaca, NY: Cornell UP, 1985.

Greenwood, James. *In the Wilds of London*. New York: Garland Publishing, 1985.

Haggard, H. Rider. *Ayesha: The Return of She*. New York: Ballantine Books, 1978.

———. *She*. 1887. World's Classics. Ed. Daniel Karlin. New York: Oxford UP, 1991.

Le Fanu, Sheridan. "Carmilla" in *Through a Glass Darkly*. World's Classics. Ed.Robert Tracy. New York: Oxford UP, 1993.

Lindfors, Bernth. "Ethnological Show Business: Footlighting the Dark Continent."In *Freakery: Cultural Spectacles of the Extraordinary Body*. Ed. Rosemarie G. Thomson. New York: New York UP, 1996.

Stoker, Bram. *Dracula*. World's Classics. Ed. A. N. Wilson. New York: Oxford UP, 1983.

Virey, J. J. "Negre." *Dictionarie des sciences medicales*. 41 vols. Paris, 1819, 35: 398–403.

Chapter 16

"A Girl Like That Will Give You AIDS!": Vampirism as AIDS Metaphor in *Killing Zoe*

Jeane Rose

In Roger Avary's 1994 film *Killing Zoe*, a vampire subtext resonant with pop-cultural conceptions of vampires, AIDS, and homosexuality functions as a means of encoding character and propelling the narrative. Set in contemporary Paris, the film traces the events surrounding a Bastille Day bank heist.[1] Zed, played by Eric Stoltz, arrives in Paris on July 13th as the robbery's official safe-cracker. Upon his arrival, Zed hires a prostitute for the evening, the title character, Zoe, played by Julie Delpy. Zoe's entrance introduces a vampire motif that stigmatizes those individuals outside the sexual parameters of "conventional" morality and depicts them as emblems of sexual perversion. While not a vampire film proper, *Killing Zoe* draws on a wealth of popular associations between vampirism and the spread of HIV infection. According to these contemporary allegories, a person infected with the virus becomes the metaphorical vampire. The popular rationale underlying *Killing Zoe*'s vampire imagery, in turn, establishes the infected person as a monster who seeks to infect others.

Significantly, this danger is a sexual one, as in traditional vampire lore where the vampire affects a sexual conquest through a bite to the neck, turning his (less frequently her) victims into fellow vampires when an exchange of blood occurs. The vampire "infects" the victim through his tainted blood. A blood-borne infection, the vampire's bite bears an obvious similarity to AIDS transmission. The AIDS virus enters the body through the bloodstream or through sexual contact. Both modes of transmission resemble the vampire's bite, which is simultaneously an exchange of blood and a symbolic sex act.

Like the tales in which the vampire poisons his victims with the taint of vampirism, appalling stereotypes about people with AIDS continue to circulate—particularly media images of prostitutes and homosexuals who intentionally infect their partners. In his impassioned study of the AIDS crisis, *And the Band Played On*, Randy Shilts identifies French Canadian airline steward Gaetan Dugas, known as "Patient Zero," as allegedly being responsible for all the AIDS cases in North

America. Jan Zita Grover points out in "AIDS: Keywords" how sensationalized tales depicting "carriers" as active disease-spreaders achieve mythic proportion:

the unspoken model is Typhoid Mary, who symptomatically infected with the typhoid bacillus— in popular fancy *willfully* continued to work as a food service handler after her infected state was made known to her (the fact that Mary Mallon was untrained for any other kind of work does not enter the fable). (22)

As another example of the fear of AIDS "carriers," a Florida court ordered an HIV-positive prostitute to wear an electronic collar to alert police whenever she left her house (Zita Grover, 25).

In keeping with these apocryphal tales about people with AIDS, the vampire's sexual conquest of a virgin—with the virgin signifying purity free from sexual stain— bares a resemblance to reactionary myths about AIDS and forms of contraction: that people with AIDS or HIV are unclean, that one can contract the virus from toilet seats or handshakes, that people with AIDS engage in unorthodox sexual acts. As late as 1988, *Cosmopolitan* reported that for heterosexuals "there is almost no danger of contracting AIDS through ordinary sexual intercourse," with ordinary sex excluding homosexual sex or sex with a prostitute (Gould, 146).[2] Operating within a heteronormative framework, reports like these have constructed homosexual practices and prostitution as responsible for the spread of the virus. It is important to point out that, in contrast to *Cosmo*, "one of the very few sources of up-to-date information on all aspects of AIDS has been the gay press" (Crimp, 237).[3]

With Francis Ford Coppola's 1992 Dracula film and its intrusive shots of red blood cells as one of the most blatant examples, the AIDS epidemic brings new resonance to vampire stories. *Interview with the Vampire* and Anne Rice's subsequent series connects vampirism with the gay community, who comprise a large part of Rice's cult following—no doubt because of her nonjudgmental treatment of sexual freedom. According to Linda Bradley, "*The Vampire Chronicles* offered on the one hand a, bisexual and homoerotic utopia and coping ritual for our plague years" (121). Linda Haas and Bob Haas, who detail Rice's treatment of "boundary creatures" who lack acceptance within the dominant culture, suggest that Rice's vampires possess a liberating sexuality because Rice withholds moral judgment (65).

Rice features gay relationships throughout her series, particularly the relationship between Louis and Lestat, respectively played by Brad Pitt and Tom Cruise in the 1995 film version of *Interview*. Rice's vampires often grant an immortality through the spread of vampirism such as Lestat's "gift" of vampirism to his dying mother Gabrielle, which can be read as an antidote to stories about predatory homosexuals who spread HIV. More complex than a simple act of salvation, however, the spread of vampirism sometimes becomes a curse for the new initiate, a kind of death in life, particularly for Lestat's young initiate Claudia.

Released one year before the film version of *Interview with the Vampire*, *Killing Zoe* entered a cultural milieu with popular associations that linked vampirism with threatening sexuality. The film's narrative posits Zoe, the prostitute who represents sexual danger, as the metaphorical vampire or AIDS-carrier. The worldly Zoe marks a contrast to Zed, whom the film constructs as an innocent abroad: he doesn't speak

French, fails to understand the French monetary system, and is on a trip to Paris to visit his boyhood best friend. Significantly, the two have sex while F. W. Murnau's 1922 silent film *Nosferatu*, based on Bram Stoker's *Dracula*, plays on the hotel television set. According to J. Gordon Melton's *The Vampire Book*:

Nosferatu is a modern word derived from the Old Slavonic word nosufur-atu, borrowed from the Greek nosophorus, a 'plague carrier.' Vampires were associated in the popular mind with the spread of disease (such as) tuberculosis whose cause was otherwise unknown and by extension with the idea of spreading the infection of vampirism through its bite. (435)

Cutting back and forth between Zoe—who is on top during the sex act and imaged as the aggressor—and Murnau's plaguespreader, Avary's montage creates an equivalence between Zoe and the vampire. The film juxtaposes Zoe's implied act of fellatio with scenes of Murnau's vampire biting his victim's neck, likening oral sex to the vampire's bloodsucking. Describing the vampire's oral fetish in relation to aberrant sexuality, Linda Bradley says, "The vampire has always covertly implied a perverse or displaced sexuality—that is, displaced from the genital to the oral stage and combining phallic penetration with 'feminine' morality and nurturing" (123). By performing oral sex, Zoe wields a displaced phallic power, depicted as an act of aggression akin to the vampire's bite.

Zoe further embodies oral aggression and phallic monstrosity when she bites Eric, Zed's best friend, who storms into the room and throws Zoe into the hallway. Eric then maligns Zoe: "She's a dishrag whore. . . . She's dangerous. . . . A girl like that will give you AIDS! Go out to the suburbs and find yourself a nice girl." Featured in contrast to Zoe, Eric appears to be a protective and trustworthy friend who will guide Zed around Paris. The first half of the film downplays the criminality inherent in the bankrobbing scheme, focusing instead on the nostalgia of two childhood friends who want to re-experience the thrill of stealing from the local mini-mart.

As the narrative unfolds, it becomes apparent that Eric poses a danger to Zed, and the film alludes to Eric's own potential for monstrosity. Unbeknownst to Zed, who came to Paris primarily for a reunion with Eric, Eric has scheduled the bank robbery for the following day. When Zed panics, Eric informs him: "You don't need to know shit. Just let the rest of us take care of it." Under the pretext of showing Zed "the real Paris," Eric drags him out for an evening of cocaine, heroin, and other assorted narcotics. Eric and his band of merry thieves delight in driving under the influence, racing on the highway, visiting a divey bar that plays Dixieland music, and pressuring Zed into substance abuse.

Throughout the evening of pre-robbery glee, Eric makes numerous homoerotic advances toward Zed, overtures that the film juxtaposes with Eric's admission that he actually has AIDS. Driving by a group of male prostitutes, Eric encourages Zed to offer himself to them—in French, so Zed doesn't understand what he is saying. Immediately after, Eric leans over to Zed and whispers, "You know, I have AIDS," pausing and then adding "from the needles," as if to dissociate himself from the homosexual prostitutes, thereby exhibiting a homophobia contradictory to his flirtations with Zed. Denouncing the gay prostitutes enables a homosocial bonding that Eric uses as a covert seduction tactic. At the bar, Eric physically assaults a woman who had been flirting with Zed, following his pattern of exhibiting aggression toward any woman who exhibits a sexual interest in his friend. Although the entire group engages in homosocial male bonding and dances together with their arms around one another, Eric's behavior stands out as he strokes Zed's face, whispers in his ear, and keeps his arm around him when the dancing has stopped.

In a chilling scene, Eric drags the drunk and nearly somnolent Zed into an alley, pries open his mouth, and forces a pill down his throat, while telling him: "I have here the only other man I can trust in the world. My very good friend who I look up to. You are the one Zed." On the verge of nausea from substance overload, Zed utters a prophetic "I'm going to die." He then passes out and wakes to see Eric sodomizing and beating a man a few feet away in the alley. While it seems plausible that Eric gave Zed a sleeping pill, the film offers no evidence that Eric used the drug as a means of sexually assaulting Zed. At the same time, however, the mere possibility of rape combined with Eric's behavior during the evening clearly establishes him as representing a danger of sexual contamination akin to Zoe's implied vampirism.

Culminating in the bank robbery scene, the film adopts the "search-for-and-destroy-the-vampire" narrative appearing in vampire films as diverse as Francis Ford Coppola's adaptation of Bram Stoker's *Dracula*, the teenage comedy *Once Bitten*, and Joel Schumacher's *The Lost Boys*. Avary applies this search narrative on a metaphorical level throughout the bank robbery scene, lending it a new spin: we learn that Zoe works at the bank, and we now have two metaphorical vampires on the loose. Zed finds himself in the position of having to choose whether to remain loyal to Eric, who engages in unprovoked shooting of the bank employees and customers, or to ally himself with Zoe, a prostitute he has known less than twenty-four hours.

While working underground in the bank's vaults, Zed eventually realizes that the police have surrounded the bank. With no regard for Zed's safety, Eric had permitted Zed to continue safe-cracking. Aware of his own impending death, Eric would have willingly sacrificed Zed, an intentional death-sentence metaphorically akin to giving him AIDS, an act that makes Eric guilty of vampirism in the film's terms.

The "search" for the vampire complete, only his destruction remains. In a showdown between Eric and Zed, Eric scorns Zed for his loyalty to Zoe, saying she "has already fucked with your mind" and asks how Zed can love her. Jealous, and consistent with his pattern of violent behavior toward women attracted to Zed, Eric holds a pen knife to Zed's face, slashing it while warning "never let a girl come between two men."

In a sequence involving gratuitous gun violence, the gang members are shot by the police or inadvertently shoot one another until only Eric and Zed remain. Zed manages to stumble away with Zoe, who has blood smeared across her lips after kissing his facial wound and appears very vampiric. Planning to lock themselves into an empty vault, they run into Eric, who punches Zoe, knocking her unconscious.

Eric and Zed, neither of whom have any weapons at this point, engage in a very sexualized, physical struggle, rolling around on the floor among dead bodies and pools of blood. Eric manages to acquire an uzi from one of the dead robbers. Standing poised over Zed ready to shoot, wielding the gun's masculinity and phallic power, Eric says "I give you a little kiss my friend." Fortunately, the gun is empty, and the Parisian

SWAT team riddles Eric's body with bullets. In slow motion, Eric's blood spurts out of his body, bathing Zed's open wounds with blood. Zoe tells the authorities that Zed was an innocent customer, and the two ride off, bruised and bloodied, into the proverbial sunset.

At this point, the film's seeming resolution, the viewer may be tempted to relax. Zed, however, utters his most crucial line: "It was mostly his blood." Zoe then replies, "I'll take you to my flat. You will get well. I'll show you the real Paris." That the film directs our attention to the fact that Eric's blood has covered Zed, and in light of the scientific assumption that one can contract HIV from blood-to-blood exchanges, the film suggests that Zed has contracted HIV. As the two ride off into a supposed "happily-ever-after," one can assume they will continue to be lovers. Given the title, "Killing Zoe," the film seems to intend that the viewer read beyond the film to consider what actually kills Zoe, the probable answer being sexual contact with Zed.

After Zoe reveals herself to be Zed's savior from Eric, whom the film establishes as the "vampire" who seeks to contaminate Zed, we have a clever reversal of the film's initial suggestion about Zoe as a sexual predator. This remains problematic, however. Despite the prostitute character's redemption, *Killing Zoe* associates AIDS and HIV with monstrosity. Although the prostitute figure appears innocent of vampirism, and the film negates a stereotype of sexual deviance on one level, the film's portrayal of Eric relies on a wealth of homophobic discourse and reifies stereotypes of depraved and predatory homosexuals who irresponsibly spread HIV. *Killing Zoe* establishes the person with AIDS as someone deserving of the disease, depicting Eric, an IV-drug user as well as a violent and misogynous homosexual, as a morally inept individual who will implicate others in his orgiastic lifestyle of drug abuse and crime and infect them with the AIDS virus.

NOTES

1. Avery's film bears obvious similarities to the "bank robbery gone bad" of Quentin Tarantino's *Reservoir Dogs*, an unsurprising similarity considering that the two collaborated on scripts while working together as video store clerks at Video Archives in Manhattan Beach, California, and went on to win an Oscar for best screenplay for *Pulp Fiction*.

2. When asked about the high incidence of HIV infection among heterosexuals in Africa, Gould, a psychiatrist, maintained that African heterosexuals have violent intercourse that causes ripping and tearing of vaginal tissue, creating a port of entry for the virus.

3. Crimp points to the educational campaigns originating in the gay community since the beginning of the epidemic. He describes the *New York Native*, which has published news about AIDS virtually every week since 1982, as perhaps the most acclaimed (237–8).

WORKS CITED

Bradley, Linda. *Writing Horror and the Body*. Westport, CT: Greenwood Press, 1996.
Bram Stoker's Dracula. Directed by Francis Ford Coppola. 1992.
Crimp, Douglas, ed. "How to Have Promiscuity in an Epidemic." *Cultural Analysis/Cultural Activism*. Cambridge, MA: MIT Press, 1991.
Gould, Robert. Reassuring News about AIDS: A Doctor Tells Why You May Not Be at Risk." *Cosmopolitan*, January 1988.

Hass, Linda, and Bob Hass. "Living with(out) Boundaries: The Novels of Anne Rice." In *A Dark Night's Dreaming*. Eds. Tony Magistrale and Michael A. Morrison. Columbia: U of South Carolina P., 1996.

Hoberman, J. "French Connection." *Premier*, September 1994.

Killing Zoe. Directed by Roger Avary. 1994.

The Lost Boys. Directed by Joel Schumacher. 1987.

Melton, J. Gordon. *The Vampire Book: The Encyclopedia of the Undead*. Detroit: Visible Ink Press, 1994.

Nosferatu. Directed by F. W. Murnau. 1922.

Once Bitten. Directed by Howard Storm. 1985.

Rice, Anne. *Interview with the Vampire*. 1976. New York: Ballantine Books, 1977.

Shilts, Randy. *And the Band Played On*. New York: St. Martin's Press, 1987.

Zita Grover, Jan. "AIDS: Keywords." In *Cultural Analysis Cultitral Activism*, Ed. Douglas Crimp. 1988. Cambridge, MA: MIT Press, 1991, 17–30.

Selected Bibliography

Apter, T. E. *Fantasy Literature*. Bloomington, IN: Indiana UP, 1982.

Arata, Stephen D. "The Occidental Tourist: *Dracula* and the Anxiety of Reverse Colonization" *Victorian Studies, 33* (1990): 621–45.

Auerbach, Nina. *Our Vampires, Ourselves*. Chicago: U of Chicago P, 1995.

———. *Woman and the Demon. The Life of A Victorian Myth*. Cambridge, MA: Harvard UP, 1982.

Auerbach, Nina, and David J. Skal. *Dracula: Authoritative Text—Backgrounds. Reviews and Reactions, Dramatic and Film Variations, Criticism*. Norton Critical Edition. New York: Norton, 1977.

Bradley, Linda. *Writing Horror and the Body*. Westport, CT: Greenwood Press, 1996.

Bataille, Georges. *Theory of Religion*. Trans. by Robert Hurley. New York: Zone Books, 1989.

Berenstein, Rhona. *Attack of the Leading Ladies: Gender, Sexuality and Spectatorship in Classic Horror Cinema*. New York: Columbia UP, 1996.

Booth, William. *In Darkest England and the Way Out*. New York: Funk and Wagnalls, 1890.

Brantlinger, Patrick. *Rule of Darkness: British Literature and Imperialism, 1830–1914*. Ithaca, NY: Cornell UP, 1988.

Bunson, Mathew. *The Vampire Encyclopedia*. New York: Crown, 1993.

Cawelti, John G. *Adventure, Mystery, and Romance: Formula Stories as Art and Popular Culture*. Chicago: U of Chicago P, 1976.

Dalby, Richard. *Bram Stoker: A Bibliography of First Editions*. London: Dracula Press, 1983.

Day, William Patrick. *In the Circles of Fear and Desire*. Chicago: U of Chicago P, 1985.

Elrod, P. N. "Caretaker" in *Tales of Ravenloft*, Ed. Brian Thomsen. Lake Geneva, WI: TSR, 1994.

Farson, Daniel. *The Man Who Wrote Dracula*. London: Michael Joseph, 1975.

Gelder, Ken. *Reading the Vampire*. London and New York: Routledge, 1994.

Gilman, Sander. *Difference and Pathology: Stereotypes of Sexuality, Race, and Madness*. Ithaca, NY: Cornell UP, 1985.

Glover, David. *Vampires. Mummies, and Liberals: Bram Stoker and the Politics of Popular Fiction*. Durham, NC: Duke UP, 1996.

Golden, Christie. "The Birth of a Vampire." *Dead of Night*, 9 (April 1994): 42–44.

Greenwood, James. *In the Wilds of London*. New York: Garland Publishing, 1985.

Guileryl, Rosemary Ellen. *The Complete Vampire Companion*. New York: Simon & Schuster/Macmillan, 1994.

Haggard, H. Rider. *She*. 1887. *The Annotated* She*: A Critical Edition of H. Rider Haggard's Victorian Romance with Introduction and Notes*. Ed. Norman Etherington. Bloomington, IN: Indiana UP, 1991, 3–209.

———. *Ayesha: The Return of She*. New York: Ballantine Books, 1978.

Hutchings, Peter. *Hammer and Beyond: The British Horror Film*. Manchester and New York: Manchester UP, 1993.

Irigary, Luce. *Speculum of the Other Woman*. Trans. Gillian G. Gill, 1974. Ithaca: Cornell UP, 1985.

King, Stephen. *Danse Macabre*. New York: Everest House, 1981.

Le Fanu, Joseph Sheridan. *In a Glass Darkly*. New York: Oxford UP, 1993.

Le Guin, Ursula K. *The Language of the Night: Essays on Fantasy and Science Fiction*. Ed. Susan Wood. New York: Harper Collins. 1994.

Lowder, James. *Knight of the Black Rose*. Lake Geneva, WI: TSR, 1991.

———. *Ravenloft: Realm of Terror*. Lake Geneva, WI: TSR, 1990.

Ludlam, Harry. *A Biography of Bram Stoker, Creator of Dracula*. 1962. London: New English Library, 1977.

Maturin, Charles Robert. *Melmoth the Wanderer*. London: Oxford, UP, 1968.

MacAndrew, Elizabeth. *The Gothic Tradition in Fiction*. New York: Columbia UP, 1979.

McCormack, W. J. *Sheridan Le Fanu and Victorian Ireland*. New York: Oxford UP, 1980.

Melton, J. Gordon. *The Vampire Book: The Encyclopedia of the Undead*. Detroit: Visible Ink Press, 1994.

Otto, Rudolf. *The Idea of the Holy: An Inquiry into the Non-Rational Factor in the Idea of the Divine and Its Relation to the Rational*. Trans. John W. Harvey. 1928. London: Oxford University Press, 1958.

Praz, Mario. *The Romantic Agony*. Trans. Angus Davidson. London: Oxford UP, 1970.

Ramsland, Katherine. "The Lived World of Anne Rice's Novels." In *The Gothic World of Anne Rice*. Eds. Gary Hoppenstand and Ray B. Browne, 13–33.

———. *The Vampire Companion: The Official Guide to Anne Rice's "The Vampire Chronicles."* New York: Ballantine Books, 1993.

Riccardo, Martin. *Vampires Unearthed: The Complete Multi-Media Vampire and Dracula Bibliography*. New York: Garland Publishers, 1983.

Rice, Anne. *The Vampire Lestat*. New York: Ballantine Books, 1985.

———. *The Queen of the Damned*. New York: Alfred A. Knopf, 1988.

Riley, Michael. *Conversations with Anne Rice*. New York: Ballantine Books, 1996.

Sage, Victor. *Horror Fiction in the Protestant Tradition*. New York: St. Martin's Press, 1988.

Senf, Carol A. *The Critical Response to Bram Stoker*. Westport, CT: Greenwood Press, 1993.

Shilts, Randy. *And the Band Played On*. New York: St. Martin's Press, 1987.

Skal, David J. *Hollywood Gothic: The Tangeled Web of Dracula from Novel to Stage to Screen*. New York: Norton, 1990.

Stoker, Bram. *Dracula*, 1897. Garden City, NY: Doubleday, 1973.

———. *The Lair of the White Worm*. London: Peter Owen, 1991.

———. *The Jewel of Seven Stars*. 1903. Westcliff-on-Sea, UK: Desert Island Books, 1995.

Sullivan, Jack. *Elegant Nightmares: The English Ghost Story from Le Fanu to Blackwood*. Athens, OH: Ohio UP, 1978.

Todorov, Tzvetan. *The Fantastic: A Structural Approach to a Literary Genre*. Trans. Richard Howard. Cleveland: Case Western Reserve UP, 1973.

Tremayne, Peter. *Irish Masters of Fantasy*. Dublin: Wolfhound Press, 1979.

Tropp, Martin. *Images of Fear: How Horror Stories Helped Shape Modern Culture (1818–1918)*. Jefferson, NC: McFarland & Co., Inc., 1990.

Varma, Devendra P. *The Gothic Flame*. Metuchen, NJ: Scarecrow Press, 1987.

Wilde, Oscar. *Salome,* 1894. Translated from the 1892 French edition by Lord Alfred Douglas. Repr. with original pagination and illustrations by Aubrey Beardsley. New York: Dover, 1967.

Wolf, Leonard, ed. *The Essential Dracula: The Definitive Annotated Edition of Bram Stoker's Classic Novel*. New York: Penguin, 1993.

Yarbro, Chelsea Quinn. *The Saint Germain Chronicles*. New York: Timescape Pocket, Simon & Schuster, 1983.

———. *A Flame in Byzantium*. New York: Tor, 1987.

———. *Crusader's Torch*. New York: Tor, 1988.

———. *A Candle for d'Artagnan: An Historical Horror Novel*. New York: Tor, 1989.

———. *Out of the House of Life: A Novel of the Count Saint Germain*. New York: Orb, 1994; Tor hardcover, 1990.

———. *Darker Jewels: A Novel of the Count Saint-Germain*. New York: Orb, 1995; Tor hardcover, 1993.

———. *Mansions of Darkness: A Novel of St. Germain*. New York: Tor, 1996.

———. *Kelene: The First Bride of Dracula*. n.p.:n.p., forthcoming: 1997.

Index

About the Contributors

MARGARET CARTER is the author of numerous works about vampires, including the well-known *Dracula: The Vampire and the Critics*. She also publishes a yearly bibliography of vampire fiction. She is an officer of The Lord Ruthven Assembly was a guest scholar at Dracula 97.

TERI ANN DOERKSEN teaches at Hartwick College at Ostego, New York. She has an interest in feminist theory and horror literature, and she has often presented papers at the International Association for the Fantastic in the Arts Conference.

TONY FONSECA is a systems administrator at the State Library of Louisiana. He has a Ph.D. in English from the University of Southwestern Louisiana. He has co-written an annotated bibliography/readers' guide entitled *Hooked on Horror: A Guide to Reading Interests in the Genre*, which will be part of the Genreflecting series. In addition, he writes reviews for *Necrofile: The Review of Horror Fiction*.

KATIE HARSE is a doctoral student at Indiana University who has published extensively on Gothic and Victorian literature. She is an officer of the Lord Ruthven Assembly and has presented numerous papers at the International Association for the Fantastic in the Arts Conference. She was a guest scholar at the World Dracula Congress and at Dracula 97.

JAMES CRAIG HOLTE teaches film and literature at East Carolina University. He is editor of the *Lord Ruthven Assembly Bulletin* and author of *Dracula in the Dark: The Dracula Film Adaptations*. He has presented numerous papers at the International Association for the Fantastic in the Arts and was a guest scholar at the World Dracula Congress and Dracula 97.

RAYMOND T. MCNALLY is the author of numerous works about Vlad Tepes and Dracula, including the influential *In Search of Dracula*; *Dracula, Prince of Many Faces*; and *The Complete Dracula*. Professor McNally teaches history at Boston College, a founder of the Lord Ruthven Assembly, and a guest scholar at the World Dracula Congress and Dracula 97.

ELIZABETH MILLER is the past-president of the Lord Ruthven Assembly and the Canadian chapter of the Transylvanian Society of Dracula. She teaches English at the Memorial University of Newfoundland, and has published extensively in the field of vampire studies. Professor Miller was one of the organizers of both the World Dracula Congress and Dracula 97.

STEPHANIE MOSS teaches at the University of South Florida and has interests in vampire studies, Shakespeare, and theater. She is president of the Lord Ruthven Assembly and a frequent presenter at the International Association for the Fantastic in the Arts Conference. She was a guest scholar at the World Dracula Congress and Dracula 97.

HEIDI L. NORDBERG teaches at Emory University and has interests in vampire studies, theology, and twentieth-century literature. She has often presented papers at the International Association for the Fantastic in the Arts Conference.

SUZANNA NYBERG teaches at New York University. She has presented her work on Victorian literature and feminist theory at the International Association for the Fantastic in the Arts Conference.

WILLIAM PENCAK teaches history at Penn State University and has interests in film, opera, and mythology. He has presented several papers at the International Association for the Fantastic in the Arts Conference..

BETTE ROBERTS teaches English at Westfield State College in Westfield, Maine. She has an interesting the Gothic Novel and has presented numerous papers at the International Association for the Fantastic in the Arts.

JEANE ROSE teaches at the University of Rochester. Her interests include twentieth-century literature, cultural studies, and postmodern theory. She often has presented papers at the International Association for the Fantastic in the Arts.

SHARON A. RUSSELL teaches film and literature at Indiana State University and has published extensively on vampire fiction and film. An officer of the Lord Ruthven Assembly, Professor Russell was a guest scholar at Dracula 97 and often presents papers at the International Association for the Fantastic in the Arts Conference.

LESLIE TANNENBAUM teaches English and American Literature at Ohio State University. Professor Tannenbaum has interests in film and popular culture and has often presented papers at the International Association for the Fantastic in the Arts Conference.

SCOTT VANDER PLOEG teaches at Madisonville Community College in Madisonville, Kentucky. He is a frequent attendee at the international Association for the Fantastic in the Arts Conference and has interests in fantasy, Gothic literature, and film.